CONTEMPORARY
DANCE IN CUBA

CONTEMPORARY DANCE IN CUBA

Técnica Cubana as Revolutionary Movement

SUKI JOHN

Foreword by Elizabeth Zimmer

McFarland & Company, Inc., Publishers
Jefferson, North Carolina, and London

LIBRARY OF CONGRESS CATALOGUING-IN-PUBLICATION DATA

John, Suki.
    Contemporary dance in Cuba : técnica Cubana as
revolutionary movement / Suki John ; foreword by Elizabeth
Zimmer.
        p.   cm.
    Includes bibliographical references and index.

    ISBN 978-0-7864-4901-9
    softcover : acid free paper ∞

    1. Dance — Cuba.   2. Dance — Social aspects — Cuba.
3. Cuba — Social life and customs.   I. Title.
GV1632.C9J64 2012
793.3197291— dc23
                                            2012022463

BRITISH LIBRARY CATALOGUING DATA ARE AVAILABLE

On the cover: Idalmis Arias, Tomas Guilarte, and members of the
Compañia de la Danza Narciso Medina rehearse at the Teatro Mella
in Havana, 1996. Photograph courtesy of David Garten.

Manufactured in the United States of America

McFarland & Company, Inc., Publishers
  Box 611, Jefferson, North Carolina 28640
    www.mcfarlandpub.com

For Veronka, Horacio, Rafael
— and the rest of my extraordinary family —
biological and otherwise

Table of Contents

Acknowledgments

This book has had many incarnations. I am unable to acknowledge all of those people who inspired and encouraged me, but I will make an attempt. Elizabeth Zimmer, Wonder Woman of dance writing, groomed me at the *Village Voice* and then encouraged me to leap into these pages. *Mil gracias.*

At Texas Christian University Dean Scott Sullivan, Bonnie Melhart, chairwoman extraordinaire Ellen Page Shelton, The School for Classical & Contemporary Dance, my fantastic colleagues, enthusiastic students, and the administration have indulged this project from the beginning, when I arrived fresh from my dissertation defense, insisting I had a book to write. At the University of Connecticut I was fortunate to have a rigorous and endearing trio of scholars to advise me: the creative Lucy McNeece, the eminently cool Robert Stephens, and the sultry and scintillating Jacqueline Loss. For their unstinting support I am also indebted to Anke Finger, Samuel Martinez, Osvaldo Pardo, Guillermo Irizarry, Ed Benson, George de Kay, Constance Sutton, Charlotte Marzani, Paule Marshall, David Moore, Laurin Raiken, Gigi Bennahum, Ninotchka Bennahum, Allison Parker and Patti Parlette.

Dancers and friends in Cuba have made this project possible since before its conception. Narciso Medina, collaborator, host, pied piper, *cocinero* of audacious projects, opened the doors of Cuban dance for me like Elegguá opening the roads. My gratitude to him and his wife and partner Idalmis Arias is enormous. Pedro Valdés, Maria Luisa Bringas and their wonderful daughter Marihue have always been my second family in Cuba, eager to share their *chicharos* and rum while talking politics, science and art. Ramiro Guerra, father of Cuban modern dance, honored me with his confidence and collegiality, which I will always strive to merit. Miguel Cabrera, esteemed historian of the Cuban National Ballet, brought me into that rarified world with unwavering certainty, earning my undying thanks. Alicia Alonso, my idol as a young girl, treated me with respect and dignity, giving me the chance of a lifetime to work with her wonderful company. Manolo Vasquez, patient and demanding master teacher of *técnica*, gave me the keys to understanding an entirely new dance form. The amazing composers, designers, and dancers whom I have been privileged to work with at Danza Contemporánea, the Ballet Nacional, and Compañía de la Danza Narciso Medina, have humbled me with their outstanding virtuosity and otherworldly artistry. I have learned so much from so many in Cuba that I hesitate to name just a few. But I can't omit these muses: Yamilé Socarrás, Cándido Muñoz, Béti Fernandez, Armando Martén, Ivan Rodriguez, Ramón Ramos, Alaya "Juancito" Rodriguez, Mario Aguila, Ernesto Márquez, Gladys Acosta, Rafael Rivero, William Castro, Alihaydée Carreño, Lorna and Lorena Feijoo, Gisela Gonzales, Tomás Guilarte, Miguel Iglesias, Eduardo Arrocha, Lino Angel, Bon Bon, Severin Nkeshimana, Viengsay Valdes, José Manuel Carreño, Carlos Acosta, *el caballero* Marcos Portal, my hosts, Gabi, Ileana and Camilo Diaz, and my own *quatro joyas:* Maggie Alarcón, Marlene Carbonell, Marnia Diaz and Mildred Gonzales. Stateside, *mil gracias* to Susan Jaffe, Lourdes Lopez, Tina Bernal, Rachel Faro, Tom Miller, Joe de Cola, Danny Bellas, Ned Sublette, Robert Johnson, Amy Jacobus, Sheriden Booker, Gabri Christa, Susanna Sloat, Louis Head, the Herzog Law Group and Bill Martinez. Joel Diamond and David Garten have made it possible for me to continue my work on and in Cuba with the best music and most exquisite photographs possible.

And now the usual suspects. My parents — all of them — have given me constant support during this long process. Roy sent me to Cuba, took me to Cuba, and shared his love of Cuba with me. He insisted I could write this book; how I wish he could read it now. Veronka taught me to think critically and to czardas heedlessly; her courage and brilliance inspire me every day. Miriam saw me dancing around the living room and encouraged me to choreograph, as did Stan, much-missed, my biggest and most honest fan, who essentially taught me how to write. Leslie ransacked the attic for my lost walking shoes, trying to save my dancer's feet when the *camello* didn't run. Sándor put up with a noisy and uncool younger sister, schlepping to and from consulates, airports and most indulgently, the National Ballet in Havana. He also reviewed and corrected passages of this text with un-big-brotherly patience and generosity. My other siblings Andi, Penny, Sasha, Joshua, Pablo, and Josh; *cuñados, tios,* nieces, nephews, and cousins have gotten me back on track the many times I fell off. All of them have taught me so much about how to live. Richard dared me to write this book, and arranged that first, fateful press junket to Finland. This is all his fault. Janet edited countless early versions; Laurita sweetly endured my writing in the kitchen. My posse Anastasia, Bill, Carlos, Elizabeth, Heidi, Ilene, Jaima, Joey, Jonathan, Joshee, Keith, Kellye, Kris, Larry, Linda, Lisa, Maggie, Mary, Monica, Nancy, Pallas, Raúl, Robin, Ryoko, Shannon, Timi, The Yarovays, Zoe, and Jack have kept me sane by indulging my craziness and keeping my faith in this process. Johanna, moon sister, shared her love, humor and enthusiasm with me for 39 years. She celebrated when I crossed the 200 page mark; may she celebrate now on her cosmic journey.

And my beautiful machos Horacio, Sebastian and Rafael keep me dancing.

Foreword by Elizabeth Zimmer

Suki John is that rare creature, a person deeply committed to both dance and progressive politics. She knows that in a cubicle-bound universe, merely to be dancing is a political act.

I feel like I've known Suki all my life, but it's probably only been 20 years since I went to work as the dance editor at New York's *Village Voice* and she presented herself as a journalist with expertise on dance in Cuba, particularly, and on the political and economic issues facing choreographers around the world, in general. Discovering that she could write clear, muscular sentences, I was happy to assign her the stories she requested, about Cuba, about creeping right-wing sentiment in France and the struggles of immigrant choreographers to survive there, about flamenco and other forms of Latin dance.

Good scholarship in Latin dance is only recently coming into its own. Thirty years ago, I was superintending a project to produce curriculum materials for New York State elementary school teachers eager to introduce the dances of the Caribbean in their classrooms. Our writers discovered next to no reliable information written in English, and we had to recruit translators to help us with what little background we could find in Spanish. A rising proportion of New York City's schoolchildren at that time were of Latin-American heritage, and it was a real struggle to find useful materials beyond a kids' book about Alicia Alonso and a few manuals on how to do the merengue.

John's work on the history and politics of dance in Cuba goes a long way toward addressing these difficulties. She comes to the subject with decades of direct experience in the culture, fluency in Spanish, and deep familiarity with a multitude of dance forms. *Contemporary Dance in Cuba:* Técnica Cubana *as Revolutionary Movement,* evolved from her doctoral dissertation and formed by her years of study in Havana, melds the personal and the political in unique ways.

She is herself a dancer and choreographer, unafraid to tackle huge, emotional subjects in her compositions. She transformed her family's experience in the Holocaust into a ballet linking that horror with the genocide in Bosnia. A New York Jew who trained in New Mexico, teaches at a Christian university, and is married to an Uruguayan man, she has studied, performed, and taught in many countries.

She is equally at home in the studio, in the research library, and on the podium; for John, neither scholarship nor art-making is theoretical. Thus the unusual structure of this volume, toggling between personal narrative and historical commentary. She is writing about the arts (in Cuba, with its heavy admixture of African cultural heritage, it's quite difficult to tease the disciplines one from another: visual, musical, and movement arts emerge together) in a country where dancers have the cachet of football or baseball stars in the United States, and where ballet tickets are within reach of even the poorest citizens.

Documenting the history and development of an art form, *técnica cubana,* that has been in existence for little more than half a century, John writes from the perspective of someone who began observing this development when she was still a teenager. She remembers Cuba before the *periodo especial,* when people were still well fed and doctors did not choose to drive taxis to support their families. I made one visit to Cuba, in 1990, just as drastic changes were beginning to happen, and was struck by the anxiety and bewilderment of the people I met, who'd been more or less content with their relatively simple but secure lot and now faced massive shortages of the most basic products and supplies.

John has returned frequently since that time, at great personal cost, to make dances with and for the Cuban community. I remember a day in the late 1990s when she called and requested all the gently used dancewear in my bureau drawers, and all the surplus medicines and cosmetics in my cabinets, to take with her to a community where such things were simply unobtainable.

This book, alternating chapters of history and political analysis with a very personal journal of her first-hand experience in Castro's Cuba, will change the landscape of Caribbean dance scholarship, and provide a long-desired window on a resilient, useful dance technique. *Técnica cubana* is a wonderful way to train versatile dancers; they can articulate their torsos, heads, elbows, wrists, etc. in ways most contemporary dancers can't. They can, as she points out, "jump and turn and dive into the floor and recover back into the air with speed and ballon. They have great rhythmic understanding and the ability to work in polyrhythms. They use ballet principles but don't get stuck in space or verticality because of them."

Performers trained in *técnica* generate lots of audience connection and warmth. All of this is attractive to student dancers and to choreographers looking to work with people who can embody different movement dynamics according to the needs of a piece. Ultimately, as Cuban dancers integrate more with others, the style is likely to be appreciated and shared internationally.

Elizabeth Zimmer writes about the arts from her base in New York City and teaches in the Hollins/American Dance Festival MFA program. She edited *Body Against Body: The Dance and Other Collaborations of Bill T. Jones and Arnie Zane* and *Envisioning Dance on Film and Video*.

Preface

Dance, in its many guises, plays a central role in Cuban culture. This "delirium for dance," to paraphrase several nineteenth century Cuban authors, is what drew me to Cuba first as a young dancer, later as an emerging choreographer, and ultimately as a dance scholar. There are many forms of dance practiced passionately on the island by amateurs and professionals alike; this book focuses on contemporary dance, the highly unusual concert form of *técnica cubana*. As *técnica* (as it is known among Cuban dancers) was intentionally created during a key moment in Cuban history, this book necessarily engages issues of culture and politics that continue to shape the art.

In these pages it is my goal to provide a multi-faceted view of Cuban experience through the lens of dance. At no time was the power of dance more apparent to me than during my working trips to Havana during the Special Period of the 1990s, when Cuba suffered from particularly harsh economic conditions. Dance and music became sustenance for artists and audiences experiencing daily hardship and hunger. In this unlikely setting, contemporary dance flourished as a form of expression.

From the mid–1970s to the present I have traveled to Cuba through Mexico, Canada, Spain, Jamaica and Barbados, as well as Miami. The logistics of planning trips — making contact with Cubans to arrange housing, work, food, and transportation details — were never less than chaotic and uncertain. These difficulties were the product of policies and laws that continue to change constantly on both sides of the diplomatic gulf. Under the circumstances I have been most fortunate to spend a great deal of time in Cuban homes and studios. I chronicled my observations in journals, letters and faxes written over years of dancing in Cuba, studying Cuba, and dreaming of dancing in Cuba again. Some of those personal observations are included here. In this way I hope to share the experience, to open a window into the daily lives and sophisticated artistry of Cuban dancers.

In researching this book I have consulted historical accounts, political journals, speeches, periodicals in several disciplines, profiles, reviews, dance books, film, music and fiction. I have compiled interviews with some of the foremost dancers and choreographers of Cuba, including the founder of *técnica cubana*, Ramiro Guerra, and the reigning queen of Cuban ballet, Alicia Alonso, as well as prominent performers spanning three generations.

Some excellent works have been written about Cuba, dance, and Cuban dance, yet the aim of this volume is to fill a remaining gap in the literature. The scholarship on Cuban ballet and *orisha* dancing continues to grow. I was particularly inspired and informed by the works of Miguel Cabrera, John Charles Chasteen, Yvonne Daniel, Ramiro Guerra, Katherine Hagedorn, and Robert Farris Thompson. Nevertheless, little has been written on *técnica cubana*, though it continues to flourish in Cuba and abroad. I hope that by using a cross-section of perspectives in these pages I can bring contemporary Cuban dance and life closer to the reader.

This book is structured narratively, highlighting the view of *técnica cubana* as a dance form that is not only unusual artistically, but also politically, culturally and historically. The introduction presents the basic facts about this little-known form, followed by the strange but true story of my first encounter with Cuba as an island of dance. The narrative continues in this way, alternating objective information with subjective experience, offering vignettes to illustrate the lives of Cuban artists. Chapter 1 offers details about this dancing culture, and introduces one of the most important contemporary Cuban choreographers, Narciso Medina. Chapter 2 looks at the *ajiaco*—or stew—that is Cuba's cultural make up, introducing tropes of struggle, faith, and survival that continue in this volume and on the island. Chapter 3 briefly explores the political climate that led to the Cuban Revolution, and why the Castro regime actively supported the codification of *técnica cubana*. Chapter 4 details the odd collaboration between bureaucracy and art that led to the establishment of the Teatro Nacional and the three government-supported national dance companies: the Ballet Nacional, the Conjunto Folklórico, and Danza Contemporánea. Chapter 5 teases out essential Cuban dance legacies that contribute to the complex movement vocabulary of *técnica*. Chapter 6 includes interviews with the great prima ballerina, Alicia Alonso, and attempts to debunk the myth that Cuban ballet is a tropical Bolshoi, an island version of the Soviet school. Chapter 7 looks closely at the practice of *técnica cubana*, detailing daily company class at Danza Contemporánea. Chapter 8 focuses on issues of censorship, artistic freedom, and the exigencies of the 1990s Special Period. Chapter 9 asks thorny questions about race in a country that takes pride in its diversity. Chapter 10 looks at the role of ritual in Cuban dance—where it belongs, where it does not, and how practitioners keep the sacred safe for secular consumption. Chapter 11 recounts a few leisurely conversations with the wily *maestro* and father of *técnica*, Ramiro Guerra. Chapter 12 presents classic modern dance as socially conscious, and examines one particular work of Cuban dance as pointed criticism. Chapter 13 gives voice to the personal perspectives of several Cuban dancers who appear throughout these pages. Chapter 14 looks at the global influences on *técnica*, at the dance and dancer as commodity, and on the tremendous influence *técnica* may yet have on international dance.

(Note: I use the terms modern dance and contemporary dance interchangeably. This is a questionable practice, but since neither name feels truly satisfactory or accurate, I hesitate to put too much stock in the significance of the terminology.)

Juxtaposing historical information with personal perspectives, I tell collective and individual stories simultaneously, allowing one perspective to illuminate the other, distinguished by a change in point of view and past and present tense. Examining the place of dance in a creolized culture, I realized that I had to write a creolized book. History contextualizes personal experience, and personal experience enlivens history. As a participant/observer in the dance life of Cuba, it is likely that my presence, with camera and notebook at the ready, has at times influenced what I have observed. What is certain is that my fortunate immersion in the world of Cuban dance has influenced me profoundly.

Introduction

Cuba is an island of dance. From improvisational salsa party to presentational rumba, from religious celebration to revolutionary commemoration, from aficionados to ballet stars, Cubans dance. Nevertheless, the virtuosic contemporary dance form, *técnica cubana,* is barely known outside of Latin America.

Since 1973 I have had the strange good fortune to continue traveling to Cuba as a dancer, choreographer, and journalist. It was not until my second trip to Havana, in 1988, that I first witnessed *técnica cubana.* By then a professional modern dancer, I thought myself well versed in the styles of contemporary dance. I was shocked to discover that an entire dance form existed about which I knew nothing.

In retrospect this is not surprising. Since the Cuban Revolution of 1959, few Cuban dance companies have performed in the United States, and only a small number of dance professionals from the U.S. have worked in Cuba. Though *técnica cubana* dates back to shortly after the Revolution, it is only beginning to gain currency in international dance circles.

To study Cuban dance is to study Cuba. Cuba's unique political, geographical, and economic circumstances make context central to understanding the art of the island. All dancing is performed within, without, before, after, because of, or in spite of the Revolution. Every meal reflects current domestic policies and external realities. The inter-relation between art and politics, the links between creativity and social change, make this study fascinating and rife with conflict.

For decades, contact has been extremely limited between Cuban and United States citizens (I don't use the term "American" lightly: Cubans rightly insist that they, and all citizens of the Americas, are Americans). The U.S. embargo of Cuba (or "blockade," depending on one's political affiliations) was imposed in partial form in 1960. It became a near total embargo shortly after the Cuban missile crisis of 1962, and has remained in place since then. Cuban economic, political and technical restrictions — combined with U.S. Treasury Department Office of Foreign Assets Control (OFAC) guidelines on "trading with the enemy"[1]— have severely limited interactions between citizens of the two countries. Travel, phone, post, and e-mail communication, not to mention inter cultural exchange, have long been enormously difficult.

The rules and regulations governing U.S. and Cuban relations are in constant flux. The rise of Raúl Castro, the Obama administration, and any number of other variables have restructured the complex dance between our two countries. Restrictions on travel have loosened over the last few years, as have laws allowing Cubans to own private property, such as their homes, and to operate small businesses. Cultural exchange, tourism and communication that seemed impossible just a few years ago are now feasible. Economic and social policy within Cuba continue to change. Raúl's daughter, Mariela Castro, has been an outspoken advocate for LGBT rights. In a country that once jailed homosexuals for *peligrosidad* (dangerousness) and went on to quarantine those who tested positive for HIV, it's a marvel that things have changed so radically. Today, Cubans desiring sex change operations can get them free of charge, just as they receive the rest of their health care. It's anyone's guess as to how these trends will continue or reverse over time.

As a longtime visitor to Cuba I have had the privilege of comparing slices of life from a few key — and wildly different — historical moments. This has given me some perspective on connections between life inside and outside of the dance studio. I first traveled there in the 1970s, again in the 1980s. With the help of press credentials and an academic research license in the 1990s and 2000s, I traveled frequently to work in Cuba for longer periods. Over the course of many extended visits I became increasingly fascinated by Cuba's rich dance culture.

When in 1988 I first found my way into the airy studios of the national modern dance company, Danza Contemporánea de Cuba, I felt as if I had discovered a new continent. I wrote in a letter to a fellow dancer:

> *I sat in that studio for two days, my jaw hanging open. I have never seen dancers so versatile, so able! They soar and spin and dive to the floor, spiral swiftly back to standing, vibrate their torsos, and stretch their legs in sculpted lines. They'll finish a flying tour jeté with a daring plunge to the shoulder. They perch on one leg, head cocked to the side like tropical birds, listening. They dance with such rhythmic complexity, such sensuality, such confidence — they are unlike any dancers I have ever seen!*

This book is my effort to bring this marvelous dance form into the international spotlight it deserves.

Cuban contemporary dance is based on a highly evolved hybrid of ballet, North American modern dance, Afro-Cuban tradition, flamenco and Cuban

Water surges over Havana's famous seaside drive, the Malecón, onto Soviet Ladas and buildings needing repair, January 1997.

nightclub cabaret. Unlike most other dance techniques, *técnica* was created intentionally, with government backing. At the time of the Revolution, Cuba already boasted a national ballet company of some stature — the Ballet Alicia Alonso was soon to become the highly respected Ballet Nacional. For a country with such sophisticated movement lineage it was natural — and highly effective — to link national image with the visceral power of dance.

This tactic was in keeping with the Castro government's effort to develop Cuban artists.[2] After the Revolution, the new regime consciously engaged culture as a means to unite the population. The state-supported Teatro Nacional appointed the accomplished dancer/choreographer Ramiro Guerra as the director of the newly created Department of Modern Dance, charged with creating a national company with a new, essentially Cuban, dance style. This indigenous modern dance form would reflect Cuba's diverse population and strong dance heritage, and be showcased in original repertory that would speak to a Cuban audience. Cuba, a dancing culture, was ripe for the experiment.

Flash forward to a unique moment in Cuban history, the *Período Especial* or Special Period of the 1990s. The timing of my most substantial working visits to Cuba coincided with what Castro publicly predicted would be a time of economic hardship for the Cuban people. In 1990 "Comandante Fidel" famously stated,

> What does the Special Period in time of peace mean? That the economic prob-
> lems would be so serious — because of relations with the countries of Eastern
> Europe or because of factors or processes in the Soviet Union — that our country
> would face a situation in which obtaining supplies would be very difficult.[3]

The fall of the Soviet Union and the withdrawal of its financial support to Cuba indeed precipitated a time of extreme difficulty. When I arrived in Havana in 1992, four years had elapsed since my last visit. I was staggered to discover the circumstances under which Cubans worked and lived. Basic items of everyday use, like cooking oil, shoes, and paper, were increasingly scarce. People complained constantly of hunger, of the lack of transportation, of "*el Período Especial.*"

There was almost no food or gasoline, but there was art. While hardship had increased, so had the ease and freedom with which Cubans expressed themselves. The desperate need to find immediate solutions to material crises created a climate of overwhelming change, provoking artistic regeneration. The need to create, to be seen and heard, was stronger than ever. Young artists displayed a sense of inventiveness and purpose that ranged from commercial ambition to inspired experimentation.

While many aspects of Cuban life withered, dance flourished. The material lack that resulted from the Special Period engendered a particular sort of creativity in Cuba. Artists accustomed to having access to the basic tools of their craft — ballet slippers, costume pieces, lighting fixtures, sets, props, etc. — learned to do without, to recycle, to invent. In fact, the term *invento cubano*, Cuban invention, was used for everything from makeshift fan belts to tofu croquettes. *Invento cubano* became, colloquially, a subversive yet proud reference to popular ingenuity in the face of profoundly restricted resources.

This inventiveness was manifest in the arts as well as in daily life. Cuban choreographers and directors were accustomed to commissioning sophisticated costumes, props and stage sets from accomplished designers. In the face of technical and material paucity, dance makers returned to the raw material of the body in order to create theater art. Because the practitioners of *técnica cubana* are extremely versatile and accomplished, the lack of material resources did not deter choreographic creativity. Instead, the use of choreographic tools — movement vocabulary, use of space, grouping of dancers, theme and variation, dramaturgy, and of course, musicality — were developed even more keenly during this period. While *tanztheater*[4] took hold in Europe and prop-driven, multi-media dances came into vogue in the United States, Cuban choreographers were forced to expand their basic dance language and find ways to make it speak.

Accustomed to live performance, Cubans are keen to watch and participate in dance events. During the Special Period there were precious few diversions from the daily *lucha,* or struggle. Theater and dance were easily affordable and ubiquitous at a time when few families owned VCRs or televisions (which offered only four channels: Cubavisión, Tele Rebelde, Canal Educativo 1 and Canal Educativo 2). Dancers, trained for eight years in institutes of art across the country, did what they knew: they danced. Audiences, hungry and frustrated, were eager for entertainment.

Contemporary dance is by definition an open-ended art form without obligation to tradition. This makes it an ideal conduit for evolving personal, generational, and national expression. Synthesizing dance forms from diverse sources, *técnica cubana* was created in part as a symbol of national identity. While it remained rooted in Cuban multiculturalism, *técnica* became a vibrant tool for individual artistic expression. During the Special Period, as Cuba struggled, contemporary dance transformed that struggle into eloquent, topical art.

Cuban contemporary dance continues to evolve, influenced by social dynamics, musical and theatrical innovation, the availability of cooking oil and — to a limited degree — international dance trends. From the uncertainty following the Revolution, through the hardship of the Special Period, to the battle between flux and stasis that characterizes Cuba today, *técnica cubana* continues to provide dancers and audiences with an immediate, visceral means of expression in vertiginous times.

My hunch is that dance could be the ping-pong of Cuban-American relations. Just as table tennis helped open communication between the U.S. and China during the Nixon administration, dance has the potential to ease diplomacy between Cuba and its northern neighbor.

As they say in Cuba, *ojalá,* let it be so!

Prologue: Havana 1973

My fascination with Cuba began when I was fourteen, which was a long time ago (I am the same age as the Revolution). My father, a neurophysiologist with ties to a Cuban laboratory, engineered an exotic summer vacation for my brother and me: he shipped us off to Cuba. I arrived on that verdant island of humid dreams and sacred dances thinking I was going to study ballet with the great Alicia Alonso. My brother Sándor, three years older and a linguistic prodigy, planned to perfect his Spanish. Instead, we were delivered into the hands of a man we called Brito, a bored bureaucrat who schooled us in the Cuban art of waiting.

After several languid hours in José Martí Airport, we emerged into the faded seduction of Havana. My father had sent us blithely off through Mexico City, where we had gotten lost several times trying to obtain our Cuban visas. The Mexican capital had jarred me with its overt desperation, its tiny children selling chewing gum under a thick blanket of air pollution. Havana seemed wholesome by comparison.

The sky was a torrid pink that first evening, alive and endless beyond the seaside drive, the Malecón. Waves crested over the seawall, splashing cars built before the Revolution. Bougainvilleas bloomed on the crumbling walls of once-elegant mansions. Nature's vivid colors shamed the dull, cracked buildings. Huge palm trees reigned over parks where old men played dominoes and children cavorted noisily. Across the Malecón from the boundless blue of the Caribbean, a row of colonial houses stood shoulder to shoulder, their arches and columns tired and defeated.

Magnificent Havana needed a coat of paint.

We spent the next afternoon waiting for Brito on a dusty curb in Central Havana, watching the vintage cars clatter by. Clunky Chevys and Pontiacs with tail fins and rounded hoods: we had entered a time warp. Civil and determined despite the stifling August heat, Brito had trundled off dutifully to who knows where to find out who knows what in order to get our marching orders. The atmosphere was thick and heavy, the air dense with gas fumes and dust. Our bodies were covered with a thin film of greasy sweat. We passed the time making up songs about our slow moving guide. In our discomfort we were wickedly unforgiving of poor Brito, who no doubt saw us as the spoiled yanquis *we were. The next day he carted us off to the countryside, where we joined a Cuban brigade that was building a school. If Brito hadn't been such an apparatchik, I'd say he enjoyed the last laugh. As it was, I don't think he knew how.*

The Julio Antonio Mella Brigade was part of the Ejército Juvenil del Trabajo, the Youth Labor Army, also called the Seguidores, *or followers, of Camilo y Che. (Julio Antonio Mella was a famous student revolutionary who founded the Cuban Communist Party.) There had previously been a handful of foreigners in the brigade, mostly from other parts of Latin America, but when we arrived we were the only ones. My brother and I were accepted as a strange but thoroughly welcome addition. The Cubans on the brigade were a breed apart: handsome, energetic and irreverent. The men were muscular and the women curvy. Everyone was loud. There was non-stop teasing and singing, handholding, backslapping and cackling. The sexual exuberance was palpable; the winking, grabbing, flirting and smiling flew past me but never in my direction. I had barely reached puberty and spoke almost no Spanish; I was a fish completely out of water. The women I worked with called me* la niña *(the little girl) and made it their business to take care of me. They fattened me up on the avocados and condensed milk they kept stashed in their metal lockers. Mid-morning and mid-afternoon, we were served frosted layer cake and sweet soft drinks called* refresco. *In those glory days the Soviet Union was still helping to keep Cuba pleasantly plump.*

Gloria, a boisterous bottle blonde in her late twenties, harbored a maternal instinct that she practiced on me. Gloria hadn't gone to school when she was young and was just learning to read. "That's why," she told me proudly, "I volunteered to build schools with this brigade." She taught me the words to a popular torch song, "Te Vas Amor," scribbling the lyrics in her unpracticed hand so that I would not forget them, or her.

> "Algo de mí, algo de mí, algo de mí se va muriendo
> Quiero vivir, quiero vivir, saber por qué te vas, amor..."[1]

The operatic quality translates to mere soap opera:

> "Something in me, something in me, something in me is dying
> I want to live, I want to live, to know why you are leaving, my love..."

The school we were building was the pilot project of a new modular design. Open stairways and heavy balconies flanked concrete slabs painted in solid colors: Eastern Bloc chic. The school was almost finished when we arrived, so there was very little work left to do on that building. We women swept and painted lethargically in the damp summer heat, while the men began the heavy work of starting a new school down the road. Sometimes we walked dirt roads to the building sites, past fields of sugar cane that swayed above our heads. The tall thin cane was new to me, as were the stout banana trees, their wide dark leaves crowning clumps of green fruit. As we walked down the road, one of the compañeros *would invariably cut a stalk of sugar cane for us to pass around, sucking the sweet essence out of the pulpy center. Today Sándor recalls "two of the guys pointing me east and showing me railroad tracks, then north and showing me cane fields, then west and showing me a sugar refinery, then south and showing me something else, and saying: 'Before, all that belonged to the* yanquis. *Now it all belongs to us.'"²*

Occasionally we would ride in rickety school buses to a new building site further away. We were always accompanied by live music when we took the bus. The men clanked spoons against their tin trays, beating out percussion to lusty songs spiced with laughter and improvisation. The women harmonized and vamped in the aisle as the bus rattled down bumpy roads past campesinos *driving horse-drawn carts laden with produce. It sounds like a Dolores del Rio movie, but it's true. My brother tried to decipher the songs; one was about a spider woman, he said, and another about salty cod. Though the innuendo whizzed by me, once again the songs stuck.*

Toward the end of our stay the men started digging foundations for the new school they were preparing to build nearby. Sándor, The Intellectual, gloried in the discovery of his muscles. I found myself voluntarily washing his clothes by hand, bemused by my rustic efficiency and our unprecedented teamwork. I would stand over the open-air trough where we cleaned our faces, teeth and clothes, scrubbing his t-shirts with yellow bars of Soviet soap. The huge concrete sink divided the men's and women's privies—cold water showers and seatless toilet bowls—no frills and no doors. Modesty was not a useful virtue on the Brigade.

The Cuban brigadistas *were my teachers, gently correcting my grammatically tortured Spanish. Always well groomed, even in bandannas and plastic sandals, the women taught me the words for combs, brushes, nail polish, tweezers, razors, deodorant, eyeliner and all sorts of other items they deemed essential. They offered their friendship and humor with a generous warmth I now recognize as very Cuban.*

At night, cocooned in mosquito netting, I listened to the beat of Afro-Cuban drums. Fire burned, voices mingled, a musical incantation brewed just outside. My new friends—a few years older and a culture apart—drank and danced and sang deep into the night. I was too timid to investigate those rum-soaked rumbas, though today I can't imagine how I stayed away. Chants, melodies and syncopations

The iconic image of Che Guevara overlooks a 1950 Dodge driving on Avenida 23, at the east end of the Almendares bridge. The caption by Che's face reads *"Tu ejemplo vive, tus ideas perduran"* [Your example lives, your ideas live on]. Vedado, June 2004.

lulled me to sleep. By osmosis, those rhythms found their way into my dancer's bones. They resonate there still.

On the day our school was inaugurated, Fidel Castro arrived in a helicopter accompanied by Nicolae Ceaucescu, then Secretary General of the Romanian Communist Party. The Soviet chopper descended into an open patch of vegetation the men had cleared with their machetes. Our cohorts chanted the slogan we had been taught that morning, "Fidel, Ceaucescu, rra, rra rra!" My brother whispered indictments of Ceaucescu in my ear as I stood dumbfounded by the spectacle surrounding us. Our red bandannas proudly bore the stamped silhouettes of the Revolutionary heroes Camilo y Che. All around us compañeros *waved these hankies triumphantly. As if in response, an industrial-sized fresco of Che Guevara gazed back from the side of the new school building. Che's familiar profile served as a backdrop for one of "El Comandante" Fidel's endless speeches. Apparently Fidel had been told that there was a pregnant woman working among us. After an hour of impassioned monologue he gestured in our direction and, as Gloria explained to me later amidst much excitement, he said, "Look! We even have a* barrigona *(a big belly) serving the Revolution in this Brigade!" Aleda grinned and waved her arms in the air. At that time no one knew what would become of the Revolution and its lofty goals, of the literacy campaign, or, for that matter, the shadowy regime of Ceaucescu. The* brigadistas *had accomplished something tangible, and they were proud to be acknowledged for it.*

Back in Havana for the last week of our stay, Sándor and I lolled about the Protocol House of the National Science Center, known as CNIC. The ranch-style house in the Miramar neighborhood had been a luxurious private home before 1959. After the Revolution it was taken over by the government, as were many elegant buildings. The Protocol House was used to house foreign scientists (and in this case their unscientific offspring) so our father often stayed there while working with fellow neurophysiologists in Havana. According to his colleagues, our father's collaboration greatly benefited brain research in Cuba. For his part, our Dad liked snorkeling, staying up late talking politics, and working with brilliant scientists who were unconcerned about their next grant application. Cuban science, especially medical science, has enjoyed the Revolutionary government's enthusiastic support for decades. It's an investment that has paid off. Castro trumpeted the use of Cuban vaccines throughout Latin America, shamed the yanquis with Cuban infant mortality rates lower than those in the Bronx, and competed gamely with industrialized nations to develop lucrative pharmaceuticals. Every new discovery has added to Cuba's viability on the international market, even though the U.S. embargo severely limits where those inventions can be sold.

Back in Havana, the moment finally arrived for me to visit the studios of Alicia Alonso's ballet empire. Sándor dutifully escorted me on a complicated bus trip to the Ballet Nacional, where he spoke to the sympathetic receptionist at the front desk. She smiled and made a quick call. A stern assistant with a balletic bun and scary eyebrows approached us, her high heels clattering on the marble floor. Sándor was happy to let me proceed alone. I was led to a large studio where huge French doors opened above the street. Full-length mirrors reflected natural light onto soft blue walls. Perched on an indoor balcony, I watched the great ballerina take class.

Regal and raven haired, Alonso was almost blind despite several cataract operations. She squinted hard at her image in the mirror. Listening intently to the verbal instruction of her teacher and then-husband, Fernando, she led the company deftly through class. I was rapt. Alonso's ferocious concentration was contagious. All of the dancers were exceptional, the high arcs of their arabesques *as taut as bowstrings. They soared through their turns with thrilling calm, turns for which the Cuban Ballet is justly famous. Alonso herself was matchless: slowing her multiple pirouettes to a demure balance on* pointe, *she'd pause for a moment with her knee in* passé, *and only then, as if she'd changed her mind, slide her raised satin foot into a perfect fifth position* sous-sous. *When she moved across the room there was a sense of abandon matched by complete control. Her* petite allegro *skimmed the floor, her* entrechats *beating the air rhythmically as her arms carved effortlessly through space. I was witnessing the nuts and bolts of great art being forged.*

I knew then that I had to come back. Cuba had seduced me.

Chapter 1

An Island of Dance

Cuba possesses a privileged place in Latin America with respect to the dance ... along with religious dance it boasts many manifestations of folkloric and popular dances, which offer a rich panorama of dance.—Ramiro Guerra[1]

In Cuba everyone dances, even the truck drivers, and they dance well. Dance is considered an important part of life. Maybe it's because the ubiquitous religion of *Santería* is celebrated in music and dance. Maybe it's because everyone's grandmother taught him or her to dance *guaguancó, danzón, mambo* and *salsa* (except Fidel, apparently, who is notorious for NOT dancing ... among other things). Professional dance training is free and excellent, an investment the country makes in its talent. Dancers are respected, not trivialized. The materialist side to all of this is that dance, and Cuban culture in general, are lucrative exports.

Ramiro Guerra, the father of *técnica cubana*, is one in a long line of writers to affirm Cubans' love of dance. Documented in the literature, this tendency is celebrated and decried by nationals and foreigners alike. In his engaging study, *National Dances, African Roots*, John Charles Chasteen cites the nineteenth-century writer, María de las Mercedes Santa Cruz y Montalvo. Born in Havana, she married extremely well in France, and became the Countess of Merlin. The cosmopolitan Countess delighted in detailing the dances of her homeland. Merlin wrote of the Cuban penchant for partying in 1844: "The women of Havana really love to dance. They stay up all night, agitated, madly whirling and dripping sweat until they collapse, exhausted."[2] Not everyone was so keen on Cuba's dance mania. Thirty years later a U.S. war correspondent, James J. O'Kelly, would describe Cuba's popular dances as "weird and well-neigh savage."[3] A literary journal of the same period noted the "undeniable fact that Cuba is the country par excellence for dancing ... we have a kind of delirium for the pastime."[4]

Salsa dancers at the beloved dance club *Palacio de la Salsa* in the Hotel Riviera, May 1994.

"In Cuba, music and dance are like food," says music producer Rachel Faro, who has worked with the legendary Cuban timba band, Los Van Van. This *comparsa* [parade] echoed that sentiment, taking over the roadway of Paseo del Prado in February 1994.

Such a delicious "delirium" may have been unavoidable. Cuba's history is peopled by dancing cultures. Spanish Conquistadors documented the dances of the indigenous populations they decimated. Indigenous peoples participated in these dances in order to maintain harmony between themselves and their deities.[5] Though we have no remaining examples, and can never know exactly how these tropes may have been incorporated into other forms, the notes of the conquerors suggest that original Cuban dances included simple steps, processions, and zigzagging spatial patterns. Africans, transported in the bellies of the slave ships, brought with them the complex dances and rhythms of their many homelands. Crypto-Jews[6] escaping the Inquisition contributed the grapevine steps of their circle dances. Haitian colonials and creoles, fearful of the slave revolts on their own island, arrived on the eastern side of Cuba, where their versions of French court *contredanses* informed Cuban *tumba francesa*. Spaniards brought their own dances too, such as the rhythmic fancy footwork of Andalucia, *zapateo*. The Countess of Merlin described the rural Cuban, or *guajiro*, version of *zapateo* as [possessing] a "lively, ardent, and voluptuous character that lasts until the often delirious end."[7] Here again is the delirious voluptuousness that would come to characterize not only Cuba's social dances, but its concert dance as well.

Narciso Medina and his wife Idalmis Arias, founders and co-directors of the Academia and Compañia de la Danza Narciso Medina (originally *Gestos Transitorios*), February 1996.

European dance influences, from festive rural dances to measured courtly *sarabandes* (which, as it turns out, also developed in the countryside) found their way into Cuban social dance.[8] Dance was incorporated into religious ceremonies ranging from the raucous spectacle of the Epiphany to the guarded observance of *Carabalí* ritual[9]. Social dances, courtly dances, and other European dance elements mixed with a trove of Afro-Cuban movement. Cuba became home to not only one of the spiciest cabarets, but also to one of the world's great ballet companies.

From rumba circle to living room, from studio to club, café or concert hall, dance life on the island is part of daily life.

This great dance legacy remains mysterious and enticing to those of us from across the water. Over the last half century, contact between citizens of the U.S. and Cuba has been limited enough; contact between dancers was for a long time absolutely minimal. Few Cuban dance companies have performed in the United States during this period, and only a small number of dance professionals from the U.S. have worked in Cuba. For a long time there was virtually no mainstream exposure for Cuban artists in the U.S. In one of the many byzantine twists characteristic of North American–Cuban relations, the U.S. Treasury Department prohibits Cuban nationals working in the U.S. from receiving remuneration. This means that touring artists can't even earn an honorarium, but can only have their expenses paid.[10] In the last two decades the popularity and mystique of Cuban artists has increased, partially due to the release of the Buena Vista Social Club CD produced by Ry Cooder (1997) and the Wim Wenders film of the same name (1999). Though dance is less widely attended than film, the dance world has recently taken note of the rise of Cuban ballet. The Cuban National Ballet has appeared in a few major cities in the U.S. and in many locations abroad; from the ranks of that illustrious company several international ballet stars have emerged. The most important ballet companies in the U.S. now boast Cuban principal dancers on their rosters. Significantly, some of those dancers remain Cuban citizens and members of the Cuban National Ballet, while others do not.

In 2007 Alicia Alonso, Artistic Director of the Ballet Nacional de Cuba and UNESCO Goodwill Ambassador, wrote an open letter in favor of increased intellectual and artistic exchange between the U.S. and Cuba. While her letter sparked a letter-writing campaign on the part of over 500 prominent U.S. citizens,[11] official OFAC policy remained intact. Different administrations enforce the laws differently however, and moments of leniency in cultural exchange alternate with eras of increased restriction. Alonso herself has been known to restrict visits from particular dancers she chooses not to acknowledge, and to forbid others from working as guest artists abroad. Nothing is black and white in terms of Cuba — nothing except the Black Swan and her white counterpart.

In the fall of 2010, American Ballet Theater (ABT) and members of New York City Ballet (NYCB) joined the ranks of the few North American dancers who have performed in Cuba since the Revolution. These prestigious companies were represented by dancers participating in Havana's biannual International Ballet Festival. American Ballet Theater's visit was especially meaningful, as Alicia Alonso danced with ABT at various points during her exceptional career. It is also quite rare that Havana's vociferous ballet audience gets a chance to view an entire company from the U.S., as it did during Washington Ballet's well-publicized appearance in the International Ballet Festival of 2000. As Cuban contemporary dance finds a larger audience abroad we may see more international companies attending Havana's *Días de la Danza*, or Days of Dance. This spring festival of modern dance, which began in Havana's Teatro Mella in 1996 under the auspices of Artes Escénicas, is now hosted every April by the Compañía de la Danza Narciso Medina in the company's Central Havana home, Teatro Favorito.

As restrictions on travel to and from Cuba are constantly changing, intercultural exchange occurs in fits and starts. For my part, I was fortunate to have the doors of Cuban dance opened to me in an unlikely setting: a summer festival in Scandinavia.

Kuopio, Finland 1991

It was in Finland where I first met the dancers who would share the world of Cuban dance with me. It was also the first time I heard the term "Special Period." I had gone to that twilit land of lakes and saunas to write about the dance festival in Kuopio, a charming town north of Helsinki. The enthusiastic crowds, hi-tech theaters and magical northern lights make Kuopio a welcome stop on the European festival circuit.

The Finns are crazy for tropical rhythms, hungry, no doubt, for heat and color. Along with the rest of the festival audience, I was bowled over by Gestos Transitorios (Transitory Gestures), a small Cuban modern dance company led by a maverick choreographer, Narciso Medina. He is one of those electric dancers who emanate power and stage presence. Although the other three dancers all held their own, Narciso had the bearing and focus of a leader. Lean, dark, and muscular, Narciso performed a solo that rekindled the awe I had felt sitting in that studio in Havana. Then he danced a strange and sensuous duet with an exquisite woman I later learned was his wife, Idalmis. The duet was called Caverna Mágica, *and in it the couple wrapped their bodies around each other with a*

Narciso Medina's prize-winning work *Metamorfosis* in rehearsal. Cándido Muñoz, Ramón Ramos and Medina prepare for a performance at the Teatro Mella, February 1996.

proprietary hunger, climbing, rolling and walking as one, almost never letting go. Transfixed by their ability—power and flexibility, sudden changes of dynamic and direction—I was even more deeply moved by the naked humanity of their work.

In Metamorfosis, *the dancers were barely recognizable as the same artists who had moved so harmoniously moments before. They transformed themselves into animals or insects, thrashing and interlacing their bodies, yelling and twitching. Invoking imagery melding Kafka and Darwin, the three male dancers froze along the stage diagonal: one crouched, one hunched and one standing. Their postures ascended the evolutionary scale, signposts on the road to homo sapiens. Edgy and disturbing, the dance resonated in my mind as the theater emptied.*

After the show, I nervously accosted the troupe at the stage door. Tired and hungry, arms full of dirty costumes, they nonetheless seemed eager for conversation. "You are from Nueva York, Nueva York [translation: the capital of the dance world]?" asked a compact dancer named Juancito. I told him a bit about New York and asked a lot about Cuba while we walked along a narrow path, past a shallow lake and up a hill to a cluster of buildings. Arriving at their dormitory housing, Narciso invited me to share their food and rum.

Idalmis was the only female among the four dancers and, therefore, company cook. (I later learned that in most Cuban homes equality is a relative thing; no matter how exalted her career, a woman's work is never done.) Idalmis made me feel welcome in the institutional kitchen, both of us giddy with post-performance excitement. We sat down together and I dug in gratefully, relishing the familiar taste of black beans and rice. Idalmis, a gorgeous example of Afro-Cuban-Chinese intermarriage, was amused by our contrasting cultures and bad translations. We understood each other best when we focused on our common language: dance. Narciso joined in and I told them about watching class in Havana. In addition to running his new little company, Narciso was a soloist in Danza Contemporánea. He had been one of the Herculean dancers I'd seen flying through the studio three years earlier. He laughed at the coincidence, a sweet girlish giggle. I felt then that I was part of the tribe.

Suddenly a crowd from El Conjunto Folklórico, the Cuban Folklore Company, burst in. The music blasted and the party began. In the Finnish white night, embargoes were broken and time lost all meaning. Juancito took it upon himself to instruct me. "You gringos," he complained, "you let the melody distract you from the beat!" Repeating the incantation: "un, dos, tres; un, dos, tres," a thousand times, he initiated me into the sacred art of salsa dancing.

Chapter 2

Struggle and *Sabor*

The nation turns out to be a hope, a yearning, a difficult task that is taken up only to be abandoned, an agony and a struggle, a manipulation, at once something sublime and a place bound by shackles and steel.—Heredia[1]

While contemporary American culture often attempts to distance itself from the politics that surround it—either through escapist entertainment or formal abstraction—Cuban culture is bound to the politics that engender it. Whether an artist wants to espouse or eviscerate the party line, imitate or provoke the imperialist enemy, join or reject the state-sponsored conservatory, life in Cuba is too strongly shaped by politics for the arts to escape it. Even art that purports to be outside the political realm, such as classical ballet, reflects a choice made by its practitioners (most publicly, Alicia Alonso) who have taken a stand simply by continuing to practice their art form under the current system. In order to contextualize *técnica cubana* within Cuban daily life, it is important to include some background information about the island's historical, cultural and political influences. This inter-connectedness is not new to Cuban culture, or simply a result of life in a communist system. It may, in fact, go back to the Conquest.

Ajíaco—A Cuban Stew

The dance history of Cuba is inextricably linked to the mix of cultures that collided on the island, and their resulting social and political upheavals. From the earliest days of the Conquistadors, Cuba's cultural and racial integration can be seen as a metaphor for the New World. Cubans refer to this as their intercultural stew, their *ajíaco*. Fernando Ortiz, who was trained as a lawyer but went on to lay the foundations of Cuba's cultural anthropology, noted famously that cultural influence goes both ways. That is, when cultures collide both sides of the exchange are transformed into what Ortiz calls "intermeshed transculturations."[2] The peoples that found themselves together on the island were destined to intermingle and adapt, to invoke their heritage on new soil and in so doing re-create their traditions and themselves. The result is the creolized culture of Cuba, which is not African or European, Central American or generically Caribbean. In articulating his theory of transculturation, Ortiz insisted that rather than one culture simply assimilating, dominating, or mixing with another, Cuba's unique *ajíaco* produced a culture that effectively transformed its ingredients into something new.[3]

While the Special Period of the 1990s stands out as particularly trying, it is part of a long history of difficult times experienced by the Cuban people. Cuba's legacy of conquest, colonization, genocide, slavery, resistance, nationalism and revolution has determined a symbiotic connection between the country's politics and its culture.

Like most of the Americas, Cuba was home to various indigenous populations. Little is known about them, but their decimation by the European Conquest is undeniable.

> Knowledge about the early inhabitants of Cuba is generally sketchy. The Indians that inhabited the island at the time of Columbus' landing, estimated at about 60,000, possessed no written language and most of them, although peaceful, were annihilated, absorbed, or died out as a result of the shock of conquest ... sources indicate that at least three cultures, the Guanahatabeyes, the Ciboneyes and Taínos swept through the island before the arrival of the Spaniards.[4]

Early in its recorded history, Cuba was considered less valuable to the Spanish crown than some of its mineral-rich neighbors. It was mostly used as a way station for Mexican and Peruvian silver en route to Europe, and for supplies going back to the Spanish mainland. Cuba's first Spanish governor, Diego de Velázquez, ruled the island by the sword and had little respect for the body or soul of his native captives. Velázquez founded the village of Baracoa, where the first Cuban government was situated. Later it was moved to Santiago in the East, and finally in 1538 to Havana, with its superior location and excellent harbor, "one of the finest in the world."[5] By the mid-sixteenth century piracy had become rampant in the Caribbean. In 1555 the French corsair Jacques de Sores captured, plundered, and "burned Havana to the ground."[6] Pedro Menéndez de Avilés, governor of Cuba from 1568 to 1572, initiated the fortification of Havana. But it was only in the 1580s, after shattering attacks by Britain's favorite rogue, Sir Francis Drake, that construction of the fortress began in earnest. That foreboding barricade and symbol of Havana — El Morro — was not completed until the eighteenth century. Havana's harbor, its location on the Florida Channel, and its status as the main (and only legal) port for ships en route to Seville, made it an international outpost, with an economy based on shipping. But Spain was not about to allow Cuba to operate independently, to slip out of its exclusive control. From across the Atlantic, Spain prohibited the colonists from "trading with the enemy."[7] The enemy in this case was primarily England, but also any one of a number of countries with whom Spain was in competition for material and political control of the colonies. How familiar that phrase would become over the years.

> From its earliest days on the global playing field, Cuba wrestled with imposed isolation. Over the years, in so many guises, Cuba has been a pawn in the international game. This fact has played into the Cuban psyche, creating a climate that could produce someone like the patriot poet José Martí (1853–1895), and resonated again and again in what remains a fierce Cuban commitment to independence.[8]

Martí's concerns reverberate more than a century later. Both the United States and Spain continued — and continue today — to exert enormous influence over Cuba's economic and cultural life. The same could be said of the Soviet Union. Before and during the Revolutionary period, with and without the support of the Soviet Union, there has always been an uneasy balance between the dominant cultures and the insistently creative culture of Cuba. Along with its geographical location, Cuba's history as a colony has helped to brand it as a Third World[9] country. Despite the high level of education enjoyed by contemporary Cubans — including artistic, intellectual and scientific production of eminent quality — questions of colonial domination continue to impact Cuban identity, self-confidence, and culture.

Havana 1994

Lino Angel, small and muscular, climbs the narrow steps to the tiny upstairs studio where I have been rehearsing with Narciso's company. He finds me sweeping the floor before practice. He stands staring silently for a long time. Finally he says, "I never thought I'd see a yanqui *sweep a Cuban floor."*

The Dance of Survival

"There is no Afro-Cuba, just Cuba. All of Cuban culture is Afro-Cuban."[10]
—Choreographer Marlene Carbonell

From the beginning of Cuba's recorded history, Africans were brought to the island against their will. While the importation of slaves ebbed and flowed in the early years after the Conquest, by the nineteenth century sugar had become "king," and the sugar trade was hungry for new blood. Sugar production required up to three times as many people as were needed for the production of other crops.[11] King Sugar was brutal, and rather than protect the health of slaves, most plantation owners replaced failing workers with new and healthy slaves. Slave workers were supplemented by a considerable population of indentured Chinese, whose presence in Cuba became more significant between 1848 and 1874 when "approximately 124,000 Chinese arrived in Cuba under very similar conditions as those of the African slaves."[12]

The institution of slavery was fortified by an alliance among Peninsulars (those born in Spain but living in Cuba), the Creole planters, and slave traders. The Creole elite was pragmatic and well educated. While Cuba was beginning to contemplate independence from Spain, Cubans of African descent had long struggled for their freedom. Slave uprisings occurred throughout the early colonial period, and as slave numbers increased, so did the frequency of slave rebellions. The ruling class was terrified by the success of the Haitian slave revolt of 1791 and "the specter of another black republic in the Caribbean."[13] After 1825 this seemed especially imminent, as there had been a demographic shift: the black population in Cuba outnumbered the white.[14]

As Cuba's economic viability increased, so did the corruption and inefficiency of the Spanish bureaucracy. Cuba estranged itself from Spain, and the idea of annexation to the United States gained currency. After an economic crisis in 1857, reformist politics began to take hold in Cuba. By the mid–1860s the questions of slavery, separation from Spain, and annexation to the U.S. were surrounded by ambivalence. Ultimately it was the issue of slavery that made annexation attempts unsuccessful; the emancipation of the slaves in the United States brought the issue to a close with Cuban sugar barons determined to maintain their prosperous system.[15]

In 1868 the Ten Years War broke out against Spain. Cubans fought "a limited war for limited goals,"[16] in order to avoid disrupting sugar production and the destruction of property. After the failure of the Ten Years War and the subsequent *Guerra Chiquita*, or Little War (1879–1880), some Cuban thinkers began to see their goal as a larger, more comprehensive re-imagining of Cuban society. "In my view, the solution to the Cuban problem is not a political but a social one," José Martí wrote to General Antonio Maceo in 1882, "our goal is not so much a mere political change as a good, sound, just and equitable social system...."[17] These ideals were planted firmly in the Cuban national psyche.

When Cuba finally abolished slavery in 1886, Afro-Cubans continued to agitate for equality. Inspired by the anti-racist social agenda of General

Maceo (an Afro-Cuban) and Martí, Afro-Cubans hoped to earn truer economic, social and political freedom by participating in the revitalized struggle for independence from Spain (1895 to 1898).[18] Cubans of color did not experience a transformation of the racism that had burrowed deeply into their society, nor did this war give Martí the quick and decisive victory he had hoped for. The war took Martí's "own life early in 1895, dragged on for three more years, and eventually prompted the American intervention (1899–1902) that he had feared."[19] Thus, the convoluted power relations and resulting ambivalence between Cuba and Spain, Cuba and the United States, and Cuba and its own multi-cultural population continued.

"The blood of Africa runs deep in our veins,"[20] Fidel Castro would say more than a century later.

The growth of the Afro-Cuban population coincided with the deepening, and reconfiguring, of African influence on Cuban soil. The process of transformation of African tradition into African-American culture has been described eloquently in *The Birth of African American Culture,* the seminal work of cultural anthropologists Mintz and Price.[21] African traditions were guarded, remolded and passed along through *cabildos,* "fraternal mutual aid organizations for slaves in Cuba, first established in the 1500s under the auspices of the Catholic Church,"[22] and in *palenques,* secret runaway slave settlements. These links were central to the survival of African rituals celebrated in dance and music. In and out of captivity, Africans and their descendants found ways to keep their practices alive — in secrecy, in tolerated contexts such as Kings Day, or through syncretic forms,[23] through which Catholic saints were melded with non–Christian deities. In Cuba the African gods were shielded by merging with their saintly counterparts, giving each deity two identities. These veiled forms of worship helped preserve African tradition through repressive times.

The role of the *palenques* in the persistence of Afro-Cuban dance forms can be compared in some ways to that of Brazilian *quilombos* in the development of the martial arts/dance form, *capoeira.* As Barbara Browning explains in her absorbing work, *Samba,* "Blacks in Brazil trained *capoeira* for defense of the *quilombos*— communities composed of escaped slaves — and its practice was prohibited by white authorities."[24] While most Afro-Cuban ritual dances were not used for self-defense, they were proscribed repeatedly by white authorities. They owe their survival in part to the secluded protection offered by *palenques* and *cabildos.*

For its part, the *cabildo* has a long legacy, going back to fourteenth-century Spain. Local centers for politics, justice — such as it was — and administration, *cabildos* provided structure for colonial municipalities. The first governors of Cuba remained beholden to the Viceroyalty and the court, or royal *Audiencia de Santo Domingo,* on the island of Hispaniola. But on the Cuban island it was the *cabildos* that provided social, legal, and political structure.

Cabildos appear in various guises throughout Cuban history. While *cabildos* represented the local government of free white men, the Spaniards allowed African *cabildos de nación.* Community centers, brotherhoods, guilds, dance halls, and keepers of the faith, *cabildos* were a lifeline for African slaves arriving on Cuban soil. These *cabildos de africanos* enjoyed relative autonomy, playing a crucial role in preserving and protecting African traditions. Africans of like national and tribal origin gravitated to *cabildos* where their shared heritage could be acknowledged. Through the mingling of similar — but not identical — traditions and the forces of necessity, hardship and happenstance, rituals were transformed from African to African-American. Each nation group developed recognizable music and dance structures.[25] In preserving and passing down these evolving forms, dance emerged as a central feature of Afro-Cuban identity.

From colonial times to the Batista years, the rituals of Afro-Cuba were discouraged and at times punished. Slaveholders were legally bound to instruct and convert slaves to Catholicism, according to the 1842 *Reglamento de Esclavos* [rules for slaves].[26] Despite centuries of repression, Afro-Cuban rituals persisted. Just as the deities of the Yoruba were syncretized with the saints, so were traditional African feast days combined with Catholic holidays. Most notorious of these was Kings Day or the Epiphany, January 6th.

> Slaves took advantage of some Catholic celebrations, making them their own and infusing them with neo-African meanings…. Pageants at Epiphany, an old Iberian custom, provided the perfect focus for slave sociability, *especially if the get together involved black kings…*[emphasis in source]. Like any great social event, gatherings of neo-African nations called for pomp and circumstance, in this case, drums and dance."[27]

Members of the Tribe

One nineteenth-century traveler, John George Wurdemann, described Cuba as more tolerant of "religious opinion than many European Catholic communities." He was of course writing of the rift between Catholics and Protestants. Curiously, he claims that Cubans applied the term *judio,* or Jew "to all foreigners, including Spaniards, more in jest than derision, and without any particular reference to its sectarian application."[28] Indeed, there was a persistent Jewish presence on the island, one that grew significantly in the early twentieth century when various Sephardic and Ashkenazi groups immigrated to Cuba. Certain members of these congregations claim "they have been better treated in Cuba than anywhere else in the world to which their family history extends."[29]

Passover in Havana: 1994

Havana's conservative Sephardic Synagogue (October 1995) established in 1954. The current building was dedicated in 1957 at Calle 17 esquina E, Vedado, La Habana.

Boxes of donated matzo are distributed annually to the hardy Jewish community in Havana. The matzo arrives from Israel, Canada, Mexico, anywhere but the U.S., from where it is virtually impossible to send even humanitarian aid to Cuba. But this year there is a special delegation of American Jews who arrive bearing kosher treats to Havana for Passover. We are introduced at a seder at the Sephardic synagogue in Vedado. I am seated across from some Cuban ex-patriates who live in Mexico. Down a few seats is an entourage from California. On my right sits a couple with a slight twist in the common theme of Cuban inter-marriage: he's Jewish, she's black. This is only unusual because Jews are rare in post–1959 Cuba, and most interracial marriages lack an obvious religious component. The couple's baby boy chews unsalted matzo with gusto as he attracts admiration from the lively party. Spanish, Hebrew, and English merge as the ritual unfolds. We all argue and carry on just like any group of Jews anywhere. With one significant exception: the lights go off, come back on, and— God forbid!!— we run out of food. Nevertheless, the good will is undaunted and the celebration continues into the wee hours, illuminated by candles and starlight.

Despite its sparse interior, the Sephardic Synagogue attracts a dedicated and boisterous congregation. October 1995, *Centro Hebreo Sefaradi de Cuba*, Calle 17 esquina
E, Vedado.

Castro's Conversion?

Castro's regime was at first hostile to all religion. In keeping with communist dogma, it severely restricted all religious practice. Slowly this official
position changed. Shortly after the Revolution, at the same time as it formed
the modern dance *Conjunto*, the government formed the *Conjunto Folklórico*.
This company's mandate was to perform Afro-Cuban traditional dances,
including the ritual dances of *Santería*. Significantly, these dances were
redesigned to be performed in theatrical, rather than religious, contexts. The
Teatro Nacional and the *Conjunto Folklórico* have been credited with helping
to legitimize Afro-Cuban forms of expression over the years, particularly after
a mid–1960s law prohibited *Santería* initiation ceremonies.[30] That act was
revoked in 1971, although it took some time for initiates to feel comfortable
with open religious practice after years of secrecy.

Cuba's attitude toward religion has softened significantly, the most famous
symbol of that change being what had previously been unimaginable: the
Pope's 1998 visit to Cuba. With a more accepting attitude toward religion in

general, *Santería* is now openly practiced. The turnabout in official attitudes toward Afro-Cuban tradition is not just good internal politics; it's good business. By the 1990s the government had begun to capitalize, literally, on the benefits *Santería* could offer Revolutionary Cuban society. Today there exists the huge phenomenon of *santurismo*, a hard-currency generating tourist industry focused on *Santería* initiation. *Santurismo* has become big business, and international visitors arrive daily with the hope of "making saint," being initiated by Cuban *santeros*.

Santería had been censured throughout the colonial and Republican eras; at the beginning of the Castro years Afro-Cuban ritual practice was again actively suppressed. When that policy changed, practitioners did not know how to respond. The shift in official attitude, though received with doubt and caution by practitioners, was certainly pragmatic: by embracing African tradition the Revolutionary government created good will in the black community. In celebrating Afro-Cuban culture, Cuban society acknowledged the myriad contributions of those who had been disenfranchised over centuries.

It was therefore imperative — not only artistically but culturally and politically — that the rich dance traditions of Afro-Cuba be included within a contemporary Cuban dance form. This logical choice was also aesthetically sound; the dances of Afro-Cuba contain vast movement knowledge, much of that which makes *técnica cubana* unique.

Chapter 3

Fidelistas and *Yanquis*

The history of Cuba in the twentieth century, including the Cuban Revolution of 1959, has filled many volumes, not to mention late night rum-fueled arguments. For our purposes I will defer to more seasoned historians and chroniclers of Cuban politics (I confess that in writing this passage I consulted my brother, now the esteemed Dr. Steven Sándor John, professor of Latin American, U.S. and labor history).[1]

As a lucrative producer of slave-plantation sugar, Cuba was one of the last Spanish colonies to achieve independence. However, the U.S. thwarted this independence, reducing Cuba to a neocolonial condition. Most famous of the North American measures was the Platt Amendment, which unilaterally gave the U.S. significant influence in Cuban affairs as well as military control over Guantanamo Bay. This bitter experience left a deep feeling of national humiliation that conditioned politics over the next century.

The Great Depression that brought Cuba's northern neighbor to its knees arrived early on the island. By the mid–1920s the price of sugar had begun to drop, and it stayed low for over a decade. Controls on sugar production did not have the desired effect of stabilizing prices, but instead set the economy reeling further. "By 1933, 60 percent of the population lived at submarginal levels of under $300 in annual real income."[2] Cuban-American author and sociologist Marifeli Perez-Stable notes that widespread governmental corruption and instability characterized the period leading up to the Revolution:

> During the 1890s and 1930s, the United States helped Cuban elites to defuse popular challenges. Immediate successes, however, were not conducive to long-term political stability.... Among Cuban politicos, retaining or gaining access to the public treasury was the primary electoral concern.[3]

During the administration of President Gerardo Machado (1925–1933), great sums of government revenue were used to satisfy the foreign debt. Salary cuts and layoffs of civil servants ensued. The conditions were rife for political opposition and social conflict. Civil discord, armed bands torching farmlands, attacks on rural guards, and general unrest led to the suspension of constitutional guarantees in November of 1930. Repression, inevitably, stoked the rise of a new opposition, this time with leadership from student organizations and young professionals. Nepotism and chaos reigned. With the support of the student movement, Dr. Ramón Grau was appointed provisional president in September 1933. By January 1934, with the implicit approval of the United States, the newly promoted Army Chief Fulgencio Batista forced Cuba's President Grau to resign.[4] In the years that followed, Cuban leaders resorted to various means to quell the discord that had rocked the country during the 1930s. Under the presidency of Federico Laredo Brú (1936–1940) Cuba enacted progressive policies through the Constitution of 1940. But the compromise was short lived, and the constitution was in effect for only 12 years. "New politicos and political parties continued the tradition of corruption."[5]

In 1947 Senator Eduardo Chibás, a crusader against graft and gangsters, helped to found the opposition Ortodoxo party. A powerful orator with a weekly radio program, Chibás was a prominent example for students and reformists, advocating "public integrity, administrative honesty, and national reform."[6] In 1951 he shocked the country by committing suicide on the air during his radio broadcast. This surprising loss made a profound impression on a young student in Havana, Fidel Castro, who was deeply interested in the independence movements of Latin America. The opposition movement lost heart, while the political system in power remained rife with corruption and cynicism. In 1952, General Batista and his army seized power again, this time in a military *coup d'état* that preempted the constitution.

Toward the Revolution

Deep socio-economic injustice, political grievances and economic dependence on the United States fueled conflict between Batista and his opponents. Cubans depended on the U.S. for trade, but were afforded none of the social services of their northern neighbors. The Cuban middle class had increasing difficulty maintaining its lifestyle while rural workers endured low wages, poor education and unsafe housing.[7] Cuba was a playground for American high-rollers and gangsters, most famously Al Capone, who built Havana's illustrious Hotel Nacional. By the late 1950s thousands of Cuban women worked as prostitutes in Havana. *New York Times* scion Arthur Schlesinger, Jr. recalled:

I was enchanted by Havana — and appalled by the way that lovely city was being debased into a great casino and brothel for American businessmen over for a big weekend from Miami.... One wondered how any Cuban — on the basis of this evidence — could regard the United States with anything but hatred.[8]

The presence of big spenders and mobsters further illuminated the differences between the haves and the have-nots, fueling the growing revolutionary movement. On July 26, 1953, Castro mounted an attack against the Moncada army barracks. Though the rebellion failed, the attack, arrests, trials, and subsequent events spurred the movement forward. Castro delivered his famous "History Will Absolve Me" speech during his trial, and although he was sentenced to 15 years in prison, popular demonstrations contributed to his amnesty and release in 1955.

On January 1, 1959, revolutionary forces took control of Havana. Batista fled Cuba in the middle of the night. A week later Castro's 26th of July Movement triumphantly entered Havana. Myths and legends about that historic moment abound: references to the revolutionary colors of black and red (the colors of the Santería deity, or *orisha*, Elegguá, who opens the roads, as well as the colors associated with anarcho-syndicalism); the significance of a dove landing on Castro's shoulder; and the unprecedented sight of Afro-Cubans riding victoriously through the streets of Havana, shoulder to shoulder with their white compatriots.[9]

On Trading with the Enemy

While initial U.S. reactions to Castro were somewhat ambivalent, shortly after the new regime took power the U.S. rapidly embarked on a crusade to defeat the Cuban Revolution. Notoriously this involved a bizarre series of plots to kill Castro, ranging from traditional hits to more exotic means, like poison scuba gear and exploding cigars (detailed in the film *638 Ways to Kill Fidel*). These assassination attempts were accompanied by a campaign of U.S. sabotage on the island. The failed U.S. invasion of the Bay of Pigs (known as Playa Girón in Cuba) deepened and broadened Fidel's popularity throughout Latin America. Cuba came to represent David against the North American Goliath. Cuba moved closer in ideology and alliance with the Soviet Union. Anticipating another attack from the U.S., Castro accepted Soviet Premier Nikita Khruschev's proposal to base nuclear missiles on the island. In 1962 the Cold War came to the boiling point during the 13 days of the Cuban Missile Crisis; the USSR and the U.S. ventured as close as they ever would to mutually assured destruction. Once the nuclear terror dust settled, the U.S.

adopted strict economic measures against Cuba, attempting to embargo the indomitable island into involuntary regime change.

Early attempts to spread the Cuban model of revolution by guerrilla warfare narrowed down by the mid–1960s. Che Guevara embarked on a tragically flawed attempt to implant a Cuban style *foco* (nucleus of a guerrilla insurgency) in a particularly inhospitable part of the Bolivian hinterland. His tracking and assassination by the CIA in 1967 became the stuff of legend as his image became much more than a trivial icon to millions of would-be rebels throughout the world. Cuba meanwhile was becoming increasingly reliant on its alliance — despite very real frictions — with the Soviet Union. After many ups and downs and rumored softening of Washington's intransigence, Cuba entered the Reagan/Bush years still as a favored target of U.S. enmity. Many believed the collapse of the Soviet Union in 1991 would be followed almost immediately by the fall of Cuba's government; all the more surprising to many was the regime's ability to survive, while the achievements and promise of the Revolution seemed increasingly fragile. North Americans who inquire beyond the boundaries of the narrow spectrum of political discourse in the U.S. are often nonplussed to find that much of what they take for granted about Cuba is seen very differently in other parts of the world. The very survival of this small island's experiment, however flawed, under the guns of the *yanqui* colossus, is for a large number of people around the world an incalculable achievement and source of inspiration.

Enormous changes have taken place in the years since "The Triumph of the Revolution," as Cubans on the island refer to it. Particulars of the economy, political climate, and relative ease or difficulty of daily life vary enormously within short periods of time. But certain fundamental characteristics of life in post–Revolutionary Cuba seem never to change.

*"In Cuba," Idalmis is fond of saying, "don't bother to ask **why?!**"*

Although travel from the United States to Cuba continues to be extremely limited, those who visit Cuba on a regular basis report huge bureaucratic, technical, and dietary changes within short periods of time. They also pick up on the less quantifiable "mood" of the island, which changes like the Caribbean wind, depending on the availability of foodstuffs, exit visas, and transportation.

These visitors often belong to a certain class of observers who follow Cuban culture either professionally or as aficionados. Their numbers have grown since the late 1990s as a result of the increased visibility of Cuban artistic, agricultural, and scientific accomplishments. Organizations spring up with increased regularity, like the Cuban Artists Fund, U.S.–Cuba Cultural Exchange,[10] Cuba Central, The Center for International Policy's Cuba Program, the Center for Cuban Studies, and Global Exchange. Some of these organizations offer legal travel to Cuba, some lobby for an end to the embargo, and others work to increase artistic interchange.

Visa restrictions on the part of both governments continue to limit cultural exchange. During George W. Bush's administration, Cuban-Americans were only allowed to return to Cuba once every three years, even in the face of family emergencies and the death of loved ones. Despite more airtime for Cuban music, and more stage time for Cuban dancers, the lives these cultural figures lead and the luster of their talents are blurred by romance, OFAC restrictions, and visa disputes. One result of these ever-changing restrictions is that the extraordinary creativity of Cuban musicians and dancers has reached mythic proportions, but little is known about their everyday lives.

Miami to Havana, 1992

It has taken me nineteen years to prepare for this 45-minute flight. I am on my way to Havana to choreograph for Narciso's fledgling modern dance company, Gestos Transitorios. Life in Cuba is such a world apart, it feels as if we're flying to the moon.

Strapped into this stifling tube on the Miami tarmac, I put doubt, pragmatism and the law aside. Legally, Americans are supposed to request permission from the Treasury Department in order to travel to Cuba. I haven't done that because I'm not about to give them the chance to say no. After years of karmically loaded coincidences, I now have a real invitation from a real dance company. No leaden dose of reason can stop me. Sweat trickles from my temples. A chorus of female voices rises from the row behind me: "I have a lawyer who never lost a case: his name is Jesus." Hopefully they're praying for everyone on board.

I don't have the right visa, my slim wad of cash is strapped to my waist, and I'm definitely missing some crucial item I can't quite name that will no doubt be unavailable in Havana. I have left my New York life in absolute disarray in order to follow my muse. I'm sure to return penniless, just as next month's rent is due. I am fighting panic, logic, and the embargo. For some reason we're flying on Haiti Trans Air. But the crew is clearly Cuban: flirtatious and disarmingly casual. They laugh and talk, preparing a routine flight over a tiny strip of ocean. We will cross worlds of politics and culture in a hiccup of space and time.

I am lucky that my press credentials allow me to travel directly from Miami to Havana, although without an OFAC license I'm taking my chances. (Note: Don't try this at home! Some of my friends have gotten sued by the State Department.) The Marazul charter that flies three times a week at the crack of dawn is restricted to passengers with special passports or affiliations that sidestep the myriad travel restrictions to Cuba. As a tourist or choreographer, they'd never have let me on the plane. I'd have to go illegally through Canada or Mexico. I tend to assume, being born American, that I am free to travel as I please even if guidelines and politics contradict me. This attitude of entitlement opens doors and slams them in my face.

The intricacies of travel to Cuba are dizzying. This morning in Miami I played "the journalist" in order to get on the plane. To get off the plane in Cuba I will play "the tourist" and make use of my tourist visa. The tourist visa lasts for only seven days, requiring a return flight in one week! I can't possibly make a ballet in that time; instead I plan to stay for 30 days. Once in Cuba I will be "the choreographer," which necessitates a work visa, which means transforming my tourist visa into a temporary Cuban green card. I have no idea how to untangle this red tape. As the sweltering mini-plane finally takes off, I marvel that I have gotten this far.

The cabin crew comes around with trays of hard candies. Cubans love sweets. Despite the island's legendary production of sugar, I've been told to bring gifts of caramels with me. Coals to Newcastle. The lady next to me grabs handfuls of the sticky wrapped sweets and stuffs them in her purse.

Last night I slept on the floor of a friend's Miami apartment. Just back from Cuba, she kept me up late with tales of running out of gas and food from Santiago to Matanzas, cheerfully adding that, "in Cuba they have nothing, no delis on the street corners, not even toilet paper." Once she had me totally terrified, she took out a picture of her Congolese boyfriend, William, and handed me a stack of letters for him. I asked how she had found an African boyfriend in Cuba. African countries, she explained, educate their doctors in Cuba where the training is excellent.

Richness and lack, that's Cuba.

This morning in the airport bathroom I furtively stuffed a few extra rolls of toilet paper into my bag as they issued the final boarding call for my flight.

The chorus of passengers begins again; I myself could use a little divine intervention. I've been heavily charged for changing my flight, my tourist visa, and my overweight luggage stuffed with dance clothes and vitamins I plan to give away. The airline clearly doesn't care about my humanitarian intentions. Narciso will pay me, of course, but he will pay me in pesos. I can't use moneda nacional, or pesos, for air travel or practically anything else, since I am not Cuban and do not legally have access to rationed goods. I see my meager food and emergency dollars dwindling rapidly.

Queasily, I realize that I am embarking on this adventure in an extremely tenuous state. I picture myself stranded in Havana, broke, without food, unable to make an international phone call or get a return ticket. I breathe deeply and tell myself it will all work out. I will fly first and legalize later. I remember a *phrase from Narciso's letter of invitation,* "todo se resuelve," *everything gets resolved.*

The flight is laughably short. Suddenly the island is below us: lithe palm trees, dirt roads, smoke rising from factories, coral reefs in the azure coastline. Our winged shadow glides across the emerald countryside. As the wheels touch down, my fellow passengers cheer and I join in their applause.

Chapter 4

Birth of an Art Form: *La Técnica Cubana*

In the postcolonial world, national culture is considered strategic, is mobilized, becomes a political issue. — Fernando Martìnez Heredia[1]

Shortly after the Cuban Revolution of 1959, Fidel Castro's government appointed Ramiro Guerra as director of the Department of Modern Dance within the Teatro Nacional in Havana. The goal of this project was the creation of a dance company with original repertory based in a new, indigenous Cuban modern dance style and technique.[2] The new *Teatro Nacional* was founded, funded and fully supported by the Revolutionary government, which consciously engaged culture as a means to unite Cubans after the Revolution. The *Teatro Nacional* was the parent organ-

Ramiro Guerra, historian, choreographer, and father of contemporary Cuban dance, at the barre in his apartment on the top floor of a crumbling Vedado building, April 2006 (photograph by the author).

ization of the Departments of Music, Modern Dance, Theatre, Chorus and Folklore, and its buildings housed a library and research organization in addition to the burgeoning performing companies. The fact that contemporary dance was considered a vehicle for strengthening national identity brought the art form out of obscurity and into the cultural dialogue. This is not to imply that contemporary dance enjoyed financial or critical support on a par with that of ballet — then or now. But contemporary dance was seen as a vibrant, eloquent part of the new Cuba. In the U.S. modern dance is often dismissed as incomprehensible, experimental, or "downtown." The idea of a national "Department of Modern Dance" is enough to make the North American dancer's head spin.

As it was, Cuba's Department of Modern Dance was formed "amid the effort to define that which is Cuban."[3] This movement encouraged nationalist sentiment in a country long defined and dominated by Spain and the U.S. The new regime capitalized upon and stimulated this trend to unite Cubans via cultural symbols. The ongoing tradition of Cuban dance, with African, Spanish and indigenous origins, made dance a logical tool for bringing together Cubans of varied backgrounds. "Seeing how passionate Cuban people were about their traditions, the government recognized the value of connecting these traditions with the state."[4] The attempt to link national image with the visceral

Marianela Boán, a preeminent Cuban choreographer of contemporary dance, and founder of DanzAbierta. She is shown here during a question and answer session after a performance at the Teatro Mella, February 1996.

power of dance was a logical choice for a country with such strong dance lineage. In 1962 Rogelio Martínez Furé founded the *Conjunto Folklórico* to present Afro-Cuban dances in theatrical settings. In *Divine Utterances,* Katherine Hagedorn's informative book on Santería performance, Furé explains that the *Conjunto* was founded to "satisfy the need of the Cuban people for an institution capable of retrieving Cuba's music and dance traditions for integration into the new national culture."[5] Cuba already boasted a ballet company of some stature; after the Revolution the Ballet Alicia Alonso became the Ballet Nacional de Cuba. With Guerra's Conjunto de Danza Moderna, as the new modern dance company was originally called, Cuba now funded three high-quality, high-visibility national dance companies.

While celebrating and preserving traditional culture, the Revolutionary government also encouraged new Cuban art forms and artists.[6] In dance that translated to an unprecedented mandate: the development of an indigenous modern dance form that would reflect Cuba's artistic influences, mixed population, and strong dance heritage. The reigning modern dance aesthetic of Europe and the United States was not the standard to which the new dance form would be held. The Department of Modern Dance was charged with creating a national dance company with a new, essentially Cuban dance style, and with building an original repertory that would speak to a Cuban audience.

Dance has played a large role in Cuban lives and self-concepts, contributing heartily to what is known as *cubanismo, cubanidad* or *cubanía*—all of which loosely translate as "Cuban-ness." John Charles Chasteen, in studying national dances and their social function, sees dance as "a basic social mechanism for group solidarity, [an] agglutinative force in world history."[7] He contends that dance helped to develop the Cuban sense of identity; I believe that is true in defining Cuban experience both before and after the Revolution. In this context it is logical that those in the National Theater—at that time under the auspices of the Consejo de Cultura, in turn directed by the Ministry of Education—perceived the need for a theatrical dance form that truly expressed the many aspects of Cuban culture. By providing a forum for Cuban cultural expression and presenting Cuban concerns in a uniquely Cuban way, the state encouraged nationalist sentiment.

"Dance is permeable to all influences, from high culture or low, without any social prejudice," says Guerra.[8] He modeled this process of inclusion while creating *técnica cubana*: borrowing popular traditions off the street, combining them with academic dance elements, and raising them to the level of national expression. It was not necessary for the content of the new dances to be overtly "revolutionary" or political; the medium was in large part the message. In creating a contemporary dance form from the many rich sources

Narciso Medina dancing his *Diálogo con el vacio* in his company's home, a former movie theater, Teatro Cine Favorito, Centro Habana, December 31, 2001.

of Cuban movement, modern dance and dancers became integral to the new *cubanidad.*

The Conjunto/Danza Contemporánea

Promotional materials from what is now known as Danza Contemporánea de Cuba state that the national modern dance company was formed on September 25, 1959.[9] The first recorded performance, featuring choreography by Guerra, took place on February 9, 1960, at the Salon Covarubbias in the Teatro Nacional, the newly constructed National Theater on the Plaza de la Revolución. "According to Ramiro Guerra, it was just a half-finished building. It was the outside shell but inside it was still empty."[10]

Ethnomusicologist Argeliers León, a former student of Fernando Ortiz, was the founding director of the Teatro Nacional's Department of Folklore. Uniting his well-developed musical talents with enthusiastic support of the Revolution, León was particularly committed to fighting racial and class divisions within Cuban society. Bringing Afro-Cuban artistic traditions to the fore at the Teatro Nacional, León helped promote the study of folklore alongside Western academic forms. In so doing, he spurred the inclusion of African tropes into hybrid artistic movements. León was one of many intellectuals and artists who combined their professional and political energies in the hope of creating a bright, new Cuba.

The powerful but uneasy role of art in revolutionary society was evident to Ernesto "Che" Guevara, who discussed it in his seminal letter to the editor, "Socialism and Man in Cuba." Writing to *Marcha,* the Uruguayan newsweekly, Che, as he is now universally known, opined that there were "no artists of great authority who also have great revolutionary authority."[11] The assumption here was that not only did the artist have an obligation to uphold the new society, but that there existed a right way and a wrong way to participate as artists in the new framework. Che's reference to the arts underscores the influence and importance given to cultural production in the early years of the Revolution:

> The likelihood that exceptional artists will arise will be that much greater because of the enlargement of the cultural field and the possibilities for expression. Our job is to keep the present generation, maladjusted by its conflicts, from becoming perverted and perverting the new generations. We do not want to create salaried workers docile to official thinking nor "fellows" who live under the wing of the budget, exercising freedom in quotation marks. Revolutionaries will come to sing this song of the new man with the authentic voice of the people.[12]

There is a spooky prescience to Che's words, as he describes a nationwide malaise of salaried workers that he would not live to see. But more on that later... What he did see was a need for supporting those Cuban artists who could speak to a population that varied greatly in education, culture, and familiarity with the arts. In the all-out effort to create a utopian Cuba, the arts were enlisted to play a crucial part. Professional organizations, unions, schools and theaters were established to train and present the new generation of artists to the newly educated, socially engaged workers.

In the realm of literature and literacy, the Revolutionary regime was remarkably robust. Literacy campaigns utilizing over 270,000 teachers and

Narciso Medina and Marlene Carbonell rehearsing Medina's *Caverna Magica*, with company members looking on, March 1998.

volunteers around the country dropped Cuba's illiteracy rates from 42 to 4 percent in the first three years of the Castro regime.[13] With a new and expanded audience, the regime showed a powerful commitment to establishing homegrown literature that reflected and supported the Revolution. Jean Franco, writing about the relationship of society to the artist in Latin America, explains that new authors were connected with an expanded class of Cuban readers:

> New writers have emerged to provide for this readership, encouraged to write and helped to publish by the official Union of Artists and Writers [UNEAC], and by the prizes offered by the Casa de las Américas, which acts as a cultural clearing-house.... It is the writers who have been at the head of the "cultural revolution."[14]

What is omitted from this and most other analyses is the role of dance in this "cultural revolution." Dance is hard to interpret and prone to metaphor. It is also ephemeral in nature, existing only in the moment instead of preserved on paper, canvas or film for repeated consumption and study. Videos are a poor substitute for the experience of live dance, especially old-fashioned documentary videos. These simply record dances that have not been made to fit the camera, and they don't use the electronic medium in active interplay with dance. Dance notation is often unwieldy, inadequate or expensive, and usually requires the skills of specially trained interpreters. For these reasons, historians and theorists cannot read dance "text" in the same way as they can a script or score. Though notable dance works are shown repeatedly on national television, the copious literature on the Cuban Revolution rarely mentions dance as a major player in revolutionary culture. It is not surprising, therefore, that most cultural critics have neglected to include dance in their analysis of the transformation of Cuban society.

Despite this gap in historiography, dance has played a large role in Cuban lives and self-concepts, contributing heartily to *cubanía* in practice, if not in theory.

Narciso's Company, Teatro Nacional 1992

Choreographing for the exquisitely voluptuous dancer Yamilé, I ask for more sinuousness in the torso and arms as she makes a long diagonal across the stage. Yamilé struggles for a while to embody the liquid quality the choreography lacks. Suddenly she says, "Ah! You want more cubanía!" I can't define the word yet I know it must be right. ¡"Sí!," I say emphatically, "that curvy undulating Cuban thing you do... ¡Cubanía!" From that moment I begin to seek a quality of Cuban movement that still doesn't translate into English.

Birth Rights

Modern dance was and is an art open to experimentation. Cuba had a modern dance maverick and leader in Ramiro Guerra. Prior to the Revolution, he was already experimenting with ideas of *cubanía* in what was initially a North American dance form. Guerra had prepared himself as an artist with deep inquiry into various dance forms including modern dance, ballet, the folkloric dances of Cuba and other Latin American countries, and various forms of theatrical show dancing. Guerra had impeccable credentials: after performing in Cuba with his Russian ballet teacher, Nina Verchinina, he studied in New York with Martha Graham, José Limón, Doris Humphrey and Charles Weidman.

In 1956, Guerra directed the Teatro Experimental de Danza under the auspices of Alicia Alonso's ballet school. The mere fact of being associated with Alonso, the matriarch of Cuban ballet, suggests that Guerra had achieved a high level of stature and competence early on. Alberto Méndez, a major choreographer for the Cuban National Ballet, began his dance career as a member of Guerra's troupe. In 1957, Guerra founded the chamber group, Grupo Nacional de Danza Moderna, and created choreography "in search of

Lorna Burdsall, one of the founding members of the original Conjunto Nacional de Danza Moderna, seen at her home overlooking the mouth of the Almendares River, March 26, 2004.

a certain *cubanía* in his style of dance."[15] This evolving movement style was already evident in his piece *Sensemayá*, originally choreographed for the Alonso group, Teatro Experimental. Guerra continued to define and refine his maverick style in *Tres danzas fantásticas* and *Rítmica*, which the Grupo premiered in 1957 at El Sótano [the basement] Theater in Havana.

Guerra and his core group of collaborators considered questions of characteristic Cuban movement with the work of their small Grupo. In order to maximize the experiment, to truly hybridize Cuban, European and African movement tropes, they needed institutional support and a school in which to train dancers. In 1959, with the support of the Revolutionary government and the Teatro Nacional, Guerra's Grupo was renamed the Conjunto Nacional de Danza Moderna — the National Modern Dance Ensemble — giving *técnica cubana* a mandate and a context in which to grow. The nature of this inception is in itself noteworthy: *técnica cubana* was intentionally developed as a state-supported, multi-cultural dance form, a pluralistic representation of the new Cuba.

Guerra had the foresight to bring together an eclectic group of amateur and professional ballet, modern, Afro-Cuban, and nightclub dancers. He held open auditions from which he chose 12 white and 12 black dancers,[16] consciously putting into practice his theory that dancers from different cultural backgrounds move differently. Guerra's objective was to incorporate distinct physical tendencies into the new technique. Guerra collaborated with and led, among others, the North American dancers Elfreide Mahler and Lorna Burdsall, who were living in Havana at the time. He invited Mexican dancers Elena Noriega and Manuel Hiran to join the experiment. The group culled their resources and training, and began to synthesize previously diverse dance forms into a truly Cuban *ajíaco,* or stew. Together they constructed a technique that is tremendously athletic and expressive, a reflection of the African, Spanish and Caribbean roots of Cuban culture within the theatrical tradition of modern dance. Eduardo Rivero, artistic director of Teatro de la Danza del Caribe in Santiago de Cuba, is one of the most exquisite dancer/choreographers to come out of Danza. He has explained, "We dance with a multitude; with the Africans, the Europeans, the Chinese, the Indigenous peoples. We dance with the world in our blood."[17]

Growing Pains

The process of creating a new dance vocabulary, building a repertory and establishing a system for training dancers was inevitably trying and uneven. Shortly after the founding of the new state sponsored company,

Guerra stopped performing and devoted himself fully to directing the new troupe. Although he came out of retirement occasionally to reappear in roles he couldn't resist, Guerra knew that his directorial eye and leadership were crucial to the success of the group. "During the first years of existence of our Conjunto, we moved within a radius full of contradictions as far as a cohesive technical point of view was concerned," Guerra told writer Fidel Pajares, who also danced in the company. "Almost the only thing that united us was an abstract concept of modern dance, something different from an academic vision, but full of individual contradictions in terms of aesthetic and technique."[18]

Working in this fashion, ironing out everything from warm-up strategies to choreographic details, the Conjunto forged a style and evolved a technique. Slowly, parsing differences in training, belief systems, language and artistry, they developed a system of pedagogy. Guerra and his colleagues used their vast movement knowledge to create a dance language that reflected Cubans' experience and history while holding space for their rapidly changing culture.

Despite the initial lack of codification or consensus on the fine points, the dancers enjoyed the advantage of state support, which allowed them to invent, research, and reinvent the new dance form. Unlike dancers in many modern dance companies that operate in the United States and beyond, members of the Conjunto were able to devote themselves exclusively to dance work without relying on outside jobs for income and without searching for funding to produce concerts, finance theater rentals or rehearsal space, disseminate publicity, build costumes, commission compositions or construct sets. The Conjunto focused on designing a movement language and creating choreography that would meet their aesthetic criteria and speak to a Cuban audience. Guerra believes that they were successful in that endeavor. Here he describes the new dancer, trained to communicate to the New Man (and Woman) of Cuba:

> It was necessary to create new dancers who would see modern dance not as a frivolous game, but instead as responsible work that serves a social function. We had to make them understand that the dancer isn't just an individual who dances, but also someone who thinks while dancing. In this way I think we have arrived at a nationalistic approach to the arts, in which we take folklore and elevate it to a universal category.[19]

The Conjunto successfully married Cuban cultural experience with theatrical spectacle. In the 1962 documentary film, *Historia de un Ballet (Suite Yoruba)*, produced by the national film institute, ICAIC, director José Massip interweaves dance footage of "ordinary" Cubans with shots of the Conjunto. In Havana's *solares*, or tenements, residents are shown dancing for the *orishas*.

These stunning images of non-professional dancers are intercut with scenes of Guerra's troupe preparing for opening night of his fusion masterpiece, *Suite Yoruba.* The award-winning film illustrates how Guerra translated Afro-Cuban ritual into the compositional elegance of modern dance.

Historia de un Ballet (Suite Yoruba) 1962
Documentary Dance Film

A tiny girl moves in time to the trio of sacred batá *drums. Imitating the adults around her she steps from side to side, her shoulders punctuating the rhythm, her lips pursed in concentration. A wizened old man pounds the two-headed drum resting on his lap. He assesses the ritual unfolding around him: pairs of feet shuffling in unison, a dapper carpenter leading the chant for Elegguá, a rapt young woman lost in song. A mature woman in blue and white steps forward to dance Yemayá, the maternal goddess of the salt sea. Lowering herself onto the patio stones, she drops a coin in front of the drummers, then kisses each of the three drums. Standing, she holds her skirt in her hands, evoking the waves of the ocean as her footwork becomes increasingly complex. The women behind her mirror her swinging elbows, her swaying hips, but leave room for this seasoned dancer to work her subtle magic. Their hope is that the deity will join them, "mounting" this believer's receptive body.*

Backstage at the Teatro Nacional, a female soloist in golden robes prepares for the curtain to rise on the final dress rehearsal of Suite Yoruba. Crowned with a cross as Cuba's patron saint, the Virgen del Cobre, she is simultaneously the flirtatious freshwater goddess of love, Ochún. A shirtless young man dangles a cigarette from his lips as he lifts her onto the backs of three crouching male figures. She extends an exquisitely pointed foot high above her head, accompanied by the poetry of Nicolás Guillén: "Ochún has learned well the secrets of her savage libido." She smiles broadly as she teasingly encircles each of her cavaliers, embracing them briefly before she moves on.

Filmed from above, six women surround Yemayá. They spin around her in a counter-clockwise circle; Yemayá rotates clockwise, her steps swift, her gestures regal. Skirts swirling, the women genuflect and reach upward toward the camera. This unexpected angle gives the syncopated sequence a strange Busby Berkeley feel. Yemayá flashes her black eyes; her torso dissects the rhythm as she throws her head back. "It is important that we don't betray Yemayá, her color, her ostentation," intones the baritone voice. "It is important that we betray neither the waves nor the oars of Yemayá."

Changó, the lightning-thrower dressed in red and white, stomps furiously across the stage, his spine rippling in response to his thunderous steps. A diagonal line of lanky men follows in his wake, a visual trail of testosterone. The camera jumps to images of dancers in the studio stomping in the same linear pattern. Dressed in rehearsal clothes they pound the wooden floor until their bodies resonate, heads jerking and shoulders bouncing. The narrator asks, "Changó of the rehearsal studio, who makes the floors vibrate, how will you appear on the stage, Changó of the rehearsal studio?" Large plate glass windows reveal gardens and traffic outside the Teatro Nacional. The young Ramiro Guerra graces the screen: compact and confident, with a head full of dark hair. His body is coiled with energy, his sharp features focused in concentration. Guerra consults with the designer Eduardo Arrocha, nodding at sketches of elaborate costumes.

Cigarette break finished, the shirtless smoker has transformed into Oggún. Machete in hand, this fierce god of iron and war is the archenemy of Changó. The two figures clash on the stage, mingling balletic ballon *with spinal percussion. Oggún hovers in classical* relevé, *deftly turns in* attitude, *then assumes the equally classic stance of an African warrior. Changó flicks his hand high in the air, a pantomimic gesture signifying a bolt of lightning. The battle between Oggún and Changó dissolves in a dizzying whir of bodies, one rolling over the other, Oggún's grass skirt tumbling over Changó's head.*

Opening night. The camera turns to an elderly man sitting in the packed theater. "Like many in the audience, Andres is coming to the theater tonight for the first time in his life," the narrator explains. Elegant and attentive, Andres watches the battle between Oggún and Changó, though he knows the outcome of this famous wemilere, *or myth. The dueling orishas flash onto the screen as the narrator speaks of Andres, "grandson of Africa, grandson of a slave. How will his ancient eyes view this spectacle, where his venerated deities are the protagonists?"*

The question remains unanswered. The film leaves Andres behind, focusing instead on the tumult onstage, a crescendo of stylized aggression. The ensemble evokes a Greek chorus, or the acolytes of Martha Graham and Katherine Dunham, as they shield their faces from the fierce contest between the gods. Ultimately Oggún vanquishes Changó, as he does every time the story is told. The drums reach a peak, Changó exits in shame, and Oggún stands his ground. The film ends abruptly. No analysis, no deconstruction. Just the reverberating final beat of the drum.[20]

In *Suite Yoruba* Guerra crystallized the goals of the Conjunto with the material of *técnica cubana*. As his collaborator Elfreide Mahler explained, "It wasn't that Ramiro was the only one to synthesize modern [dance] and Afro-Cuban religious traditions, but that everyone felt that he did it right. You couldn't feel where the traditional left off and the contemporary began."[21]

Intentional Art — By Committee

The intentionality of *técnica cubana* is in itself quite rare. While art forms and stylistic movements, like Impressionism and Cubism, may find official government subsidies once they have established their place in the competitive world of commercial art, it is unusual for a government to sponsor a form before it truly exists.[22] In contrast, *técnica cubana* was created in order to fill a perceived need in a society accustomed to viewing and participating in dance. The idea of creating a dance form because one is needed is highly unusual if not unique in dance history. Because Cuba is highly attuned to dance as both a participatory and a spectator art, the creation of *técnica cubana* was a logical step in the cultural life of the island, as well as in the propaganda campaign of the new regime.

A significant factor in the creation of *técnica cubana* is that it was designed to incorporate the great range of Cuban movement intelligence, as opposed to expressing the artistic genius of a single individual. In the lore of modern dance, famous iconoclasts like Martha Graham and Isadora Duncan are revered for having rebelled against the institutions and academies of art to create their own ways of dancing. It could be said that Graham set out intentionally to create her own technique, while Duncan found her style, which is not a codified system but rather an approach. Neither artist created her dance form with state support (the Graham company, which ultimately became one of the most important modern dance companies in the world, has notoriously lost state funding even in recent years).[23] These dancers created their art outside and in reaction to the establishment long before they were accepted by the great institutions of culture, let alone the state.

Most modern dance styles and techniques were developed by, and thus associated with, a single individual. Duncan described sitting still for hours, searching for the spot from which her body initiated movement. She ultimately located this "crater of motor power" in the solar plexus, and founded her school on the spiritual theory she developed from that discovery.[24] In keeping with the idea of choreographer as auteur, Duncan went so far as to give some of her protégés her surname. Even today some Duncan dancers refer to themselves as "Isadorables." For her part, Martha Graham felt that life, energy, and movement came from deep in the pelvis. The powerful "contract and release" of the torso became synonymous with Graham technique and the way that radical choreographer expressed emotion through movement. Alvin Ailey culled exercises from Graham and Horton (another technique designed by and named for an individual) in order to train dancers in what became the Ailey style. Paul Taylor has an eponymous company and technique, as did Merce Cunningham. It could be argued that all of these techniques share basic structural and kinesthetic information that has been developed by academies, dance masters and performers over the centuries. Nevertheless, these forms are taught as distinct techniques bearing the names, artistic imprints and aesthetics of their progenitors. In contrast, *la técnica cubana*, though it enjoyed the leadership of Ramiro Guerra, was created by a group of people rather than by an individual. Here Guerra describes the group's conscious synthesis of movement principles:

> This technical base had two fundamental aspects: one, that it did not constitute a personal point of view beyond the modern dance, instead its technical material was an assimilation of principal tendencies in the modern techniques of the time. The techniques of Graham, Limón, Sokolow, Humphrey and others were included.... This gave us a solid foundation for the creation of new teachers. From that point, with an understanding and profound study of this course, we developed the actual technique of the *Conjunto*. We were thus able to resolve contradictions that had hindered our work in earlier years.[25]

Cuban modern dance is linked to its North American roots through the technical contributions of Martha Graham, Merce Cunningham and others. Like certain other contemporary dance styles enjoying increased visibility throughout the world, *técnica* has evolved its own signature, taking and leaving aspects of North American aesthetics and form.[26] Modern dance is often cited as one of the three art forms indigenous to the United States, the other two being jazz and musical comedy. (I would add hip-hop as a fourth art born in the U.S.) It is ironic, though unsurprising, that in the self-proclaimed birthplace of the art of modern dance, there is almost no knowledge of the powerful form *técnica cubana*.

Chapter 5

Cuban Dance Legacies

From the late fifteenth to the mid-nineteenth century, Cuban dance percolated with tremendously varied ingredients until it solidified culturally.... By the end of the nineteenth century, many different ethnic groups from both Europe and Africa had replaced Cuba's native populations, and most of these nations left their mark in terms of dance style and music-making traditions. — Yvonne Daniel[1]

Técnica's founders called upon their experience not only in modern dance, but in the many movement styles embodied in Guerra's motley group of dancers. Borrowing from eclectic sources, the young company created a national dance form designed to represent a highly diverse culture. Cuban tradition offered a complex and sophisticated dance trove from which to choose.

Ritual dance, *guajiro* [country] dances, cabaret, and classical ballet all contribute to Cuba's enormous cache of movement knowledge. In this equation racial and cultural diversity combine with "Cuban-ness" to create the broad range of Cuban dance. Within that range there is a quality of movement that is intangible yet recognizable. In his earliest forays into choreography, Ramiro Guerra began to look for ways to identify "how the Cuban body moved."[2] This concept of a Cuban way of moving is packed with implications. That a nation could house people who move in a certain way, a way that differs from how people move in another geographical location, suggests a pervasive influence on physicality coming from social mores, recreational activities, cultural practices, religious observance, climate, clothing, and myriad other factors.

In his book, *The Repeating Island*, Antonio Bénitez-Rojo plays with the idea of *de cierta manera* [in a certain way]. He uses the phrase to describe a particular feel, the "magical loam of civilizations that contributed to the formation of Caribbean culture,"[3] and the insistent presence of polyrhythms in everything Caribbean. This concept of going through life "in a certain way"

57

reflects back on the idea of *cu-
banísmo or cubanía*. Cubans get
profound aesthetic pleasure from
creating and consuming dance and
music. They can, and often do,
take sensuous pleasure in the constant presence of sun and sea, the
extreme heat and profuse life of the
island. Languor and vigor coexist
in every step. Cubans enjoy looking at each other, and being looked
at. They dress to be seen, not to
blend in. Despite great frustrations, politics and poverty, Cubans
are intensely social. They are well
educated, animated and creative.
Movement — from gesture to walking to dancing — reflects these
influences. It's almost as if there is
a song playing in everyone's head,
and although the songs are different, with varied tempi and
rhythms, the whole population
hears music as they move through
the day. Guerra describes this in
simple kinesthetic terms: "As a

Aleida Tamayo dancing the *orisha* Yemayá
with Los Pinos Nuevos, directed by Lazaro
Noriega Aguirre. Restaurante La Mina,
Calle Obispo, La Habana Vieja, May 1998.

young man in New York I was fascinated with the athletic way Americans
walk. We in Cuba seem to walk more sensuously, and both these styles are
translated into our dancing."[4]

In a country as diverse and large as the United States, one would be
reluctant to make generalizations about national ways of moving. We might
refer to an urban tempo, a Southern saunter, a no-nonsense New England
stride, but we'd be hard pressed to categorize regions by their movement styles.
In Cuba, however, it can be argued that there are elements of Cuban dance
tradition that have found their way into the national profile. Just as our social
and physical environments affect the ways in which we dance, dance affects
our physical approach to daily life.[5] Social dance is part of the structure of
social interaction. It is part of the education of the young, the recreation of
adults. It is physical education, and just as swimming, biking and soccer leave
their imprint on the body, so does dance. Gestures, manners, gait and posture
are all influenced by the experience of dancing.

The Conjunto Folklorico performing traditional *orisha* dances adapted for the stage. Teatro Mella, Havana, January 2000. The dancer in front depicts the deity Oyá.

Writing of the nineteenth century craze for social dance, Chasteen notes, "being Cuban meant dancing frequently, and in a distinctively Cuban way."[6] I contend that this has affected not only dance but pedestrian movement as well. Through dancing and being exposed to dance, people change the way they view and perceive the body. Our experience on the dance floor influences social mores, ideas of appropriate and inappropriate behavior, and styles of dress. On my first working trip to Cuba I was stunned to see young children dancing with bumps and grinds we might see on MTV, moving their hips in ways most North Americans would consider sensuous and therefore inappropriate. But those children were just practicing their salsa moves and learning folkloric dances. There was nothing lascivious about them. Historically, the lack of a puritanical presence on the island translates into less ambivalence about pleasure and the body. Cubans for the most part seem less troubled by sensual suggestiveness than many North Americans. Many a popular song incites the listener to *mueve la cintura* [move the waist]. The children I saw wiggling their hips were simply adding to their movement repertory, which includes the flowing undulations of the *orishas*, the complex arm tangles of *casino*, and the spatial trigonometry of *salsa rueda*. An anthropologist would describe this phenomenon in different terms than a kinesthesiologist, ethnomusicologist, or Laban movement analyst. In dance theory we might say they were assimilating the tropes of Cuban dance. In short, these children were learning how the Cuban body moves.

The Special Period: Havana 1992

The doors of José Martí airport slide open to reveal a steamy tropical morning. Outside, amid a crowd jostling for a glimpse of long lost relatives and potential taxi fares, I spot Narciso. He is thinner, weathered and ropey with muscle. He greets me as if welcoming me home, kissing me on the right cheek. I ask about his wife, Idalmis, and he holds his hands out in front of his stomach, grinning his goofy grin. "Está bien."

The air is different in Cuba, velvet, the atmosphere almost viscous. Flowers are everywhere. Blossoms dangle next to overflowing dumpsters. The heat is equatorial, an exotic cousin to the heavy haze that shrouds New York in summer. As we drive into town from the airport I revel in familiar sights: boxy Chevys, pastel houses with proud little columns, horse-drawn carts filled with bananas, children in their red school uniforms.

Company rehearsal for Medina's *Caverna Magica* in the tiny upstairs loft that once housed the Medina family (and the author), March 1998.

Narciso's home on Calle 8 is a broken-down building where, a plaque states, José Martí's mother once lived. A crumbling cast iron fence separates the tiny front yard from the sidewalk. A stone walkway leads into the house. On the right a garden grows wild; on the left a concrete slab covers an ancient water pump. Narciso teases me about my heavy luggage. I feel like a conspicuous consumer and consequently protest too much. In his letters he asked me to bring bits and pieces of costumes and stagecraft unavailable in Cuba; I quickly promise to produce useful items out of the depths of my leaden bags. We drag them down the walkway, up three steps to the patio, past the historic plaque and down a long dark corridor where a naked child eyes me with curiosity.

Idalmis greets me with a big smile and a bigger belly. She is very pregnant, insouciant as ever. A skinny little girl surveys me from the stairway. She wears a white shirt with a bandanna from the Pioneers — the Communist youth — tied around her neck. Her kinky hair is braided and adorned with barrettes. "You must be Dislaidys," I say. That's all it takes. This wiry seven-year-old clearly has no fear of strangers. She jumps off the stairs and kisses me — right cheek again. A little white dog runs in circles around my feet, blissfully hysterical.

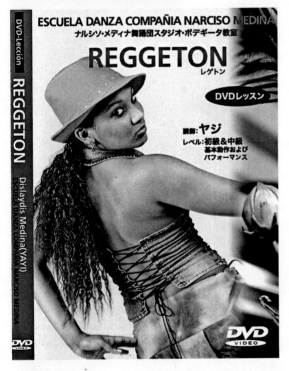

Top: Dislaidys Medina in her school uniform and Pioneer bandanna, 1992. **Bottom:** Dislaidys Medina on the cover of a Japanese Reggaetón DVD, Tokyo 2005 (photographs courtesy of Idalmis Medina).

"¡Lassie, basta!" Dislaidys has quite a yell. Lassie? Yes, Narciso confirms, Lassie.

When I look at the apartment they share with Dislaidys, I marvel that this family has invited me to stay with them. The tiny kitchen/living room/dining room has a small window that opens two feet away from the next building; a wooden door leads to the minuscule bathroom. A few ragged plants wilt above a small window seat. A narrow flight of steps leads to a second-floor loft Narciso constructed himself. The first room is draped with wet laundry. This is where I will sleep with Dislaidys. Idalmis and Narciso sleep in a small adjacent room with slatted wooden blinds that allow air to enter from the building corridor. The little apartment has no running water and the gas gets cut off constantly. Nevertheless, they seem undaunted by the prospect of sharing their limited space and rationed food with me.

Welcome to the "Special Period." The U.S. embargo is even more effective since the fall of the Soviet Union; the combined forces are squeezing Cuba's economy dry. The island nation tries to buy time with austerity and sacrifice, saving resources in the hope that something will change.

No more Soviet subsidies. No food, no gas, no paper. It's a world away from my visit in 1988 when my dad's friend, Alfredo, took me to Lenin Park and encouraged me to devour an entire roast chicken on my own, without napkins. That was the Golden Age. This is The Special Period. It's becoming a mantra.

Nevertheless, Narciso lives much better than most Cubans do. With the money he earns abroad he is able to purchase certain "luxury" items from the government, like his car, a Soviet Lada—a real sign of status in Havana. Narciso explains that it is illegal for Cubans to possess dollars. The law insists he trade the bulk of his hard currency for trade vouchers. He asks me to hold onto some of his contraband "fula." Seeing my confusion, Narciso laughs. "Fula is slang for dollars," he clarifies. "It's risky for me not to give the government all my fula, but...."

I don't want to reveal how hungry I am. As Dislaidys sits down to a snack, my eyes give me away. Idalmis hands me a small bowl of a root vegetable called boniato, sweet and starchy. Idalmis and Narciso don't join us. The dish barely scratches the surface of my traveler's appetite, but that's clearly all there is. Welcome to the hungry new Cuba. I wonder if one ever gets used to it.

Less than an hour after my arrival on Calle 8, Narciso and I backfire off to rehearsal in his funky Lada. We're headed to the Teatro Mella in the Vedado section of Havana. "Vedado is Havana and Havana is Cuba," Narciso says. He grunts when I ask if he's from Havana. He's "guajiro," which means he's from the countryside.

We drive through streets filled with ornate houses crumbling behind cast iron fences, boxy cars from the '50s, theater marquees, empty restaurants and women sauntering through the heat in Day-Glo Lycra. This urban landscape is mesmer-

izing. I spot a man on a bicycle with two passengers — one on the handlebars, another behind the seat. "No gas," shrugs Narciso in explanation.

At the theater I am introduced to Narciso's company in its current entirety, seven dancers full of questions I barely understand. They dress in colorful clothes that show off their buff bodies, young women with hair piled on top of their heads, guys with smooth chins, everyone fresh with flowery cologne. They speak rapid-fire Spanish, eating their consonants and gargling their vowels. Irma, pale, petite, and vivacious, has dark hair down to her hips. She's brought a plastic bin filled with homemade sweets, and gives each dancer a tiny treat made of rationed bread and hoarded sugar.

"They don't say hello to me," she brags. "They say, Irma, what did you bring for us to eat?" The other dancers nod appreciatively, savoring their goodies as if they were Belgian chocolates. The treat tastes like breaded caramel.

Now comes the real introduction. To my chagrin I realize I'm menstruating. Impeccable timing! I've left all of my carefully packed supplies back at the apartment. Although it's not what I had in mind, I am suddenly one of the girls, whispering pleas for help. Irma clearly enjoys the role of den mother. She takes me into an unlit loo without running water and hands me a wad of sterile cotton. The doors to the stalls don't close; clumps of sticky newspaper litter the floor. I am getting an idea of the conditions under which these artists live and perform. I tell Irma how grateful I am for her precious gift. "We don't have much," she says, "but we share what we have."

In this one day of travel from Miami to Havana, I've gone from English to Spanish, capitalism to communism, commercial overload to material lack, marginal modern dancer to welcome guest artist. Narciso says "trabajamos," let's work.

And so we do.

The *Orishas* Dance

Santeros today suggest that the *Orishas* of *Lucumí*[7] made the trip across the waters from Africa in the songs of their devotees... — Robert Stephens[8]

When Africans crossed the Atlantic in the bellies of the slave ships, they carried their deities with them. This act of faith was not accomplished with trinkets or texts; the gods were carried within the bodies of the believers. It was the muscle memory of dance and rhythm, the tonal memory of song, that constituted the bodily temple. In this way, just as an actor remembers a monologue he hasn't performed for years, or a dancer recreates choreography upon hearing familiar music, the essence of worship — and a vast movement knowledge — was preserved within the worshippers.

Ana Pérez of Los Muñequitos de Matanzas performing the *orisha* Ochún at a benefit for the Afro Latin Jazz Association, Metropolitan Pavilion in New York, May 18, 2011. Visible in the background are Sandy Pérez and Roman Diaz.

Four major African dance traditions have survived in Cuba: Yoruba, Kongo-Angolan, Arará, and Carabalí.[9] In a process consistent with Ortiz' theory of transculturation,[10] and Mintz and Price's theory of African-American culture as a whole,[11] the dances of Africa mingled and evolved in the new world, becoming something new, linked to tradition but separate in identity and practice. Scholars describe specific influences that brought heterogeneous African groups together in Cuba: the lack of critical numbers of worshippers, the confluence of distinct cults cohabitating in urban settings, and a desire to overcome differences in a foreign environment.[12]

> African retentive elements in Yoruba music and dance in Cuba are related to the fact that the Yoruba were among the last to arrive during the slave trade, sometime between 1820 and 1840.[13]

The late arrival of large numbers of Yoruba from modern Nigeria, Benin (formerly Dahomey) and Ghana, accounts in some part for the survival and hegemony of distinct Yoruban cultural elements. Because they were among the last to arrive, Yorubas survived the sugar boom in greater numbers than some other African peoples who had the misfortune to arrive earlier. Africans were classified into groups called *naciones* with distinctive names. "Originally there was no comprehensive term for all Yoruba subgroups. In Cuba those from the Yoruba subgroups mixed with those from West and Central Africa."[14] Although there were many Yoruba nations, they were combined into one *cabildo;* similarly there was one *cabildo* for the Carabalí nation.[15]

Descendants of the Yoruba and some of their neighbors became known as the *Lucumí* nation. The origin of the term *Lucumí* is unclear. Some scholars believe it came from the Yoruba greeting, *OLoKu Mí,* meaning "my friend."[16] Between 1850 and 1870, the slave population of Cuba became heavily *Lucumí.*[17] Members of the Yoruba tribe exerted a strong influence over the developing Afro-Cuban culture. When African traditions were syncretized, Yoruban names were often used for the deities for whom dance was an essential form of worship.[18] Spanish names and foot patterns also found their way into the dances of Afro-Cuba. Spanish *zapateo* was integrated into certain secular and ritual dances, most notably dances for the female *orishas* of water, Yemayá and Ochún.[19] On the eastern part of Cuba, especially in Santiago, clear French-Haitian influences can be identified as coming from Vodún and Gaga ritual, *contredanse* and *tumba francesa.*

Haiti, Brazil and Cuba are home to deities with clear Yoruban origins. The gods share certain characteristics but are manifest differently in each country. Their worship developed distinctly in these places, reflecting languages, working conditions, and a host of other diverse influences. Music and dance are the cornerstones of *orisha* worship, practiced under different names and conditions in Africa, Haiti, Brazil and Cuba. While the essence of the songs and dances associated with each deity persisted in the diaspora, daily challenges created a blurring of tradition. As more of the Yoruba arrived in the Caribbean, the practice of their worship was reinforced, even as it was swayed.

What we today call *Santería* includes components of Spanish Catholicism and Yoruban *orisha* worship. Author George Brandon notes the surprising inclusion of "Kardecan spiritism, which originated in France in the nineteenth century and became fashionable in both the Caribbean and South America."[20] Many African elements were syncretized with Catholic tradition, which is why each of the *orishas* in Cuba today corresponds to a Catholic saint. The same process may explain why the Turtle and Buffalo dances of the Rio Grande Pueblos in the American Southwest occur today during Christian holidays. Oppressed peoples have long survived by assimilating religious symbols of the dominant culture. Yet while indigenous and slave populations were forced into conversions and baptisms, they succeeded in integrating small and some-times surprising ritual elements of their original religions into local Catholic practice.[21]

Most *orishas* had devoted followers, or "children," in the Yoruba home-land. When believers reached the New World they didn't always have critical mass to maintain original forms of worship. Members of distinct African groups now found themselves mingling in urban proximity. They overlooked differences in practice in order to build larger congregations and unite in a foreign environment. People began to look for commonalities between *orishas* in order to continue practicing. Followers of Oggún, the war-making god of iron, would team up with followers of Changó, the lightning-throwing god of thunder. For this reason some *santeros*, as well as initiates, can be seen wear-ing the colored beads of four or five different *orishas*.[22]

In the microcosm of African-American worship that is the north coast of Cuba, we can see how varied African influences may have conjoined in the New World, creating new ritual forms that are African-American as opposed to purely African. Matanzas, a city east of Havana, has a deep-water port where large ships can easily dock; this aided both the importation of slaves and the export of sugar. Matanzas became a center of Afro-Cuban worship. *Santero*[23] practices differed, and continue to differ, between Havana and Matanzas (not to mention the eastern city Santiago de Cuba). Over time, *creyentes* [believers] merged separate traditions for reasons of practicality or necessity. Drummers would travel from one city to another, sharing drums and teaching each other rhythms from different African and Caribbean sources.[24]

Centuries of shared experience, improvisational exchanges, and everyday

Altar to Obatalá on the occasion of the end of a new *Santería* initiate's (*iyawo*) first year as a *santero* (*yaboraje*). It represents the first observation in a lifetime of annual anniversaries of the *santero*'s initiation. The other *orishas* are represented by the cloths below those of Obatalá. On the floor there are offerings to all the *orishas* including cake, fruit, cigars, merengues, and popcorn. At the front in the center are artifacts of communication (bells, maraca) and slices of coconut for use in divination. La Habana Vieja, March 1999.

expediency continue to have tangible effects on the rites of *Santería*. A living practice, the dances and songs celebrating the *orishas* continue to evolve.

Despite variations in practice, the principal goals and beliefs of *Santería* persist. Divine union is sought through *orisha* dancing. At its ecstatic height, the believer falls into a trance, dancing furiously, "ridden by the god."[25] The Yoruba pantheon is vast, and each divinity is said to enter the body of its acolytes and cause them to dance in a distinctive way. Each of the *orishas* has his or her specific colors, rhythms, gestures and dietary preferences. While some rhythms are traditionally associated with one particular deity, at times those rhythms may be played for other *orishas* as well. There is an element of pantomime to the dances, slightly abstracted but still recognizable. The gods' gestures evoke specific actions: cutting cane, fanning oneself, turning a key. Knowledge of these particulars is pervasive in contemporary Cuba. School-children sing songs in the Yoruba language honoring Changó, the god of lightning, and Yemayá, the goddess of the sea. Changó, the King, jabs the air, lightning-like, with one hand. Yemayá dances in a 2/4 against 3/4 rhythm, evoking the waves of the sea as she swirls her blue and white skirt hypnotically. Ochún moves sinuously as she mimes looking in a mirror and laughing, covering her body in honey. The gestures, footwork, torso isolations and rhythmic patterns of the *orisha* dances allude to specific legends, struggles and beliefs. These tropes are incorporated — literally taken into the body — synthesized, and passed down from one practitioner to the next, creating a treasure trove of movement knowledge.

Class in *técnica cubana*— Danza Contemporánea de Cuba — Havana 1992

The music is soul-shaking during técnica cubana *class: tobacco-flavored melodies and dense rhythms, traditional folk and country tunes, and the haunting songs of the* orishas. *The gods of* Santería *hold great sway over the Cuban soul. Despite official calls to materialism and atheism, they stand their spiritual ground. They demand tribute in song and dance, rum and cigars. Each deity has his own steps, her own colors, tunes and tempi. Ochún, the goddess of fertility and sweet waters, dresses in yellow, laughing as she performs her undulating steps. Oyá, the crone, swirls her arms violently above her head, summoning the winds of change.*

The orishas are serenaded in the language of the Yoruba. A jungle of percussion punctuates the strange words of that distant language. It's music that serves as incantation, relying on rhythm, not melody. It is the heartbeat of Cuban dance.

Most of the musicians wear the white clothes of the initiated. These santeros *seem untouchable, shrouded in mystery. The band's size and shape is constantly shifting. Unfamiliar musicians sit in with friends while others disappear for days at a time. I imagine them as victims of Havana's notorious transportation crisis: standing by the side of the road, instruments in hand. Usually one drummer will start the class; an hour later he'll be surrounded by percussionists, a flautist, and maybe a guitarist. Most days, the singer is a wiry old man whose white beret offsets his coal black skin. The band's infectious songs buoy and drive the dancing.*

We dancers slip into a state of active meditation: artistic and analytical, yet primal, on the verge of trance. Dripping sweat, we absorb the insistent beat into our bodies. Class becomes like church, or temple, or a bonfire in the countryside: a ritual that goes beyond mere steps and counts. The gravitational pull of these songs is undeniable. Waiting their turn to fly across the floor, many dancers lift their voices in the strange African tongue of the Yoruba, singing melodies they've known since childhood.

Rumba

> *Rumba* developed during the 1850s and 1860s in places where free blacks gathered to communicate their feelings or comment on their struggles and where enslaved Africans were permitted to congregate after work ... [they] expressed their frustrations, as well as their joys, through dance and music.— Yvonne Daniel[26]

Cuban *rumba*—which is about as distinct from ballroom rumba as it could be — evolved as a disguised form of protest among African slaves. *Rumba* dance and music reflect African influences that evolved and melded in urban *solares*, housing centers where large numbers of Afro-Cubans lived. *Capoeira* and *samba* developed in much the same way among the hillside slums and runaway slave settlements of Brazil.

The many variations of *rumba*, which are primarily secular, are understood to be part of a group of dances known as the *"rumba* complex."[27] The

Rumba aficionados join in at a weekly event known as *La Peña del Ambia* held at UNEAC (*Unión Nacional de Escritores y Artistas de Cuba* [the National Union of Cuban Writers and Artists]), an important organization and meeting place in the world of Cuban culture. Marta Galarraga is dancing with Eloy "*El Ambia*" Machado, a poet and well known personality. The man seen in profile behind Marta is the late Harold Williams Hernández Estrada, often known simply as Harold Williams. Vedado, January 1995.

Grupo AfroCuba de Matanzas, professional *rumberos*, performing at Teatro Miramar, Miramar, February 1995. From left: Dolores Pérez Herrera, Ramón "Sandy" Garcia, and Enrique Mesa Céspedes (1942–1997).

rumba complex includes improvisational solo dances within many different forms, where the most virtuosic and humorous performers are often men. As in many West African dance forms, *rumba columbia* includes highly competitive and martial examples. *Guaguancó,* a playfully suggestive male-female dance, provides easy entertainment for Cubans teaching *rumba* to foreigners.

Party at Irma's Apartment, Centro Havana 1992

Unable to even pronounce the word guaguancó, *I am dragged onto the dance floor by Narciso's soloist, the insouciant enfant-terrible Cándido Muñoz. Trying desperately to keep up with his rollicking steps and gyrating knees, I am shocked when he aims a salacious jab directly toward my crotch. To the riotous derision of Narciso's dancers, I have cluelessly failed to protect my dignity. Several dancers yell that I should know better! The woman is expected to quickly close her knees and bat the man's hand away, without showing dismay or losing the beat. Cándido laughs uproariously at his triumph. I accept defeat, determined not to be humiliated again.*

The stance used in *rumba* combines the elongated Spanish torso with African flexed posture: the body inclined forward from the hips, knees bent.[28] In this way even the alignment of the *rumba* dancer was synthesized to differ from the posture of the traditional African dancer. Despite the social and secular bent of *rumba*, there are instances where the danced elements of *orisha* worship have been included. This can happen unintentionally, when dancers participate in many forms of dance, or intentionally, when dancers allude to other styles while performing *rumba*. A mixed version of *rumba*, which acknowledges *Santería* influences, is called *batarumba*. This form combines chants, rhythms and pantomimic gestures from Yoruba *orisha* dances with the racy jabs of *guaguancó*, and the twisting, turning, hand-held partnering of *casino.*[29]

The Afro-Cuban dance canon is a gold mine of historical references, physical skill and rhythmic versatility. The range of movement styles that it encompasses, and their influence on other dance forms, is enormous. Dance elements from many of these rich sources are quoted, reflected, or subtly referenced in *técnica cubana.*

Trans-Atlantic Dance Influences

"Something new and powerful happened when couple dancing met the liberation of the lower body to create the *dance-of-two.*"[30] — John Charles Chasteen

From colonial times onward, key elements of style and behavior were passed back and forth across the Atlantic, effecting change in both the New World and the Old. Fashions in clothing, cuisine, and language were shaken and stirred, transforming dance in the process. Transcultural shifts occurred across racial and socio-economic lines. European and African dance traditions mingled to produce what is known as the Trans-Atlantic dance tradition, the progenitor of *danzón, tango* and *salsa.*

Dances of the street found their way to the ballrooms and salons of Europe, only to come back to the Americas transformed. Many African peoples were accustomed to dance etiquette that eschewed physical contact between the sexes. In traditional African settings the embrace of two dancers face to face — European dance position — was considered unseemly. But the New World was not the Old, and traditional patterns were broken down as peoples and customs intermingled. Colonists and sailors imported European partner dances to the islands, where stiffly formal postures were relaxed and embellished. Often these dances acquired a pronounced shift from hip to hip, a fluidity in the pelvis that incited scandal and delight when danced in Europe.

Some historians attribute lateral hip movement to West African sources, others attribute it to traditional Spanish dance.[31] Breaking the upright line of the body, this emphasis on the hips was called *quebrar* [to break] and it often resulted in a freer, more sinuous torso. In Cuba, this popular torso ripple was named for the snakes it evoked: *culebreo*.[32] Inevitably dances that emerged in the Americas and traveled back to Europe were considered salacious. Occasionally they would be banned. In keeping with tradition, whether it was grinding or the twist, the *sarabande* in sixteenth-century Spain or the Bacchic dances of ancient Greece, banning a dance only made it more popular.

In the colonies, European court dance had a strong and subversive influence. On plantations across the Americas, slaves would watch and imitate the dances of wealthy slaveholders, who themselves were often attempting to copy the dances of European aristocracy. Appropriated by the oppressed, these dances became exaggerated and satirical. While whites traveling through the antebellum South expressed "amazement (or was it envy?) at the dancing ability of the enslaved Africans,"[33] the irony of these imitations went unrecognized by the powerful. A good example of this subversive mimicry can be seen in the courtly dances of Eastern Cuba, including what is known as *tumba francesa*. French colonists fleeing the slave revolts of Haiti brought the roots of *tumba francesa* to Cuba in the late 18th Century. *Tumba francesa* includes performative aspects of African dance, a significant inclusion of courtly manners from both European courts and African royalty, and a healthy dose of parody where French couples-dancing is concerned. Folkloric groups specializing in these dances (such as the Cuban troupes Ban Rra Rra and Cutumba) can be seen performing quaint courtly formations reminiscent of *minuets* or *gavottes*, and complex sequences intertwining ribbons around huge maypoles. Rupturing the courtly allusions, Ban Rra Rra employs a sensational finale in which a woman twirling flaming wands in both hands stands on a table that four men lift into the air — with their teeth.

Historically, the most important public dances took place during Catholic holidays, even as the dances themselves were African in style and origin. *Cabildos*, so central to Afro-Cuban life until the twentieth century, regularly staged dances and prepared celebrations. Epiphany was known as a time for raucous excess, when enslaved peoples could practice drumming and dances that were often suppressed and periodically banned. Recurring prohibitions from the eighteenth and nineteenth centuries limited dancing and drumming to only a few hours on Sunday; however slaves were given Kings Day off, when the *cabildos* converged in joyous cacophony. Kings Day provided an accepted outlet for subversive and outsized creativity. Guerra describes seeing travesty dancers during his youth, including a cross-dressing father and son who proudly performed during the carnival atmosphere of *día de los reyes* [Kings

Day].[34] Each January 6, huge crowds took to the streets, with enslaved peoples of the neo-African nations crowning a king, or sometimes a queen, of their own. Within the context of Catholic celebration, members of the *cabildos* gathered to dance and drum, to dress outrageously, satirizing Europeans and wealthy Creoles. With feathers and beads, flashes of mirror, painted faces and royal regalia, they danced their national dances on the street in the biggest celebration of the year. The spectacle was described admiringly by several local publications, attended and appreciated by citizens of all stripes, and attracted a fair amount of tourists.[35] But by 1887 official tolerance for the exuberance of Epiphany had eroded, coinciding with the abolition of slavery. African dance influences, long nurtured by the *cabildos*, made their way into mainstream Cuban dance, and thus the culture at large.

Spanish art forms, already inflected on the Iberian Peninsula with Arab, Indian and African elements, found new life in the Americas. Social and courtship dances of Spanish origin transformed as they added postural, gestural and rhythmic elements from both sides of the Atlantic. Practitioners may not have been aware of the sources of new steps and spatial patterns, but just as Castilian speech transformed into new dialects in the New World, so were dances reconfigured and reinvented.

Dance historian Ninotchka Bennahum cites Hindu, Muslim, Catholic and Sephardic Jewish influence on the Gypsies who developed flamenco in Andalucia. She sees a classical influence from European *danse d'ecole,* on the "upper body carriage in flamenco, the erect spine, the torque in the middle back, the proud, elegant forced extension of the chest and diaphragm outwards, into space."[36] Flamenco's complex footwork, *taconeo* or *zapateo,* is infused with percussive rhythms contrasted by delicate intricacy of the arms and hands snaking around the torso. These elements may have found their way into flamenco from the Kathak dances of India.[37] Settlers of Andalusian origin brought versions of flamenco to the New World. Other Spanish tropes made their way into Cuban social dance, including the give and take of partner dances like *Sevillanas,* and the liveliness of folk dances like the *Jota.* There was also the aforementioned Spanish hip emphasis. That hip action became decidedly more lateral and pronounced in Cuban dance over time.

In rural areas of Cuba one can still see a percussive form directly linked to flamenco: *chancletas,* which literally means sandals. Some Afro-Cuban folklore groups perform *chancletas,* which features *zapateo* danced in floppy sandals. While the upper body carriage in *chancletas* borrows little of the stylized torso of flamenco, the footwork is a direct descendant. This surprising hybrid, showcasing rhythmic sophistication with upper body ease, is taught alongside classical flamenco in Cuban dance academies. *Chancletas,* like other Cuban dances, expresses transculturation through the realm of movement.

What is known as *contradanza cubana, danza cubana* or *danza* is "a far cry from contredanse, originated by the English, disseminated by the French, and imported to Cuba by the Spanish in the late 1700s."[38] In the Cuban version, courtly music was interpreted by black musicians and syncopated, which once again invited lateral movement of the hips. It is my belief, and that of other dance scholars,[39] that Cuban national identity emerged thanks in large part to a national fervor for dancing. In the mid-nineteenth century many elite Habaneros danced in ways that were considered transgressive. Some danced in styles that were overtly sensual, and perhaps more provocatively, many crossed racial and class boundaries. These questionable practices involved taking inspiration from the dances of the *cabildos,* the use of *danza* rhythms that blacks played on drums, and of course, close physical contact between dancers. This truly Cuban way of moving, *danza,* had style, danger, and *sabor* [flavor]. During the struggle for Cuban independence in the 1860s, Creole elites wanted to differentiate themselves from Spanish loyalists. Despite their original hesitations, upper class Cuban nationals began to celebrate African-inflected social dances — though not, of course, religious dances. These social dances, part of the Trans-Atlantic dance tradition, usually took the form of flirtatious dances for couples, the predecessors to *danzón, salsa, mambo* and *cha-cha-cha.* Their popularity signaled a break from traditional Spanish dance forms, heralding a New World identity that embodied African influences within a transgressive gumbo of movement ingredients.

Elements of social dance, Afro-Cuban folklore and theater dance find their way into Cuban cabaret dancing. Part Moulin Rouge, part *rumba,* the aesthetic of the famed Tropicana nightclub has filtered its way into the Cuban zeitgeist. The pinnacle of this form can still be seen at the Tropicana, which after a short stint catering to Cuban nationals after the Revolution is once again a tourist magnet in Havana. Guerra admiringly describes the work of Roderico Neyra (Rodney) who began synthesizing this particular combination of high heels, outsized headdresses and hip rotation in the 1950s:

> This choreography was the first to put onstage the batá drums and stylized movement of the African dances, acclimated in Cuba, in the heat of religious syncretism known as *Santería.* Dancers, men and women, whites, blacks and mulattos, displayed in Rodney's productions a strong and erotically expressive style.... [Productions] include a high level of technique and professionalism displayed as much through skill in dancing as in scenic design, theatrical resources, costumes, music, lighting — stagecraft which amplifies the effect of these splendid bodies in movement.[40]

While Afro-Cuban and contemporary dance elements were included consciously in the creation of *técnica cubana,* the cabaret dancers who collaborated with Guerra most certainly brought a sense of showmanship to the mix. A bit of that outrageousness surfaces in the otherwise sincere and earthy form, connecting the grounded modern dance style to another part of its heritage — the exuberant kitschy excess of the *día de los reyes*. You can see this connection also in the conspicuous lack of modest costumes; Cuban dancers frequently wear revealing and sensational outfits onstage and off. Cuban contemporary dancers, while serious and focused on their art, indulge in competitive flash, jumping higher, splitting their legs faster, and doing more multiple turns than their peers — inventing pyrotechnical trademark steps that reveal a bit of the floorshow spirit that forms part of their legacy.

Dance, always central to Cuban culture, transformed as the country grew and changed. Music and movement sources from Asia, Europe and Africa bloomed in the Caribbean heat, bursting with hothouse hybrids. *Técnica cubana,* a fortunate progeny, provided fertile ground for the intertwined dance legacies of Cuba.

Chapter 6

Cuban Ballet: Soviet Import or Sovereign School of Art?

"Los cubanos son los nuevos rusos del ballet..." [In ballet, Cubans are the new Russians] — Isis Worth[1]

The formidable technique of Cuban ballet is a major ingredient in the training of dancers in *técnica cubana*. Cuban ballet, with its unlikely predominance and stellar accomplishments, exerts as strong an influence on contemporary Cuban dance as Afro-Cuban tradition.

Many observers — in the dance world and beyond — presume that Cuban ballet is just a Latin mirror of the Soviet art form, a reflection of Cuba's longtime political and economic dependence on the USSR.[2] In the mainstream press, casual conversations, and travel journals, it is not unusual to encounter statements like this one from a blog about Cuba: "How remarkable that this supposedly nationalistic revolution has replaced Cuban folk music and dance with the elite Soviet sport of ballet!"[3]

The implication here is that Cuba inherited its ballet tradition from the Soviets, along with modular architecture and a fleet of rusting Ladas. But the truth, inevitably, is more complicated. Cuban ballet is very much the product of its own school and style, linked in its formation and future to both Soviet influence and North American pressure, rooted in European tradition and creolized on Cuban soil ... in other words ballet is an art form as Cuban as *rumba* or *danzón*.

La Reina Alicia

Today, Cuban dancers perform with major ballet companies around the world. Their artistry is testament to the strength of the Cuban school of ballet.

(Note: the word "school" is used here to connote a comprehensive system of training and a clear artistic perspective, not just an institution or style of dance.) The school that educated these artists, and the company that nurtured their talents, owe their existence to the lifework and legacy of Cuba's *prima ballerina assoluta*, Alicia Alonso. The indomitable artistic director and *raison d'etre* of the Cuban National Ballet, Alicia Alonso, built the Cuban school in collaboration with her former husband and brother-in-law, Fernando and Alberto Alonso respectively. Alicia Alonso is as dominant in Cuban ballet as Fidel Castro long was in Cuban politics. Her prominence and power are absolute and unprecedented, her image is iconographic, and despite training countless acolytes she has no heir apparent.

The seeds of Cuban ballet were planted long before the Revolution. Born in Havana in 1920, Alicia Ernestina de la Caridad del Cobre Martínez Hoya, whose nickname was Unga,[4] began her studies in the 1930s at the Sociedad Pro-Arte Musical de la Habana, where she met Alberto and Fernando Alonso. Alicia (as she is known throughout Cuba) became engaged to Fernando and

Caridad Martinez (standing), founder of the Ballet Teatro de la Habana and former principal dancer with the Ballet Nacional de Cuba. Here she participates in an event on Cuban ballet held at the Bildner Center for Western Hemisphere Studies, Graduate Center, City University of New York, February 4, 2011. Also visible (from left to right) Ana Maria Hernández (LaGuardia Community College), Octavio Roca, author of Cuban Ballet, and Mauricio Font, director of the Bildner Center.

went to New York, where she debuted on Broadway in 1938. Fernando and Alberto soon followed, studying with many of the great international ballet teachers then residing in the city. Alicia went on to earn her place on the world stage as one of the major ballerinas of her time. She danced with Ballet Caravan, the predecessor of Balanchine's New York City Ballet, and with Ballet Theatre, now American Ballet Theatre (ABT). Alicia worked with the major ballet choreographers of the twentieth century: George Balanchine, Léonide Massine, Agnes de Mille, Antony Tudor, Jerome Robbins and Bronislava Nijinska. She originated the lead roles in Tudor's *Undertow* and *Fall River Legend*, and most famously, in Balanchine's devilishly difficult *Theme and Variations*.

After studying and performing abroad, the Alonsos parlayed their extensive experience into developing Cuban ballet. They founded their Cuban company in 1948, and began a school in 1950. Miguel Cabrera, the official historian of the Cuban Ballet, writes in his *Ballet Nacional de Cuba: Medio Siglo de Gloria* [Half Century of Glory]:

> [In 1948] in the old Teatro Auditorio de La Habana, this artistic group was born, the first of its kind in the history of the country, with the name Ballet Alicia Alonso, its principal founder and most luminous ballerina, who along with the brothers Fernando and Alberto Alonso, and with the progressive and valiant collaboration of the Ballet School of the Society Pro-Arte Musical of Havana, and a group of dancers from Ballet Theater in New York, gave themselves the job of taking the art of ballet from its traditional elitism, and developed it into what it is today, to make it accessible to all sections of the populace, and to orient it toward a new path.[5]

Alonso was a ballerina at the height of her fame when Castro's guerrillas rolled into Havana. She could have worked anywhere in the world as a performer or teacher. But Alicia's priority was clear: she stayed in Cuba and built a ballet empire.

Ballet and Revolution

It is both unlikely and momentous that ballet, a quintessentially aristocratic entertainment, should survive the social and economic upheaval of revolution. Nevertheless, ballet has been remarkably resilient, enduring the revolutionary regimes of France, Russia, China and Cuba.[6] By the time of the Russian Revolution, ballet was considered an elitist art form, in danger of extinction. The great Imperial Ballet's transition to the Soviet system was anything but smooth, fraught with ideological and material struggles. Yet, in order to keep dancing, the czar's servants — as ballet dancers were consid-

Fidel Castro and Alicia Alonso at the event "*Imagen de una Plenitud Gala Homenaje a Alicia Alonso por el septuagésimo aniversario de su debut escénico en la danza*" (which loosely translates to: "The Image of Achievement Gala Tribute to Alicia Alonso on the 70th anniversary of her stage debut in dance"), at the Sala García Lorca, Gran Teatro de La Habana, December 29, 2001.

ered — transformed themselves into servants of the proletariat. They danced through the first Soviet winter of 1917–1918 without heat, performing without pay. In this way they expanded their loyal following — and their political usefulness. Anatoli Lunacharsky, the first People's Commissar for Enlightenment, helped to convince the Soviet Politburo of the economic inexpediency of closing the Bolshoi Theater.[7] In this way he justified continued upkeep of the great tradition. Ballet would become an emblem of Soviet, rather than czarist, Russia.

After the October Revolution, audiences for ballet began to change. In 1918 a St. Petersburg critic wrote, "The new audience, the masses who flocked to the ballet … took a definite stand: It valued the ballet and chose it as an accessible art."[8] In what might be seen as a playbook for Revolutionary Cuba, ballet found defenders in both Communist leadership and popular opinion: "The Bolshevik encouragement of the arts came from [a] theoretical basis, but also from the need to fulfill certain practical tasks in the realms of education, agitation, propaganda, and publicity."[9]

The idea that the arts could be central to the proletariat, not just to artists and intellectuals, fit with certain interpretations of Marxist theory. In both the USSR and Cuba, this meant including the arts as one of many resources to be distributed more equally. By popularizing a formerly inaccessible luxury, the Soviets reminded the population of their largesse. The same would later be true in Cuba. Soviet ballet also provided an additional, if unusual, medium for spreading communist doctrine; agit-prop is the basis of such stage works such as *Spartacus, The Golden Age,* and *Maiden's Tower.*

Castro and Alicia, the de facto Queen of Cuba

Whether the traditionally aristocratic form of ballet had a place within revolutionary society was a hotly debated topic after Russia's 1917 Revolution. There is no record of such a public debate in Revolutionary Cuba, quite possibly because the USSR had already shown that ballet could make itself useful. Shortly after taking power, Castro spoke privately to Fernando Alonso. In this midnight meeting the "Comandante" offered twice the $100,000 Fernando calculated was needed to operate what was then known as the Ballet Alicia Alonso. Alicia had previously made a public refusal of support from the dictatorial regime of Fulgencio Batista; her association with the communist regime that replaced him would become even more notorious. With the support of the Revolutionary government, the Alonsos transformed their private Escuela Nacional de Ballet Alicia Alonso into a state-sponsored institution, La Escuela Provincial de Ballet de La Habana. Fidel Castro became something of a balletomane, attending ballet festival premieres well into his eighties, according to the leader of the National Assembly, Ricardo Alarcón.[10]

The marriage made in Havana — ballet and revolution — was quite successful. "To match its funding, the company also had a revolutionary zeal. With the same passion Alicia rejected Batista, she embraced Fidel."[11] Although the classics remained most popular, as they did in the USSR, the repertoire came to include examples of Revolutionary agit-prop. Most notable was a piece called *La Avanzada,* in which Alicia appeared dressed in military fatigues. Azari Plesitski, the Russian choreographer of the work, partnered Alicia as El Comandante, the name by which the elder Castro brother was universally known. Although the dance fell out of the repertoire — after being performed in the countryside, factories and schools — its symbolism could not have been clearer.

Despite strong precedents in the USSR, the motives for Fidel and Alicia's powerful and lasting collaboration are most certainly their own. After the Revolution, Alicia could have worked anywhere in the world. In fact, she continues to tour and work internationally into her tenth decade. In light of the economic realities of dance, Alicia's accomplishments on the island would arguably have been impossible in a culture less attuned to dance and without the enthusiastic support of the government. The Revolution has given Alicia financial, public, and moral support. For his part, Castro gambled on the

Miguel Cabrera, historian of the Cuban National Ballet, standing on the balcony of the company's large studio overlooking Calzada street, November 2001.

Viengsay Valdés rehearsing Odile, the Black Swan, in the downstairs studio of the Ballet Nacional, May 2002. Viengsay means "victory" in Laotian; Valdés's father was the Cuban ambassador to Laos when the ballerina was a baby. Valdés is now the prima ballerina of the BNC, a great stylist and stellar technician with a loyal Cuban following and admirers abroad.

popular appeal of a traditionally elitist European art form, spearheaded by a genuine Cuban superstar. Although at the time of the Revolution most working class Cubans had probably not seen Alicia onstage, they knew who she was: a world-class artist, proudly Cuban, who brought her cachet to the nascent regime she openly supported. By supporting the ballet, the regime was strengthening the peoples' sense of national identity and culture. Castro and the Alonsos united in making ballet accessible to audiences and potential students; they also re-branded ballet as a truly Cuban product that Cubans could be proud of. It could be argued that Cuba has appropriated and outmaneuvered the hegemonic U.S. and USSR at their own games — baseball and ballet.[12]

There have been a few other examples of agit-prop choreography beyond Alicia's foray in fatigues. But for the most part the Revolutionary impulse has been expressed through state support for dance education and a concerted effort to bring ballet to the masses. "The government declared that ballet was 'one of the most elevated and beautiful manifestations and that it would strive to make it available to all social classes, preferably to workers and other popular sectors.'"[13] The Ballet Nacional de Cuba (BNC) made extensive tours of the provinces, performing on makeshift stages in cane fields and cigar factories. Most Cubans are familiar not only with the name of Alicia Alonso, but with her famous rendition of *Giselle*, which is shown regularly on the state-run television stations. Tickets to the ornate Gran Teatro de la Habana are priced low enough that Cuba's numerous ballet fanatics can afford them. The bi-annual Ballet Festival of Havana,

Alicia Alonso onstage at the Gran Teatro de la Habana, December 29, 2001, performing a solo at the gala marking 70 years since her stage debut.

and the regular Havana season of the Ballet Nacional, routinely sell out. Ballet has become an art form loved and appreciated by the average Cuban.

Everyone's a Critic: Havana 1993

In Cuba of the Special Period, picking up hitchhikers is considered the duty of every revolutionary with a car and a thimbleful of gas. One night my legs are too tired to carry me up the steep hill to Narciso and Idalmis' house. For the most part it feels safer here in Havana than it does in New York, so I wait at the bottom of Paseo Avenue where I've seen others get a "botella," or a ride. A middle-aged guy in a tinny yellow sedan stops at the light. I stick my head in his open window and ask if he is headed up the hill. He nods. He has to reach his hand through the passenger window to open the door, squeezing the handle from the outside. Once I am in the car the questions begin. He tries to place my accent.

"Canadian? English? French? Italian?" The fact that I might be from the U.S. doesn't occur to him.

"No," I say, "I'm from New York." It's easier than trying to pronounce "esta-dounidense," while "American" is politically incorrect and geographically imprecise.

The driver is clearly surprised.

"Are you sightseeing?" he asks dubiously.

"No, I'm working."

"Working! In Cuba? Who do you work with?"

"Narciso Medina and Danza Contemporánea."

"Oh yes," he beams, "we have great dancers in Cuba."

"Are you in the arts?" I ask.

"No, no," he laughs, "I'm an engineer. But I am un fanático—*a fan*—*of the great Alicia."*

We talk about the iconic Alicia Alonso, her blindness, and her career.

"She has always done the best Mad Scene," the engineer says knowingly, referring to one of the great challenges for a ballerina, the climax of Giselle's *first act. His appreciation for our misunderstood art form is impressive, but I am learning that it is not unusual in Cuba. When we reach the top of Paseo, the engineer reaches through the window, opening my door from the outside.*

"Sigue bailando," *he says heartily.* Keep dancing!

First, a School

Upon close inspection it becomes clear that the Cuban school is not simply Soviet ballet in tropical clothing. The Cuban method of teaching ballet employs a systematic approach, reflecting the Alonsos' experience working with some of the great teachers and choreographers of their time: Balanchine, Fokine, Mordkin, Zanfretta, Vlamiridov, Muriel Stewart and Alexandra Fyodorova. "In the U.S. I had teachers from the Danish and English schools," Alicia wrote in her book, *Diálogo con la Danza,* "and one of my principal professors, Enrico Zanfretta, represented the old Italian school which is characterized by rapidity in the feet."[14]

Alicia, Fernando, and Alberto Alonso shared the conviction that they had to create a new system of pedagogy. They molded a method of ballet training that makes Cuban dancers noticeably different from ballet dancers elsewhere. The school was founded on what Alicia calls "my own taste that comes from our national heritage, our culture, our idiosyncrasy."[15] That taste translated into specific stylistic choices in the realm of classical ballet, choices that were filtered intentionally into the system of training dancers. Fernando Alonso codified aspects of Alicia's formidable skills into the technique: multiple turns, lingering balances, fast footwork, and what she has called "an accent directed up."[16]

Here Ms. Alonso writes of her experience as a young dancer:

> We were convinced that this was the moment to start our own school, the Academy of Ballet ... [with] Alberto as the choreographer, with Cuban themes and Cuban music and with our folklore. We used Cuban elements, enriching the world of our ballet technique and our artistry. Later, with the triumph of our Revolution, we were able to develop the technical part and the artistry.[17]

The Alonsos created the ballet curriculum for the National School of Art, la Escuela Nacional de Arte (La ENA), where generations of teachers and performers have been trained. "We studied the Italian school, which imparts excellent *batterie* [beats] and balance," Fernando Alonso explained to me during a 1996 interview in New York, "We were also greatly influenced by the Russian and French schools."[18] In *Diálogo con la Danza*, Alicia addresses the rise of the Cuban method of training, which later became institutionalized in an educational setting. She notes some of its essential influences, emphasizing the international roots of ballet:

> No school of ballet comes out of nowhere, but comes of others that have already existed. Ballet was so developed in Russia, and later the Soviet Union, that sometimes people think that ballet arose there, that it is a typically Russian art form.... But that is not the case. Ballet arose in Italy and from there passed to France. Afterwards the old [Imperial] Russian school arose, incorporating French, Italian and Danish elements....[19]

Alicia acknowledges a strong connection to the Imperial ballet school, predecessor to the Soviet school, stating that one of her "essential teachers was Alexandra Fyodorova ... an important connection to the old Russian school."[20] Of course another student of "old Russian" ballet, George Balanchine, had a great influence on Alicia when he created *Theme and Variations* on her. Loipa Araújo, a renowned Cuban ballerina who now acts as ballet mistress for the BNC and teaches internationally, adds "the newly-born American school" to the list of crucial pedagogical sources. This would include the quick and challenging footwork of Balanchine, as well as the clean, athletic style associated with American Ballet Theater. The results of this direct lineage were still apparent in 2004 when Cuban ballerina Lorna Feijóo danced Balanchine's *Ballo della Regina* with New York City Ballet. Her performance earned accolades from *The New York Times* critic Anna Kisselgoff for her clean rapid footwork, musicality, and understanding of the Balanchine style.[21]

Loipa Araújo, former principal and one of the "four jewels" of the Cuban Ballet, teaching ballet class at the Ballet Nacional de Cuba, March 25, 2004.

The Alonsos groomed young dancers to emulate the rigorous way Alicia approached interpretation of character. This resulted in individual performances of great strength by dancers who in no way mimicked Alicia's characterizations.[22] Beyond institutionalizing the predilections of the company's star, the National Ballet included aspects of Cuban culture in both the training of dancers and the development of repertoire. Traditional Cuban social dances are part of the syllabus, and pieces reflecting Cuba's rich mixed heritage have been commissioned over the years. While Afro-Cuban tropes are infinitely more apparent in folkloric dances such as *guaguancó* and the *orisha* dances of Santería, Cuban ballet reflects elements of national music and culture in subtle ways that contribute to the stylistic stamp of the Cuban school.

Given the long Soviet influence over Cuban politics, and the long Russian reign over the international ballet scene, it is understandable that some balletomanes and laymen outside Cuba assume that Cuban ballet is molded in the Russian image. But Cuban ballet professionals vehemently dispel this notion. As Fernando Alonso insisted, the Alonsos forged a new school drawing on diverse pedagogy and the strengths of the Cuban body, climate, musicality and "way of moving."

"Free of the obstacles that in the past interrupted their development, the company began a vertiginous climb," writes BNC historian Miguel Cabrera,

Lorna Feijóo, former principal dancer of the Ballet Nacional de Cuba, now principal dancer with Boston Ballet. She poses here on the roof of el Gran Teatro de La Habana, April 2001.

"elevating its quality, incorporating new works into the repertory, and forming new dancers."[23] Today the codified technique is taught in highly selective, tuition-free schools in all 14 of Cuba's provinces. After five years in the provincial schools, pre-professional students living west of Villa Clara continue their training at Havana's prestigious national school, La Escuela Nacional de Ballet de Cuba, directed by Ramona de Saa. Students living in the eastern part of the island (*oriente*) often finish their studies at the Ballet de Camaguey, where the same curriculum is taught. Academic classes take place in the morning, with the afternoon and evening filled with technique, partnering, variations, Cuban folklore, character dance, acting, modern dance and rehearsals. In this way students are prepared for the rigorous life of the ballet.

Ballet Nacional de Cuba, Havana 2006

I perch on a chair outside the artistic director's office in the stately Calle Calzada home of the national ballet company. Strains of piano music filter through the glass doors, Chopin, Bizet, Tchaikovsky. I make light conversation with Fara, Alicia's omniscient assistant. Though I have been here before I am inordinately nervous, wondering exactly how to conjugate verbs and ask questions. After a long wait, I am ushered into the inner sanctum. The grand dame Alicia sits in her cool and shady office, her head wrapped in a bright scarf, her face carefully made up. She wears dark glasses. I hesitate, unsure of whether or not to kiss her on the right cheek, as I do everyone else in Cuba. She smiles as her husband Pedro Simon announces me; she can't see me, but that is not revealed by her demeanor. I take her smile as a signal and kiss her cheek carefully.

Alicia has written a letter to President Bush calling for international artistic exchange. I have brought a letter of support for this initiative, signed by over 500 international artists and intellectuals. She takes the letter, without looking at it. Her husband hands me a statement she has written to the U.S.–Cuba Cultural Exchange. It reads: "I believe in dialogue, in understanding between all human beings of good will. And also in the strength of artistic creativity and individuality. A combatant who utilizes culture in his battle, and looks to the future, will never be dissuaded."[24] She signs the statement and pushes it across her desk. It seems significant that she has used the metaphor of battle, but then again she was La Avanzada, dressed in fatigues, dancing for the Revolution. Alicia speaks proudly of a recent audition, where thousands of children around Cuba vied for entry into the ballet academies. Competition is fierce. "Young people in Cuba know that ballet is a high career," she says, tapping manicured nails on her desk.

My audience is over. I thank her and back carefully out of the room.

Soviet Legacy

What Cuban ballet did unquestionably borrow from the USSR was the model for a school system designed to educate dancers of the highest caliber. The Soviet Union had built on the Imperial school, recruiting students from all backgrounds, basing admission on a stringent set of physical, musical, and qualitative standards. On admission to the school, students were provided with room and board, dance clothes and shoes, and an education in dance, drama, music and academics.[25] Alonso had visited the USSR in 1957 and 1958, before the Cuban Revolution, and toured the training facilities.[26] With the support of the Castro regime, the basic structure of the Soviet school was adopted and still operates in Cuba: a free and inclusive education for applicants who show the most promise. From grueling auditions and daily ballet classes to Stanislavski acting lessons and French language instruction, Cuban students are classically groomed for the world of dance. During our 2006 interview Alicia instructed me to visit the attractive new school building the BNC had opened on the Paseo del Prado; the airy facilities belied cutbacks facing the rest of Cuban society. She bragged that 4050 students had auditioned for pre-professional ballet schools across the country, among them 1,600 boys, proportionally a very high number.[27] As in the Soviet schools, students are professionally placed upon graduation. Seniors are told whether they will be accepted into the national company, the highly respected Ballet de Camaguey, into a smaller regional troupe, or steered into teaching. Not all dancers are happy with the placement they receive, but unlike dancers across the capitalist world, most students of the state arts academies can expect employment within their field upon graduation. Most dancers comply, accepting the position they are assigned with the understanding that they will receive a steady salary from the state, commensurate with their ongoing level of achievement.[28]

While Cuban dancers are likely to have several Russian, Romanian, or Hungarian teachers during their years of training, the aesthetic to which they aspire is very much molded in the image of the *maestra*, Alicia Alonso herself.

Men in Tights

In addition to analyzing Alicia's stylistic and technical gifts and building them into the pedagogy, Fernando Alonso also applied a strong focus to the development of the Cuban male dancer. The BNC gives big kudos as well to Ari Plisetsky, one of Alicia's long-time partners and a respected instructor in the school. Plisetsky's contribution was noted in *The New Yorker* in 2006:

If, today, Cuban men are standouts in international ballet — virile but dignified, athletic but elegant — that is probably due in some measure to Plisetsky.... He speaks of the Cubans with a special love. "Temperament, they have," he said. "Dynamism." They also have strong popular dance traditions, which beef up their ballet... "No one is so naturally gifted in dancing as the Cubans." [29]

Plisetsky's contribution, while celebrated by the Cubans, was taken by the North American press to mean that Cuban ballet is a Soviet offshoot. This coincides with the assumption that Cuban ballet must have been shaped — as opposed to improved — by Soviet forces. Dance journalist Gia Kourlas wrote in *The New York Times* that "Russian-born Azari Plisetsky, who joined the National Ballet of Cuba as Alicia Alonzo's [sic] partner in the '60s, is credited, by way of his teaching, with revitalizing ballet in Cuba."[30] This sweeping statement underestimates the enormous effort undertaken by the Cubans themselves. It can be read as evidence of the hegemonic assumption that "high" art must be imported to the Third World, even where exemplary practitioners of that art already exist.

In the following passage from *Dance Magazine,* author Lisa Rinehart is more specific. She attributes elements of the Cuban style to Plisetsky according to the master teacher's own assessment of his contribution. She writes that Plisetsky himself credits Fernando Alonso with "establishing the clean lines of the Cuban National Ballet School. But he is proud to acknowledge his own influence on the regal upper body carriage, port de bras, and the sense of 'soul' that defines many of the exciting dancers emerging from Cuba today (although certainly the Cubans brought plenty of their own soul to the table)."[31] As implied here, the collaboration between the Alonsos and Plisetsky resulted in a superior form of training, one that exemplifies the hybridity of ballet to which Alicia has referred. Miguel Cabrera, an historian who has devoted himself to studying the details of Cuban ballet, suggests that Plisetsky was both shaped by and helped to shape the Cuban school. Cabrera explained, via email:

Azari Plisetsky came in 1963, and although he graduated from the Bolshoi, he matured as an artist in Cuba. His teaching was important, but he worked assisting two Cuban maestros, Alicia and Fernando. He influenced his students with the virility of his dancing, his cleanliness as a partner, and as a male dancer with stronger technique than most men enjoyed at the time.[32]

Having often heard the charge that Cuban ballet was borrowed from the Soviets, Cabrera felt compelled to add: "But during his ten years of teaching in Cuba, Plisetsky never 'Sovieticized' the dancers here." Clearly the danger of becoming a lesser version of Russian ballet existed; Cuban artists resisted that danger intentionally. In fact, Alicia did not allow many of her students to travel to the USSR to study; in this way she hoped the company would avoid

"Russianizing," or adopting the strong mannerisms associated with the Russian style.[33] Cuban society from the '60s to the '90s was inundated with Soviet elements, from canned fish to visiting apparatchiks. The well developed sense of Cuban national identity — poeticized by José Martí and championed by Fidel Castro — chafed against imperial hegemony. Ballet was no exception.

The strength of Cuban male dancers has added to the parallels drawn between Russians and Cubans, but it is also a manifestation of Cuban social and dance traditions. Ramiro Guerra has observed that in Cuban dance "the man occupies a respectable place."[34] This differs significantly from the suspicion and stigma applied to *gringos* who dance. According to improvisational dance artist and scholar Nina Martin,

> As [North] Americans, we link our Protestant heritage as a country with a fear that if we let boys dance they may become homosexual. We also must look at the inequity of power. Even though a great many more girls than boys start to dance, in the end significant positions of power in the dance world are filled by men.[35]

In contrast, Cuban men from all walks of life dance in varied settings, often with high levels of skill, and Cuban women lead several successful companies. From popular dance in the clubs, to competitive *rumbas* in the park, to the worship dances of *Santería,* dance is integrated into the Cuban way of life. The high profile success of famous male dancers — and their ability to earn hard currency abroad — has helped erode gender stereotypes against ballet.

The increased visibility of men dancing onstage and on television throughout Cuba continues to change the landscape. Carlos Acosta, who dances with the Royal Ballet of London and American Ballet Theatre, has frequently noted that his father, a truck driver, forced the young breakdancer to go to ballet school in order to keep him off the street. Acosta maintains ties with the Cuban ballet, dancing and choreographing internationally while enjoying artistic carte blanche at home and a large income abroad. He is as much a success symbol as any ball player and remains hugely popular in his native Cuba today.

Pimienta

Just as the Russian dancers Rudolf Nureyev and Mikhail Baryshnikov brought the world's attention to ballet in the 1960s and '70s, José Manuel Carreño, Rolando Sarabia, Taras Dimitro and Carlos Acosta possess the appeal and virtuosity to reach beyond today's traditional ballet audience. Cuban male dancers are appreciated for their masculine demeanor and clear command of technique. José Carreño frequently partnered Susan Jaffe, former principal

Taras Dimitro, now a principal dancer with the San Francisco Ballet, shown here taking class with the Ballet Nacional de Cuba while he was still a member of that company, March 25, 2004. Behind him are other company members, and the viewing balcony of the BNC's large Calzada street studio.

dancer and current ballet mistress with American Ballet Theatre, in some of the ballet canon's most difficult roles. Carreño's calm attentiveness had a very positive effect on Jaffe's performance. When she first started dancing with Carreño at ABT, she felt she had finally found a *danseur noble* with whom she was absolutely comfortable onstage. She went to Artistic Director Kevin McKenzie and declared, "He's mine!!" explaining that she wanted to be partnered by Carreño whenever possible. Their collaboration allowed both Jaffe and Carreño to mature enormously as artists. When dancing together, Jaffe has said, "I trust José completely."[36]

At home as well as with major ballet companies abroad, Cuban *danseurs nobles* are appreciated for this characteristic attentiveness to their partners. This gracious chivalry is built into the training and philosophy of Cuban ballet, reflecting some of the principles expounded by Fernando Alonso's pedagogy. Alicia explains a basic attribute of the Cuban approach to duet work:

> In the [Cuban] *pas de deux*, there is a continuous connection, almost as if there was a conversation between the two. The tendency with other dancers is: he holds her, he lifts her, they turn. But you don't sense that they are dancing for each other, rather that they are dancing for the public.[37]

This distinction becomes clearer the more one watches Cuban ballet. While not all Cuban male dancers can be superstars, their careers are strengthened by the focus on partnering that is central to their training. This acquired chivalry prepares them to showcase the ballerina and to communicate with her physically, visually, and artistically. This way of working creates more convincing partnerships, and avoids the unfortunate trap of the male dancer looking like a forklift awaiting his variation.

Fernando Alonso's system grooms dancers for duet work that is not only more secure, but more heated. Cuban dancers are trained to indulge more fully in the romantic interchange that is the stuff of ballet. While there exists the danger of stereotypically branding Cuban dancers as "steamy," Cuban teachers bluntly encourage strong heterosexual connections that are cultivated onstage. Fernando and Alicia Alonso's daughter, Laura, runs her own company in Havana, Pro Danza, and frequently teaches ballet abroad. She explains the Cuban *pas de deux* in this way:

> Of course with Cuba there is a little dash of that Cuban *pimienta* [pepper], the personality of the country. We are also very careful that when the boy dances with the girl, he treats her like a gentleman or cavalier, and that is very Latin. He looks at her, he is very caring toward her, and she is a little flirtatious with him.[38]

The gender rituals enacted through the ballet thus carry more metaphorical impact. Rather than seeing two ideal examples of the species perform feats that make them seem superhuman, the audience revels in their humanity. The dancers' warmth and humor amplify their connection to each other, and enhances their kinesthetic connection to the viewer. These qualities are intentionally cultivated in Cuban ballet. Whereas some schools of ballet accentuate the distancing elements of geometric perfection, Cuban training emphasizes the accessible and the sensuous. The Cuban *pas de deux* brings the ballerina back to earth despite all her perfection. The audience is reminded that the creature being rotated on her pointes, lifted high and admired, is very much a woman.

Guerra describes ballet as "an effusive demonstration of artistic domestication, where sex is converted into a game of elegant eroticism."[39] The codification of this ritualized courtship helps to dispel uncertainties about men in dance. That is not to say that a career in dance was always an acceptable path for young men. Guerra recounts being teased and humiliated at the start of what became a legendary modern dance career.[40] He has described his early days as a male modern dancer as being quite difficult, an "*auto da fe* of homosexuality before the public ... in a false canon of insular machismo."[41]

In the context of a complex communistic reorganization of that machismo, it is unsurprising that the question of the man's role in Cuban dance recurs, albeit quietly. Riding on the image of macho cavalier and extreme athlete, male ballet dancers have enjoyed increased acceptance and popularity. Thanks in large part to the Alonsos, to Ramiro Guerra and his students, and to the matinee idols of Cuban ballet, this acceptance has increased markedly over the past half-century. It is especially true in the current economy. Stellar male dancers, always welcome in the dance world, wield almost unequalled earning power, fame and freedom to work abroad.

Special Period Humor

In the early 1990s when state salaries were almost worthless, most people who were able to work in the tourist trade for hard currency chose to do so, even people with advanced degrees. A joke that circulated at that time went along these lines: a Cuban man gets drunk at a bar and starts behaving badly. His wife is unable to quiet him and finally the bouncer grabs him. The man begins to yell, "But you can't throw me out, I'm a waiter at the Hotel Nacional!!" His wife steps in apologetically, "I'm sorry, my husband is a doctor, but he has delusions of grandeur."

Ba-dum-dum.

In Cuba today, the drunk might have righteously claimed to be a ballet dancer. If only he'd had the right physique....

Ballet and Cuban Contemporary: Separate, but Not Equal

Cuban ballet shares a long list of characteristics with Cuban modern dance. Chief among these is the dedication to a state-sponsored system of education that produces dancers of the highest caliber. Ballet is included in the curriculum of all dancers studying at the national schools of art. Modern dancers study classical ballet as well as Afro-Cuban folkloric dance, Cuban social dance, and straight Graham technique. In addition to these separate classes, elements of ballet technique are integrated into the practice of *técnica cubana* itself. The strong lower body foundation that characterizes ballet is paired with contemporary use of the torso, and African-inflected use of the arms and head. A simple ballet *tendú*— stretching the leg to point the foot on the floor — can be practiced in *técnica* with any number of upper body variations. The same is true for almost all of the movements associated with the ballet vocabulary.

Specific aspects of Cuban ballet have an enormous impact on the development of modern dancers. Practitioners of *técnica cubana* are known for their ability to do multiple turns, a celebrated aspect of Cuban ballet. These modern dancers also boast exhilarating jumps, as do their balletic counterparts, and a knack for balancing for extended periods of time. Their clean classical lines complement contemporary broken angles. The gilded legacy of Cuban ballet influences the most modern of Cuban choreography along with the most traditional performance of *Swan Lake*.

The predominance of Cuban ballet has both helped and hindered Cuban contemporary dance. From the perspective of building an audience, the familiarity of the ballet image has put Cuban modern dance at something of a disadvantage. Despite the fact that ballet was originally Eurocentric, it is now deeply imbedded in the Cuban *zeitgeist*; there will always be the idealized sylph in white, the recognizable story line, the romantic image with which contemporary dance will have to compete.

Chapter 7

La Técnica Cubana: Form and Function

The troupe that Guerra founded and ran for eleven years, now known as *Danza Contemporánea de Cuba,* travels internationally and domestically. As the national contemporary dance company, it continues to work out of the *Teatro Nacional* studios in the Plaza de la Revolución. Guerra's 1960 *Suite Yoruba* (the 1962 film version is discussed in chapter 4) remains a paradigm of the cultural and theatrical synthesis aspired to by the national company. Fidel Pajares, author and former member of Danza Contemporánea, sees *Suite Yoruba* as "a great choreographic inspiration, beyond the search or preoccupation with the ritual and folkloric elements which it incorporates."[1]

Eduardo Rivero, who went on to direct the *Teatro de la Danza* in Santiago de Cuba, choreographed *Súlkary, Danza's* signature piece. This work, from 1971, is a mixture of Afro-Cuban ritual and modern dance bravado, a striking application of *técnica cubana* used to express Cuban identity. *Súlkary* draws from Yoruba tradition to depict a "fertility rite and the consecration of a chosen one."[2] Melding movement of ancestral Africa and contemporary Cuba, *Súlkary* makes theater into sacrament, transcending ethnic Otherness to evoke the universal search for partnership and continuity.

New York, 2011

Danza Contemporánea toured the United States for the first time in 2011, introducing New York audiences to a mixed repertory that included Rivero's iconic work, Súlkary. *Some critics were underwhelmed. While the dancers of Danza Contemporánea were justly lauded, the choreography was dismissed as dated. For many decades Cuban dance artists have had almost no contact with North American dance, and only limited access to European, Asian, and Latin American*

Tomas Guilarte (airborne), Alain Morales and Arneis Rubio rehearsing the author's *Microwave Suite* on the 9th floor of the Teatro Nacional, May 1998.

dance. *Cubans have created work in a separate reality from the choreographic trends and experiments that now seem old hat to a sophisticated, international audience. It's unsurprising that dance critics, accustomed to seeing dance innovation from across the globe, would place* Súlkary *within a context that includes tanztheater, post-modernism, and myriad world dance forms. Unaware of the historical fusion of movement traditions embodied in this work, some critics referred dismissively to similarities they perceived with other companies. They cited similarly "exotic" dances of the Caribbean, the Cuban dancers' sexiness, and opined the traps of "national and ethnic identity"* [3] *encountered by companies such as Ballet Hispanico and the Alvin Ailey American Dance Theater. These comparisons may have more to do with the skin color and show-biz razzle of the dancers than with their repertory, which admittedly does not reflect the dancers' full artistic range.*

There is something endearingly guileless about the company's presentation; their love of dancing is infectious. As the worldly dance critic Robert Johnson aptly put it in The Star-Ledger:

> *Danza Contemporánea de Cuba seems sure to become one of those phenomena, like mojitos and cigars, for which the island nation is justly famous ... these dancers display a freshness and immediacy all their own.*
>
> *Their skill goes beyond the hard-earned technique that confers athletic power and versatility. These handsome movers know how to connect with an audience, and with one another. They have a warmth that puts them in the room with you.* [4]

The Compañía de la Danza Narciso Medina rehearses in their Calle 8 studio, January 1997. From front to back the couples shown dancing are Tomás Guilarte and Idalmis Arias, Ramón Ramos Alaya and Marlene Carbonell, Cándido Muñoz and Dayami Brito. In the background Marcos Portal, Miladys Pedroso, and visitors.

That basic accessibility is not for everyone. Or rather, it is. It's the kind of dancing that needs no explanation. It appeals to a natural kinesthetic empathy in the public; the dancer's unrestrained joy of movement becomes our own. We have trouble keeping our seats as we watch.

The heady days of Cuba's Revolutionary zeal left a bold imprint on dance. Some members of Danza's first U.S. audience appreciated that sense of specificity, a time code clearly stamped on artistic production. New York dance enthusiast Ilene Diamond explained: "Súlkary is very sculptural; every little movement is visible. The dancers' faces morph into bizarre African masks, an iconic derivation of painting and sculpture, via distinctly modern dance.... It evokes the rhythmic power of real ritual, intense and powerfully done. It does reflect the era in which it was made—the primal energy and sexual exploration of the early '70s. Yes, it IS dated—but who cares?"⁵

Sleeping Beauty *is dated as well; we call that a classic. One could argue that the signature works of Paul Taylor and Martha Graham are dated too, but we view them within the historicized context of "classic modern dance." In Cuba,* Súlkary *is one of a handful of classic modern dances that exemplify* técnica cubana. *Guerra's* Suite Yoruba, *Medina's* Metamorfosis, *and Marianela Boán's* Chorus Perpetuus *are also considered part of that canon.*

While Danza has followed the mandate to create a style and repertoire for its multi-cultural Cuban audience, it has also sought ways to develop and attract new choreographers. Most choreographers who travel to Cuba, myself included, pay their own way, as Cuban companies have no hard currency to bring them in. Despite these difficulties, Danza's 2011 U.S. tour included works by Cuban-American New Yorker Pedro Ruiz (a long-time member of Ballet Hispanico) and celebrated Swedish choreographer Mats Ek.

Regardless of its critical reception 40 years after being made, Súlkary *retains its formative place in the development of Danza and the* técnica cubana *it wields so forcefully.*

Hurdles and Disparities

To create a new idiom, Guerra invited Elena Noriega and Manuel Hiran of Mexico to combine their expertise and experience with that of North American expatriates Lorna Burdsall and Elfreda Mahler. They choreographed new works and restaged modern dance classics, training their dancers to have technical range and expressive versatility. Burdsall mounted works by Doris Humphrey, bringing a sense of history into the repertoire, while Mahler focused on building the dance program of the original Escuela Nacional de Arte [National School of Art] in Havana.

Guerra has referred to a philosophical dualism he embraced, the Occidental "know thyself" and the Eastern "we are all part of something greater.... The first being knowledge of the body and mind that, with the daily discipline of technique class, prepares the dancer to work in optimal condition.... The second perspective trains us, during long difficult sessions of physical labor, to nurture the humanity and patience necessary to the work of creating professionalism in the dancer."[6] With references to yoga and meditation (not nearly as ubiquitous in those days as they are today) the class was structured to include many aspects of physical and mental discipline.

Technique class is the daily foundation of a life in dance; Guerra and his colleagues knew that in creating a structure for technique class they were making the blueprint for training dancers. Today a *técnica cubana* class includes a center warm up, floor work and/or *barre*, complex center combinations and locomotion across the floor, all danced to a mix of *orisha* and traditional music, played live.

Despite the ultimate success of the program, Guerra has described a certain disconnect between the *Conjunto* and the newly formed national arts school Escuela Nacional de Arte (known as la ENA). Built on the site of the former Havana Country Club in the upscale Cubanacán neighborhood, this much-heralded arts center was designed by Cuban architect Ricardo Porro in

1965 and financed by the Revolutionary regime. "In the middle of this disparity of criteria, they created the School for Modern Dance at the Escuela Nacional de Arte de Cubanacán, and the lack of a unified point of view made it possible for this basic teaching center to fall into the hands of those from outside, those separate from the modern dance work we were doing in Cuba.... They trained dancers without knowing where they were going to end up. Meanwhile, those of us in the Conjunto had to train our own dancers concurrently with making our dances."[7]

These hurdles and disparities may explain to a certain extent why outsiders — not simply foreign nationals but those dancers not trained in Cuba — were brought in to augment the teaching staff at La ENA. This includes people such as the young dancer turned journalist Alma Guillermoprieto. Guillermoprieto, a Mexican national who danced in New York, has documented her year of teaching at the nascent Cubanacán in *Dancing With Cuba, a memoir of the Revolution*. Guillermoprieto, recruited by Mahler to teach the Merce Cunningham technique at La ENA in 1970, depicts her time in Cuba as overwhelmingly negative. Guillermoprieto describes herself as "completely unaware that I was inhabiting a poisoned, almost radioactive complex that the Revolution had declared to be contaminated from its origins."[8] Her unflattering descriptions of Mahler and Burdsall, teachers revered by generations of Cuban dancers, may in part be a result of Guillermoprieto's personal turmoil coinciding with growing pains at the teaching institution. It was also undoubtedly a very difficult period in Cuban history. In contrast author Yvonne Daniel, a former dancer with the Conjunto Folklórico, lauds Mahler, who went on to found and direct Danza Libre, a company in Guantanamo.[9] Though I never had the opportunity to meet her, I have worked with dancers who spoke of Mahler with affection and reverence.[10]

Daily Class: The Practice of *Técnica Cubana*

Over time *técnica* jelled into a strong, consistent system for training dancers. It became more and more demanding, producing dancers who turn, jump, contract, pitch, hinge, undulate and balance with uncanny ease. The result is a well-read, technically spectacular corps of dancers who fill the nation's companies.

Throughout the 1990s I was lucky enough to choreograph for Narciso Medina's company on several occasions. Through Narciso I was introduced to the directors of Danza, who invited me to set a piece on their company. Ultimately I was invited to choreograph for the Ballet Nacional as well. While in Cuba, I studied the *técnica cubana*, taking private or company class on a

Candido Muñoz and Ramón Ramos Alaya rehearsing the bench scene from Narciso Medina's *Los Ultimos Exitos del Fin del Siglo* [Greatest Hits of the End of the Century] at the company's Calle 8 studio, January 1997.

daily basis with the master teacher of Danza, Manolo Vasquez. The following description is based on personal observation and participation in the dance form that enchanted me and inspired this book.

Company class at Danza often begins with a free-standing center warm-up. The dancers start in parallel with feet touching, knees pulled tightly together, hands clasped behind the back, head down. The first exercises open from contraction in parallel into first position, with or without an upward arch of the chest, or high release as it is called in modern circles. From first position, the heels pull back into a parallel second position, at which point upper body movement or hamstring stretches may be added. Often there is a variation that includes sitting into one hip and extending the torso and arms in the opposite direction. The arms have a soft, bird-like quality, as opposed to the lifted-elbow mold familiar to ballet class. *Relevés*, head rolls, parallel *tendues* and ripples of the spine can all be inserted in parallel second position. From here the exercise may return to the beginning and repeat on the other side. After some work in parallel second, the legs are turned out to a classical second position. It is not unusual for a long sequence early in the warm-up to include *arabesques*, hip rolls, changes of weight, percussive drops to *plié*, and folkloric twists of the head and neck.

Many exercises are repeated in different rhythms, emphasizing contrasting

Danza Contemporánea de Cuba principal dancer Dulce Maria Vale Pumariega (left) and master teacher Manolo Vasquez backstage at the Teatro Nacional with the author (center) after the premiere of her *Microwave Suite*, May 1998.

dynamics. One of the identifying factors of a class in *técnica cubana* is the use of a musical ensemble. Several drummers, a singer and a flute or guitar player usually accompany company classes at Danza Contemporánea. The music ranges from country melodies to the *orisha* songs of *Santería*. This attention to musical detail marries the dancing to its Cuban roots. It transforms the movement both rhythmically and kinesthetically. Take, for example, one staple in the center warm up, a series called "Merce," named for Merce Cunningham, who developed the basis of this sequence. Beginning in parallel, the legs turn out suddenly to first position and the head and palms open upward. A high contraction rolls the spine and head inwards, turning the arms over in their sockets. Then the spine is unfurled into a diagonal straight back, legs in *plié*. From here a deep contraction in *plié* can lead to an extension of the leg in any direction, a low turn or a change of direction. The Merce is used as an introduction to other exercises, including at times the rapid *degagés à la Seconde* from first position associated with the Graham technique. When practiced to the rich syncopations of Cuban music, as opposed to a single piano or drumbeat, the exercises of both Graham and Cunningham take on a rich sensuousness that invites embellishment in the head, pelvis and torso.

While the work is clean and specific, the variations in dynamic and speed afforded by the rhythmic complexity of the music affect the feeling of the movement profoundly. Rib and head isolations, directly linked to Afro-Cuban dance elements, can be added. Flourishes of the hand, called *floreo* in Flamenco, elaborate certain *port de bras*, or arm movement.

While the warm-up follows a logical sequence incorporating ballet exercises such as *pliés, tendues, degagés, rond de jambes,* and *battements,* the sequences themselves are often long and filled with previously unmatched elements. These include: hip and head rolls, which are found in many techniques; drops of the elbow, ripples through the spine from base to head, straight out of Afro-Cuban movement; shifts to the knee and back to standing; falls to the knee or floor; turns in spiral, contraction, on the bottom or on the knee — all elements of modern dance. The spinal ripple, a sort of wave from the pelvis through the head, recurs throughout the *técnica cubana,* in warm-up exercises, during floor work or at the *barre,* and as part of full body extensions. *Ganchos,* literally "hooks," are adapted from Afro-Cuban dance, and provide a good example of an unusual shape and dynamic placed into the modern-ballet vocabulary of *técnica cubana.* To do a *gancho,* the dancer extends a leg, turned in, hip lifted, with the foot flexed and sickled, usually with the torso in a spiraled contraction. The head, used extensively in creating the torsioned and exotic shapes of *técnica cubana,* gestures toward the *gancho* leg, and at the same time twists slightly away.

A floor sequence may be included in the warm-up, often in the midst of an exercise that begins and ends standing. The floor work has a distinct Graham base, but includes more rippling flexibility in the spine and folkloric pecking and twisting motions of the head. It is not unusual to go from a Graham fourth position seated on the floor to a shoulder stand to a standing *relevé* balance.

Traveling work across the floor begins with turns and extensions, with the floor pattern often doubling back on itself in space. If the musicians play a familiar folk tune or *orisha* song, the dancers often join in singing as they wait to dance. Turns in classical *attitude* are frequently practiced with a high spiral of the upper body, while *piqué* turns are usually done in parallel with a contraction into the *passé* hip. If *piqué* turns are practiced turned out, it's not unusual for the dancer to go in and out of contraction in the course of one revolution in *plié, relevé,* or forced arch (*plie in relevé*).

Often the men will elaborate on the choreographed combinations, taking a standing turn to the floor, balancing on the tops of their feet, diving to their hands and sinking slowly to the floor, ricocheting back to standing, or springing into a huge second position split jump before walking off the floor. Cuban male dancers nurture their exceptional virtuosity with good-natured competition in class. While there is not a lot of attention paid to *petit allegro*, big jumps are a highlight of the technique. Leaps, Graham buffalo jumps, *tours en l'air*, barrel turns, and all sorts of air turns without names are followed by spectacular improvisation by some of the more pyrotechnical dancers at the end of class.

Company class in the *técnica cubana* usually ends with a low traveling step that is a variation on several *orisha* images, including that of the freshwater goddess, Ochún, observing herself in the mirror. These low stamping walks are followed by a rapid shaking of the rib cage as the dancer takes tiny steps in *plié*, vibrating from the tail bone through to the top of the head.

The *técnica cubana* includes a full set of floor exercises and a complete standing warmup holding onto the *barre*. Both of these additions are used as the ballet masters see fit. Manolo Vasquez, who has trained many of Cuba's finest dancers, invokes martial arts and yoga in his teaching. Other teachers refer more specifically to Afro-Cuban sources, to Graham or Cunningham. Some focus on footwork, speed or balance, as demands of the dancers' needs and repertoire dictate.

The *técnica cubana* is a living practice that continues to be expanded and refined by teachers, choreographers and dancers working in this young and vibrant tradition. As more dancers graduate from La ENA, and others pass from performing into teaching, the technique evolves further. The fact that it was created with an agenda has not limited the dance form to the execution of that agenda. *Técnica cubana* continues to evolve, changing both in the studio and on the stage as choreographers use this articulate form in new dances that speak to changing times.

Teatro Nacional, Havana: 1992

As a principal dancer and choreographer of Danza Contemporánea, Narciso is allowed to rehearse his own small company in the Teatro Nacional studios of the national company. We work in the same room where four years earlier I had watched company class, spellbound. The slatted windows open onto tropical greenery, gracing the space with oxygen and shade. The floor is more warped and pockmarked than it was. Like everything else, materials for fixing it are scarce. Occasionally a small bird will fly in through an open window, observe the dancing briefly, and find its way out.

Outside a wall of studio windows, visible through glossy leaves of the tall trees, stands the Plaza de la Revolución. A wire portrait of Che Guevera fills the side of a three-story building. The icon's face stares across the Plaza to a huge white tower where an armed guard stands 24 hours a day. On the other side, our studio windows overlook a small pond and a parking lot where we can track who's coming and going, who's late for class and who's kissing a lover goodbye.

I begin to delve into the mysteries of técnica cubana. *It's a heady hybrid: balletic feet, high legs and multiple turns, the off-center sincerity of modern dance mixed with Afro-Cuban percussion and fluidity. It's unlike any other dance form I have ever attempted. I take company class, joyfully subjecting myself to pain and humiliation. Following along instinctively, I search for the logic of these strange, intricate movements while trying not to stumble. My childhood ballet teacher, Meredith Bayliss, used to say, "In order to pirouette, you first have to fall down." Consoling myself with that wisdom I duly accept neophyte status.*

Juancito, who taught me to salsa *in Finland, takes pity and pulls me aside to illustrate a basic principle of the technique. Planting his feet firmly on the floor, he makes his spine undulate like a flag in the wind. A Cuban flag. Then his arms ripple, snakelike. I try the move slowly as he coaches me, tracking a wave of energy from the floor, up my legs and spine, out my arms and through my fingers. The sequence has an organic feel that is overtly sensuous, but not sexy. With that sensation in my body, the technique starts to make more kinesthetic sense.*

Other dancers start to tutor me after class, demanding more just when I think I'm going to drop from heat exhaustion. Beti, who dances for both Narciso and Danza, drills me patiently. Just out of la ENA, this young soloist balances languorously, twisting and extending her slender frame hypnotically. Beautiful Beti exhibits an easy control and rhythmic acuity I can only dream of. The Cuban system of training modern dancers has clearly found its path.

Dissemination of *Técnica Cubana*

Most professional contemporary and folkloric dancers in Cuba pass through a six-year program in the National School of Art. La ENA, as the school is known, provides free, superior training in all the arts to those who show talent and determination. As in the Cuban system for training ballet dancers, students who pass rigorous auditions to enter La ENA are provided with food, housing and an extremely demanding academic and artistic education. Dancers study *técnica cubana*, classical ballet, and Cuban folklore — including social and orisha dances — along with academics, acting and music. As dancers mature they usually begin to focus either on contemporary or folkloric dance, although they continue to study many styles. Some dancers are channeled into teaching while others are encouraged to perform. Upon graduation, dancers are chosen for Danza, the Conjunto Folklórico, for one of the provincial companies or schools, or as educators. Advanced studies take place at the Instituto Superior de Arte (La ISA), the Superior Institute of Art.

Técnica cubana, fueled by Cuba's strong national identity and practiced by highly literate artists, has contributed to a vibrant dance culture that continues to flourish and expand. In the early 1980s North American ex-pat Lorna Burdsall, one of the original collaborators in Danza, founded the contemporary troupe Así Somos (The Way We Are). In the late 1980s, before the Special Period could clip their wings or squelch their ambitions, a crop of exceptional dance artists came of age: Caridad Martinez, Narciso Medina, Lesme Grenot, Rosario Cárdenas, Isabel Bustos and Marianela Boán, to name a few. In 1988 Gabri Christa, a native of Curaçao who trained in Amsterdam at the School for New Dance Development, became a founding member of Marianela Boán's DanzAbierta. Christa describes the era as an exhilarating collaborative moment in the arts:

> It was hugely creative. Everyone was hungry for new information. Dance developed not in a vacuum but as part of an outgoing and rebellious movement. A group of young artists began doing very different work, very modern. Painters Arturo Cuenca and Manuel Mendive — they are now huge stars — worked with people from Danza. There was little influence from outside Cuba, barely any foreigners. Mendive looked back to his heritage, to Wifredo Lam, European art and the Orishas to come up with new methods. That's when he began painting on dancers' bodies. There was a need for anything new.[11]

This explosion of artistic expression transformed the landscape of Cuban dance, which had been the exclusive realm of state-supported companies since the Revolution. In an unprecedented move Caridad Martinez, a Ballet Nacional principle dancer, left the safety of the classics in 1987 to spearhead the independent Ballet Teatro de La Habana [Havana Ballet Theater]. In addition to striking out on her own, Martinez' artistic concepts were new to Cuban dance, raising the hackles of the establishment. Alicia Alonso was not pleased. A year later, when DanzAbierta was preparing its debut at the Teatro Mella, Alonso played her power card. Christa explains:

> It was very tricky. After what happened with Caridad, Alonso had decided her permission was needed in order for a piece to go on. She came to our [DanzAbierta] dress rehearsal with her entourage; she was almost blind but people were telling her what was happening onstage. Alicia was the unofficial head of the Ministry of Culture and she said, "not without my permission." We were very nervous, there was one piece with nudity. We didn't know until an hour before if we could even do the performance.[12]

That performance did take place, and many thereafter. Havana percolated with new dance. Rosario Cárdenas formed Danza Combinatoria (Combined Dance) that same year, and Isabel Bustos formed Danza-Teatro Retazos (Dance-Theater Remnants). In 1988 Narciso Medina choreographed "Metamorfosis" which went on to win the prestigious Prix de Lausanne in Switzerland. He formed his small company Gestos Transitorios a few years later, even though economic conditions had started deteriorating.

As the effusive '80s gave way to the Special Period, the artistic explosion continued. Small companies burst on the scene across Cuba, even as established troupes continued to work steadily, with and without government support. Beyond the dance boom in the capital, Liliam Padrón founded Danza Espiral in Matanzas; Ladislao Navarro began Danza Fragmentada in Guantanamo; and in Holguin Maricel Godoy founded CoDanza. Despite material poverty, lighting outages, the lack of good shoes, costumes, technology and vitamins, Cuban dancers experimented with new choreography, finding ways to use their superior training to poetic and dramatic effect.

Chapter 8

Politics In — and Out of— the Studio

How was modern dance able to flourish during Cuba's Special Period, a time of sustained material deprivation? This is a question that I have asked and been asked repeatedly. What is clear is that Cuban artists were prepared rigorously for a productive life in art. Modern dance was able to grow in an environment of support in the 1970s and 1980s; it could not have taken root under the deep economic strictures of the 1990s. But once *técnica cubana* was established as part of the cultural landscape, its practitioners were able to continue making dances despite the temptations and struggles of the Special Period. While some dancers chose to moonlight as taxi drivers or waiters, most Cuban dancers found that their art continued to be of value. At times, when touring or teaching foreign students at home, dancers found economic value in their craft. At times, during the chaos of transportation and utility disruptions, dancers found value in the reassuring discipline of their daily practice.

Even in the economic depths of the 1990s, Cuban society showed a basic respect for artistic production. Modern dance has never been universally accepted or understood on a grand scale; it is not the most accessible art form. Nevertheless, modern dance was considered important enough to merit ongoing state support throughout the Special Period. Dancers continued to receive concrete economic sustenance while in school, and later through guaranteed salaries that rose with their level of accomplishment. This in itself is a ratification of the significance of dance, which has consistently been recognized by the Revolutionary government as a legitimate career. Unlike North American dancers, Cuban dancers seldom hear the refrain, "when are you going to get a real job?"

The basic assumption that society has reserved a place for them at the table has given Cuban dancers a sense of purpose, despite the ongoing frustrations and indignities of hardship. It has helped modern dancers to integrate their national identities as Cubans with their personal and professional identities. This link between daily life and artistic production was never more evident than during the lean days of the Special Period.

I believe that dancers were most suited to facing the challenges thrust upon them by becoming more creative in the studio, reaching out to foreign artists, and ultimately finding ways to market themselves as producers, teachers and performers in the newly emerging—and frequently frustrating—mixed economy. By confirming their identities as dancers within a society that valued their creative contributions, they were more prepared to adapt economically and to create strong works of art during this difficult period.

Dance, and all art in Cuba, takes place in a conscious context of state support, prioritized arts education, high standards and national visibility. Issues of artistic freedom are manifest in diverse ways specific to the artistic medium in question, and have been influenced and altered by internal and external political changes over the years. Questions of race and gender exist within the artistic milieu just as they do on the street, but they are played out in different ways. Since the fall of the Soviet Union and the withdrawal of its significant financial support, Cuba's economic situation has changed drastically. That enormous economic change has led to smaller policy changes, including a series of revolving regulations regarding the American dollar, a new reliance on tourism, and the active goal of exporting culture. Because Cuban society is controlled on so many levels by its government, there is always a strong correlation—albeit sometimes inverse—between official mandate and cultural production. These factors are among the many that have ongoing and varied influence over the shape, direction and volume of dance in Cuba.

Cuban modern dance can be seen as a laboratory where issues of culture, gender, and race are negotiated. In sharing specific observations that were made across several decades, I hope to illuminate the delicate nexus between daily life, political realities, idealistic goals, and dance.

The Special Period *ad nauseum*: Havana, 1992

Food is scarce. Narciso and very-pregnant Idalmis share their rationed rice and beans with me, stretching meager supplies without complaint. The favored black beans go first, then the brown beans, then the white. Lassie waits for the scrapings from our plates, or for yesterday's rice. They don't make commercial dog food in Cuba. I certainly don't see it when I buy spaghetti at the dollar store—where only foreigners and Communist Party big wigs are allowed to shop—and Cuban pesos are not accepted. When I bring spaghetti home, Idalmis thinks it's Christmas.

There's no toilet paper, no shampoo, no antibiotics, no tampons, no condoms, no writing paper, and no cooking oil. Except if you have dollars. Even then it depends on what happens to be in the diplomercado, *or dollar store, that week. Gasoline is only available by* libreta—*ration book—or with dollars. Thirty-odd years after the Revolution, the* yanqui *dollar is the currency of Cuba.*

I'm amazed at how Cubans live. As part of the Special Period effort to conserve resources, much of Havana has running water for only an hour or two per day. Entire neighborhoods are blacked out one or two nights a week. No one has a working toilet; they all pour buckets of water down the bowl when they can't stand it any more. Once in a while I carry the garbage out to the corner dumpster where the cats feast and the palmetto bugs flourish. Toilet paper (often last week's Granma *newspaper) gets thrown out instead of flushed. I carry the bag gingerly. Nevertheless, it strikes me how little trash we have. There's no packaging on the food, no plastic wrap, no cardboard. In Cuba there's nothing to throw out.*

After years of coasting on Soviet subsidies, Cubans are suffering the hunger pangs of independence. Nevertheless, they dance up a storm. Narciso has scheduled a program for the Teatro Garcia Lorca in Central Havana. It's a baroque palace housing several theaters and studios. The great Fanny Elssler danced there a century ago, and the Ballet Nacional performs there still.

Today, while run down, the elaborate structure is still spectacular. The theater fills up at night with habaneros hungry for the distraction only art can provide.

The 1970s

During my first visit to Cuba in 1973, the country was still in a period of upswing. When my brother and I joined the Brigada Julio Antonio Mella, Seguidores de Camilo y Che, food was plentiful and morale among the brigade members was high. It is possible that those brigade volunteers were Communist Party loyalists, chosen to interact with foreigners for their zealotry. But our brigade was not designed primarily for international members as were others, such as the Venceremos Brigade. Regardless of how they were recruited, the *brigadistas* we met seemed, to my admittedly naïve and Spanish-challenged young self, sincere and committed. I specifically recall Gloria stating that her reason for joining the brigade was to fight illiteracy. She herself had been illiterate until the "triumph of the Revolution" and its attendant literacy campaign, which brought literacy rates to above 96 percent.[1]

At the time I was unaware of the existence of the Cuban modern dance form and company. The school at Cubanacán was going through some of its growing pains, as described in previous chapters. Lorna Burdsall, one of

Danza's founders and former wife of the revolutionary Manuel Piñiero, known as Redbeard, describes the early days of the modern dance company:

> The uphill struggle of Modern Dance was reflected in meetings at the Union of Artists and Writers as well as the National Culture Council. Distinctions were made between Ballet and Dance (anything that wasn't Ballet was Dance) instead of using Dance as a generic term for all the many styles of Terpsichore. The most important political events were usually accompanied by performances of the Ballet Nacional de Cuba, so it wasn't until fourteen years later, despite excellent reviews by critics and touring internationally, that we [Danza Contemporánea] were to have the privilege of Fidel Castro in our audience.[2]

Despite the intentional creation of *técnica cubana,* government support of its attendant company Danza Contemporánea, and the foundation of an academy where the details of teaching *técnica* were hammered out, modern dance was far from fully accepted in Cuba of the 1970s. As an art form it relies on freedom in movement vocabulary, composition and content. In contrast with ballet companies, whether new or established, the repeated performance of well-known works is not a viable option for a vibrant young modern company. Renowned groups, like the Martha Graham and the José Limón companies, can continue to show works that were created over half a century ago because their repertoire has already earned a loyal following. *Danza,* by mandate, had to create its own dances incorporating its own dance form, and then build an audience to whom those dances would appeal. Dancers Eduardo Rivero and Geraldo Lastro set choreography on the company, as did Noriega, Mahler and Burdsall.

Guerra and his collaborators built the repertoire of the young company with an eye on what was happening in the rest of the world. While cut off from the modern dance mainstream in the United States, the creative team of Danza was exposed to art and artists from Latin America, China, Eastern and Western Europe. The social shakeups of the 1960s were brought home to the relatively isolated Cuban dancers in part by their interactions with international artists. Among other influences, the Peking Opera made a strong impact on Guerra, who was inspired to experiment with humor and satire as a result.

Censoring Revolutionary Voices

Introducing the piece that created a cataclysm in his career, Guerra writes, "by the end of the seventies, the worldwide sexual revolution put pressure on the national culture, which was easily vulnerable to the dialectic struggle between art and politics."[3] Guerra spent a year working with his dancers on an experimental piece steeped in the aesthetics of psychedelia, happenings, and sexual revolution. *El décalogo del apocalipsis* (The Ten Commandments of the Apocalypse) was a huge production, designed as a site-specific extravaganza on the grounds of the Teatro Nacional, adjacent to the iconic Plaza de la Revolución, The National Theater has always been the home of Danza Contemporánea, which looks out over the Plaza, its official rallies, and essential government buildings. Guerra (accidentally/on purpose?) discounted the fact that his groundbreaking psychedelic sexual odyssey was staged a bit too close for comfort to the symbolic center of communist Cuba.[4] Costumes were designed by Eduardo Arrocha (a gifted set, costume and lighting designer with whom I have had the pleasure of working), and included unitards with flowers whimsically painted in the place of genitals. Feathered headdresses, sweeping capes, and strings of beads made bold reference to what Guerra saw as the neo-Africanist themes of Kings Day and Carnival.[5] The piece was divided into ten scenes, four of which included sexual content. Guerra describes his Prodigal Son section as including "a strong erotic relationship with incestuous and violent origins."[6] The piece was highly experimental in movement style, presentation, visual statement, the use of text, and most significantly, theme. The great social upheavals of the previous decade were expressed through the breaking of taboos in the dance paradigm itself.

But the piece was never premiered. Guerra lost not only the chance to show the dance he had spent a year preparing, but also his post at the head of the company he had formed. Sitting in a Vedado restaurant in 2006, Guerra described to me the piece that was never to be shown, and the scandal that followed:

It was a special crisis in the '70s, something that occurred within Socialist systems. The famous Cultural Revolution that occurred in China, we had that here too, demanding that art had to be strictly political. The persecution of homosexuality was not only in terms of dancers, but also throughout culture, affecting painters, music, everything. In the '70s culture here was paralyzed. Literature, everything. I worked on that piece for a year, it cost a lot of money. It used the space in front of the Central Committee [he laughs] outside the Teatro Nacional. There were very strong moments. I didn't use nudity; nudity was not permitted. But it was about the ten famous commandments. And I inverted everything, I changed the prohibitions into commandments: Rob, Lie, Fornicate. So there were lots of sexual images. Not nudity, but for example the costumes were unitards in the same shade as the dancers' skin. In the place of their sex was a flower. If it was a woman, the flower was open; if it was a man, the flower was extended.... It was in the psychedelic mode, Arrocha's designs were beautiful. For the Song of Songs, the musician improvised with the texts. I did an arrangement of the words, parodies of the great poetry of the bible.

So the scandal began. There was a candelabra of a psychedelic phallus which blew smoke; lots of proscribed things. There was a scene of insults, where the dancers cursed in other languages, hitting the iron grating around the outside of the Teatro Nacional, making the rhythm. But at the end they cursed in Spanish [he laughs again].

They didn't know or understand what I was trying to do. I was not commenting on the politics of Cuba; I was speaking about the world in the 1970s. I knew I could not continue as the director, following rules I disagreed with; because at that time the directors of artistic groups were members of the Party, not artists.

I got mad. I went home.[7]

In response to this huge scandal Guerra has written sanguinely, "In the world of the dance I was the protagonist of one of these daring happenings that, of course, was not considered good for the status quo by the cultural governors of the time."[8] It is not clear whether Guerra abdicated control of Danza or whether he was pushed out; he implies it was his choice but other sources suggest he did not have a say in the matter. He turned his attention to writing and became the foremost dance scholar in Cuba, publishing books, contributing chapters to international dance anthologies and journals, and publishing a dance periodical in Havana (when paper is available). Guerra also authored and appeared in an extensive Cuban television broadcast dedicated to dance appreciation.

The underlying source of the conflict that led to Guerra leaving Danza was political rather than aesthetic. While the Revolutionary government had begun its social experiment with an eye toward the New Man and the Cuban Artist, over time it handed control of the Ministry of Culture to politicos rather than to artists and arts administrators. The lofty goals that championed a people's art movement devolved into rigid rules and regulations once in the hands of bureaucrats. Unschooled in the history and subtleties of art, these functionaries, "perceived sedition in all they did not understand," according to Melinda Mousouris, who has interviewed and written about Guerra extensively.[9] This period of censorship lasted from 1970 to 1977. Fortunately for Cuba's audiences and artists, the skilled and erudite Armando Hart became cultural minister in 1977. Hart's appointment changed the situation significantly and ultimately led to the public "rehabilitation" of Guerra.

This precautionary tale of censure in dance, while extreme, is remarkably rare in Revolutionary Cuba's dance history. Guerra's *Decalogo* seemed to irritate a raw nerve in the bureaucrats put in charge of cultural development during the 1970s. Guillermoprieto also recounts her frustration when confronting Mario Hidalgo, a revolutionary with no artistic background who had been put in charge of the arts school, La ENA, during the same period.[10] Today, as Guerra has written and as I will illustrate later, earlier taboos regarding both homosexual and heterosexual allusions are now broken with regularity in the world of Cuban dance.[11]

Company rehearsal for the "natives" section of Narciso Medina's *Genesis por un Carnaval* at the Teatro Fausto, December 1999.

Censorship experienced in other artistic media — Cuban film, theater, and literature — is well documented. Castro's infamous 1961 speech, *Palabras a los intelectuales* (words for the intellectuals) has been interpreted as a warning against unfiltered freedom of expression among artists and intellectuals. The chilling effect in literary and intellectual circles was particularly profound, both through outright censorship and self-censorship. *Palabras a los intelectuales* has been the subject of ongoing debate ever since Castro first delivered the speech.[12] Writers, including some celebrated members of the *nuevo boom* in Latin American literature, have been imprisoned, vilified and exiled for any number of supposed transgressions. Some Cubaphiles excused the country's repressive actions in this period as necessary to the success of the Revolution. But Cuba's harsh treatment of artists and intellectuals resulted in the loss of many international allies, members of the Left who had previously been sympathetic to the Revolution. The alienation of many among the vocal intellectual elite at home and abroad did not help burnish Cuba's image during a tense period which included Cold War landmines such as the Bay of Pigs and the Cuban Missile Crisis. In part due to the repression of artists and intellectuals, former "fellow travelers" such as Octavio Paz and Jean-Paul Sartre[13] ultimately became critical of Castro, whose regime they once championed. Among the most well known of Cuba's censured writers are Heberto Padillo, Reinaldo Arenas, Severo Sarduy and Guillermo Cabrera

The Academia de la Danza Narciso Medina's entrance on the side of the building at #467 Calle 8, Vedado, May 2000. The Academia was housed in the apartment previously occupied by the Medina family (photograph by the author).

Infante. Cabrera Infante, one of the most celebrated writers of his time, served as an editor of the magazine *Lunes de Revolución*, "the major literary phenomenon of the Cuban Revolution."[14] Cabrera Infante found himself at the center of a pivotal moment in Cuban culture in 1961 when his brother Saba's film *P.M.* was censored. Explaining an episode that became all-too-familiar during this period, author William Luis writes "The political and cultural concepts promoted by the *Lunes* staff became incompatible with those [who] sought to control cultural production. *Lunes* was closed because of an alleged shortage of paper."[15]

Guillermo Cabrera Infante later left Cuba and became one of its outspoken critics, along with Heberto Padilla and Reinaldo Arenas (whose memoir *Before Night Falls* has been adapted powerfully into film and opera). The censorship of *P.M.* and other works of Cuban artists initially sympathetic to the Revolution helped to fuel an articulate, impassioned opposition to the Castro regime, and illustrates what Jacqueline Loss, an expert on Cuban literature and culture, refers to as "Cuba's shifting criteria for the role of art within society."[16] In addition to squelching the creative minds that were originally supportive of the new government, these policies succeeded in making enemies out of many of Cuba's friends around the world.

Eventually the government came around to recognizing Guerra's great contribution to Cuba culture. In 1988 an apology to Ramiro Guerra appeared in *Granma*, the official state newspaper. Modern dance continued to mature in Cuba, but the art form suffered a serious blow when it lost the active participation of its founder. He never went back to Danza, though he continued to stay involved in the progress of his students, seeing new choreography and offering seasoned feedback. Today Guerra lives in a crumbling tower that overlooks the Malecón. His small apartment is filled with books and paintings, with a ballet *barre* attached to one wall. Bits of plaster occasionally fall from the ceiling. The elevator rarely works, so if he needs to descend to the street he faces the prospect of climbing nine flights of stairs. Nevertheless, the father of Cuban modern dance continues to research and write about dance with his characteristic curiosity and quickness of mind.

In Cuba the use of dance to bring audiences together across racial and social lines proved a successful experiment. Both the Conjunto Folklórico and Danza Contemporánea were able to build strong followings domestically and abroad. Whether Cuban dance has been an articulate participant in the examination of critical social and political issues of the day is another question that I will address later in this volume. Significantly, some of the most important contemporary Cuban choreographers, like Narciso Medina, Rosario Cárdenas and Marianela Boán, take provocative chances in the form and content of their art. Guerra cites the accomplishments of these and other intrepid choreographers in his assessment of the contemporary Cuban dance scene.[17] Many, including Medina, claim Ramiro Guerra as mentor and inspiration.

Dance as Provocateur

It is my contention that dance is in its own category when it comes to issues of provocation and censorship. Using the medium of the body, dance is most likely to offend in the realm of socio-sexual mores, as opposed to inflaming overt political issues. At the beginning of the twentieth century, Isadora Duncan scandalized audiences, particularly in the United States, by dancing barefoot and most shockingly, without wearing a corset. Vaslav Nijinsky enraged audiences with his onanistic ending to *L'Après Midi d'un Faun*. Guerra violated standards of taste in Cuba, a culture decidedly less puritanical than its northern neighbor. But since Guerra's *Décalogo* was never performed it is impossible to know how a live audience would have reacted, or even exactly who and how he offended. Nude performances abound in the U.S. and Europe since the 1960s, when the Broadway runs of *Oh! Calcutta!* and *Hair*, both of which contained co-ed full frontal nudity, brought the naked dancing body to the mainstream. Since then nudity in experimental and modern dance has waxed and waned. Performance art tends to be more directly confrontational to standards of decency, with artists such as Annie Sprinkle and Karen Finley pushing the boundaries of taste even further.

Political content in dance is less common. Notable examples of agit-prop, like the National Ballet of China's *Red Detachment of Women* and The Shanghai Ballet's *The White-Haired Girl*, are being reassessed as works of art and propaganda. While clearly politically motivated, these ballets remain in the repertoire and are considered Chinese classics. Early modern dancers, like Isadora Duncan, Martha Graham, and Anna Sokolow, took decidedly progressive stances in many of their dances, and were considered vanguards in a movement of socially conscious art across disciplines. The early moderns struggled with concepts of politics and justice in their dances. According to dance theorist Mark Franko, "dance is danced ideas too ... expressive without being literal."[18]

This very lack of literalism is key to my theory that dance artists can choose to engage social or political themes either head on or obliquely. Dance makers can vary the transparency of their message in keeping with the freedom and safety of the times. In more concrete art forms — especially those where a written text or script can be examined and re-examined — instances of outright censorship and subtle self-censorship are more common. Dance retains the freedom of abstraction. Choreographers can employ an intentional illegibility that renders their social commentary inoccuous. They can design movement to be understood on many levels. Underlying meanings that may have seditious content can be obscured by theatrics, technical virtuosity or by intentionally engaging the difficulty many laymen have when trying to "read" dance. The repeated complaint voiced by audience members unaccustomed to dance is, "I don't understand it." While overt sexual content is hard to miss, more subtle subversive content may be easier for the choreographer to cloak, if he or she chooses to do so, than for the writer to bury in satire or metaphor. Granted, writers such as José Lezama Lima and Severo Sarduy are perfectly capable of obscuring social criticism with their rococo style, but dance makers can be even more elusive.

At the same time, I contend it is harder for a choreographer to successfully transmit political or social commentary in a convincing manner. Dances with a social agenda often come across as too literal, naïve, corny or anachronistic. With a few notable exceptions — like Graham's *Chronicle*, Sokolow's *Rooms*, and Kurt Jooss' *The Green Table*— few overtly political dances have shown themselves to be resilient works of art over time. The obscure nature of dance is both its strength and weakness as a vehicle for ideas.

From the Golden Age to the Special Period

In the spring of 1988 I took my second trip to Cuba, this time as a tourist, not a brigadier. I traveled with my father, a neurophysiologist who collaborated extensively on issues of stroke and mental illness with Cuba's Centro Nacional de Investigaciones Científicas (CNIC), the National Center of Scientific Investigation. His friend, the Havana-based neuroscientist Pedro Valdés, refers to the late 1980s as Cuba's "Golden Age."[19] Looking back from the hungry perspective of the 1990s, the '80s seem like the end of a gilded era, the last period during which Cuba enjoyed the patronage of the Soviet Union.

One of my strongest memories from that 1988 trip was a visit to Abraham Lincoln Park. A vendor was selling barbecued chicken from a cart under a huge tree. My guide Alfredo, another scientist and family friend, insisted I eat an entire chicken by myself, without napkins. That image became iconic for me during the Special Period. I thought of that oversized meal when in 1992 Idalmis divided one frozen chicken into tiny pieces, using it to flavor rice that her family of three shared with me for several days. But back in 1988 the Soviet Union was still buoying Cuba's economy; food, gasoline, paper goods, and basic necessities were readily available for Cuban pesos. The Golden Age. *Diplotiendas*, stores accepting only hard currency, were already in operation, but their purpose was to provide specialty items to foreigners.

Cubans were not allowed to carry dollars or to shop in *diplotiendas*. These stores carried goods that a traveler from the more developed world might want — imported shoes or name-brand tanning oil, for example. But the basic goods that Cubans needed were distributed to them through government-operated stores. It was not unusual for Cuban nationals to enlist the help of foreign visitors in shopping for a particular item that they wanted, something available only in the *diplotienda*. The foreigner would have to present a passport and shop as if for herself, maintaining the fiction that the item was for her and not for her Cuban friend. This practice was fairly common, but the ruse was maintained while the clerks ignored their compatriots eagerly eyeing the goods. In significant contrast with the 1990s, the attraction of the *diplotienda* in the 1980s was the quality and range of merchandise. Later they became a way to acquire basic necessities that were absent from local *bodegas*.

The 1980s were not flush times in Cuba, but in retrospect they were far from lean. The government provided basic housing, utilities, education, health care and nutritional needs across all levels of society, from the countryside to the cities. From the '60s to the late '80s people's basic needs were assured on a modest but concrete level. Cuba still enjoyed significant advantages, especially as compared with other Latin American countries. As a member of the Soviet trade bloc Comecon, Cuba traded sugar, rum, and cigars at favorable rates. This system kept the Cuban economy afloat, but effectively limited its development as an independent nation. Cuba did not diversify its economy in ways that Che Guevara and other revolutionaries had deemed necessary: through production that would create independence and prosperity. Despite these drawbacks that would ultimately add to Cuba's woes, most Cubans remember the 1980s as a period of relative comfort and material ease. By mid-decade new economic theories were transforming the communist world. In 1986 as *perestroika* rocked the USSR, Castro began a system of "rectification." The resulting economic solutions put into place became part of the ongoing evolution of the Cuban system. Features of a mixed economy previously considered absolutely illegal, such as private enterprise or the possession of American dollars, would, over the course of the 1990s, become not only legal but common. This changed the Cuban economic paradigm and was reflected in the equations of everyday trade: recasting items as party line or illicit, available, unavailable, openly hawked or black market contraband.[20]

As if in constant reaction to the forces of global economy and politics, the rules by which Cubans live are in a frequent state of flux. On every one of my trips to Cuba I would discover that an ornate series of economic regulations — pertaining not only to complex international trade but to daily life, household goods, and the legality or illegality of possessing hard currency — had been changed by the time of my return.

The Union of Cuban Writers and Artists (UNEAC) holds congresses every five years to provide forums for cultural policy. At the Fourth Congress, which took place in January 1988, "major speeches by Minister of Culture Armando Hart, Vice-President Carlos Rafael Rodríguez, and President Fidel Castro stressed the need for youth, the evils of dogmatic approaches, and the importance of freedom in form and content in the arts."[21] I am not in a position to judge the sincerity of this call for artistic freedom. Clearly it did not undo the damage of Castro's 1962 speech, *Palabras a los intelectuales*. Dogma continued to prevail, most oppressively in the fields of literature and film. But later in 1988, when I first visited Danza Contemporánea, I witnessed a vibrant artistic community rehearsing dances with a wide range of content. I was welcomed into the studio by the company administrators. The fact that I was North American was not in any way a hindrance; at no time did I experience suspicion or resentment. In fact, as a dancer from New York, the self-proclaimed dance capital of the world, I seemed to be an object of fascination. Within hours the company brass had enlisted my help in obtaining precious items for stagecraft: Mylar, lighting gel, and glow tape. I was happy to offer to try, although I had no idea how I would actually transport any of these goods to Cuba.

In hard contrast with the 1990s, it was still not unusual in 1988 for Cubans to invite foreigners out to eat, share a cocktail, or have coffee. At that time pesos still afforded Cubans the basic luxuries of dining out, frequenting nightclubs and enjoying many types of entertainment. Cubans had access to most hotels, restaurants and beaches, paying for them with local currency. There were some locations, such as establishments frequented by Soviet diplomats, where Cubans would not be welcome, but they were the exception rather than the rule. Tourism was not yet a major source of income. The stringent economic restrictions of the 1990s had not yet begun to separate Cubans from the pleasures of their island or the fruits of their own labor. While some goods were available only in hard currency, Cuba still belonged to the Cubans; it was vastly different from the playground of foreigners and gangsters that it had been in the mid 1950s. The slow incursion of the dollar had not yet begun to divide the haves from the have-nots, effectively eroding the very real social and cultural gains of the Revolution.

The 1990s

By the mid–1990s government rations were no longer sufficient; no one was starving but everyone was hungry. I learned this first hand at the home of my friend and collaborator, Narciso Medina.

In 1991 when I met Narciso and his wife Idalmis at the Kuopio Dance Festival in Finland, they invited me to choreograph for Narciso's young company, then called Gestos Transitorios, and to stay at their home in Havana. Cubans had been told to anticipate increased hardship in the wake of the Soviet Union's fall and in light of the persistent North American economic embargo. No one knew how long that economic sacrifice would last nor, I suspect, the enormous changes that would transform Cuban society as a result.

It took over a year for me to arrange the particulars of travel. It was impossible to call Cuba directly at the time. Even if it had been possible, Narciso was one of many Cubans who did not have a phone. (He did not have one in his home until 2006 although he is one of the most celebrated choreographers of his generation). I knew that someone must have a fax machine, but I didn't know who they were or how to find their number. Even if I did know, I would have had to ask someone in a third country, like Canada, to forward the fax, since a fax line in the U.S. couldn't dial a fax line in Cuba. E-mail use, at that point still infrequent in the U.S., was a decade away from being accessible to Cubans. Mail could take as long as three months to arrive. The final confirmation of my invitation arrived with another North American dancer who hand-carried Narciso's message to me from Cuba to the United States. Within weeks of receiving his letter I was on my way to Havana.

Because I had press credentials, having written dance journalism for some time, the United States government allowed me to travel directly from Miami to Havana. The United States Treasury Department Office of Foreign Assets and Control (OFAC) bases travel restrictions on the Trading with the Enemy Act; only passengers with special passports or affiliations are able to travel directly to Cuba from the United States. Specific restrictions have changed and continue to change frequently, depending on the administration in power and the current political climate. Under the Bush administration travel restrictions were tightened even further and it became increasingly difficult for academics, professionals, and artists to engage in inter-cultural exchange with Cuba.

Upon my arrival I quickly noticed that the Cuban lifestyle had changed since my last visit. In keeping with the restrictions of the Special Period, the entire neighborhood had running water and gas for only a few hours a day. Luckily, the presence of a maternity hospital around the corner meant that unlike most of Havana, electricity was rarely shut off on our street. Within a short time I was to learn that all sorts of everyday items were strictly rationed to Cubans. Each household had — and still has — a ration book, *libreta de racionamiento*,[22] which entitles each member of the family to a specific amount of basic goods, like soap, toothpaste, beans and rum, every month. While some items were ostensibly available at the local *bodega*, supplies were so limited that families used them up early in the month. Items in short supply included paper goods from toilet paper to writing paper, cooking oil, gasoline, cotton, pencils, pens, matches, propane, and even foodstuffs manufactured in Cuba, like fruit, coffee, and ironically, sugar. While raw sugar generally was available, the refined white sugar Cubans prefer was in short supply. And coffee, a Cuban staple and point of pride, was cut with chicory. *¡Que barbaridad!*

Vedado, Havana: 1992

Narciso gives me a salary but I can't figure out how to spend it. I am paid in pesos and am quite moved by the gesture, though there's not much I can buy. Food is rationed, distributed at the bodegas where every sale is recorded. It is only on the black market that I can use pesos to purchase food items without a libreta, *or ration book. The farmers' markets have been closed since the 1980s. I'm told it has to do with the* merolicos, *or individual farmers, making a profit by selling directly to the consumer. Apparently they had to put an end to that. In lush, juicy Cuba, I can't even buy a mango. Not legally, anyway, and not in pesos. Idalmis laughs again when I ask why the farmers' markets are closed. She says, "You're so funny, always asking 'why?' and 'why not?' You're in Cuba!" As if that should explain it.*

I am thrilled to spend my pesos on the occasional illegal coconut candy, or brown sugar lollipop. Even the sale of homemade candy is outlawed as private enterprise. Otherwise, everything is sold in dollars. Moneda nacional *doesn't seem to have much value. The dollar has gone up 20 pesos since I got here—now it's 140 pesos to the dollar. It only takes a few pesos to buy subsidized food and basic supplies, but with what's left over they can't buy much of anything.*

Cubans do seem to be holding onto their social system. Idalmis is six months pregnant and she sees the doctor once a week. If she misses her appointment he comes to the house to see if she's all right. I've noticed also that people tend to be well educated. Narciso tells me his father was a truck driver in Guantánamo and his mother learned to read as an adult, as part of the literacy drive in the '60s. He says "un negro guajiro like me would probably be cutting cane if it weren't for the Revolution." *Of course he had to cut cane anyway, as a teen on the youth brigades like everyone else, but not as a career. Narciso is worldly and well read, one of the best and smartest dancers I've ever met.*

Last night it rained and we watched the telenovela. *Here in Cuba, daily life stops at 9 P.M. on Monday, Wednesday and Friday as the entire country sits down to watch the Brazilian soap opera. On Tuesdays and Thursdays they broadcast the Cuban soap, but it doesn't invoke the same allegiance. Perhaps it's because the Brazilian show, translated into sing-song Spanish with Mexican voice-overs, represents a world that is truly foreign here. Narciso says he doesn't like telenovelas, but I noticed him peeking over Idalmis' shoulder. Brazilian soaps portray a system of money, class and racial distinctions that are particular to capitalism. Not that money, class and race don't play their roles here, but the roles are different.*

On those telenovela nights, everyone in our building crowds into Vivian's house. Vivian is the lady who lives in the front apartment. It's clear that she doesn't necessarily appreciate all her guests, but people here are expected to share what they have with their neighbors. Vivian has a telephone AND a television, so she is the de facto local clearing house for information and communication. Vivian and her husband both wear uniforms and work for the CDR, the Committee for Defense of the Revolution, which is the official spy-on-your-neighbor organization. She's very solicitous when I ask to use her phone.

When it rains the phones stop working.

Transportation didn't work well in 1992 either. A bicycle or a good pair of shoes was invaluable. The plastic Chinese shoes I had seen on earlier trips were hard to find. Sneakers and comfortable sandals were highly sought after and available only for dollars. Certain *diplotiendas* were designed expressly for diplomats, as opposed to regular tourists, because they carried the most hard-to-find items. Narciso and I went to one of these specialty *diplotiendas* to buy shoes for his daughter. Once we figured out how I could gain entry into the store using my passport and some creative fictions, I was able to purchase shoes for Dislaidys, along with food staples and treats. On one occasion we bought apples, since Narciso wanted his daughter to taste the exotic Northern fruit. For normal everyday items I was able to go to a local dollar store that catered to tourists and foreign students. There I could buy powdered milk, pasta, cooking oil and tomato sauce, or sit outside at a small café that served beer, sandwiches and ice cream. This felt extremely luxurious and somewhat traitorous since my hosts were unable to enjoy the same small indulgences. They were not allowed in, even as my guests.

Some Cubans earned money by hustling, negotiating anything they could in *la bolsa*, or market, short for black market, a street trade targeting both foreigners and locals. It encompassed everything from driving gypsy cabs to any number of setups, scams, or shady deals. The brilliant dancer Yamilé Socarrás, who later defected to Spain (as have so many other artists), had a boyfriend obsessed with *bizness*. He could not lay eyes upon a foreigner without offering to sell them something. He earned the name *el negociante*, the businessman, since he was always cooking up his next deal, whether it was selling black market cigars, garlic, books, or rum. He was an ardent fan of capitalism, and his nefarious activities were considered counter–Revolutionary and highly illegal.

Santiago Pérez fought in the Revolution and then went on to work as a *lector*, a professional reader brought in to entertain the workers at the Partagás cigar factory. He is shown here outside the venerated Real Fábrica de Tabacos Partagás, on Calle Industria in Havana, July 1997.

One of the government's main sources of hard currency is cigars. The robust black market thrives on illicit *tabacos* pinched by cigar factory workers, repackaged in cardboard or wooden boxes, and sealed with precious paper rings and stamps bearing the noble trademarks of the great cigar manufacturers: Cohiba, Partagás, Romeo y Julieta. Sold at a significant discount from those at the duty free or dollar stores, these black market cigars are big business — and a thorn in the side of the Revolution. A good *negociante* can spot a likely cigar mark a mile off. Many a tourist has gambled on a cut-rate box of cigars, unsure of the quality but lured by the bargain price, a pretty paper seal, and a sweet smelling box. My own brothers enjoyed more than a few of those cigars that fell off the back of a Cuban truck....

Partagás Cigar Factory, 1992

Narciso's company gets a gig at the famous Partagás cigar factory. We will be paid in lunch, and if we're lucky, a few cigars. I don't think any real money will exchange hands. These days lunch sounds good enough. Cigar makers are among the most essential members of Cuban society. Entertainment is provided every Thursday as they roll the precious brown tubes that sustain the Revolution.

We are like a bunch of school kids taking a field trip. Cándido and Alberto clown around on the way, making noise and flirting with girls on the street. We take two buses from Vedado to La Habana Vieja, Old Havana, where the Partagás factory is housed. On the way Narciso points out the capitol building, domed and white. It's bizarre to see this loving evocation of Washington in the heart of Communist Cuba. Needless to say, it predates the Revolution. We walk up to the fourth floor of the huge factory. The open loft space is filled with seated workers, odd pressure devices, wooden cigar forms of different sizes, and round blades shaped to cut the various types, textures and sizes of tobacco leaves. Signs exhort allegiance to the Revolution. We arrive early enough to look around and talk to a few workers.

I speak at length to a young woman in a yellow headscarf. She says she's been working there for only two years. Some people spend their lives in cigar factories, perfecting their craft. The friendly novice says she makes 135 cigars a day. It's still not enough. She is expected to bring her production up. I'm not sure what will happen if she doesn't, since generally workers are not fired in Cuba for lack of productivity, and it is clear that she is working hard. I can't bring myself to ask what the ramifications will be if she doesn't improve her quotas.

She looks efficient, bunching the leaves together, making sure they're tightly aligned without gaps or hollows, then pressing them for 15 minutes in a wooden form. Afterwards, she takes a moist leaf of strong tobacco and wraps the cigar, cutting a small "pañuelo" or kerchief, for the tip, and twisting it around the end.

These cigars, of medium size, are stacked in a pile to be inspected and counted by her supervisor. She works quickly as she talks, smiling brightly as she tells me she loves to dance.

A group of musicians takes the stage before we do. They get the whole place rocking. The workers fill in the lyrics, banging out rhythms with their feet as their hands roll the precious leaves deftly. A graying percussionist elicits shouts and cat-calls as he dances like a bull in heat. He pounds out the ubiquitous Cuban clave on his guiro, *a slatted gourd he scrapes with a stick, 1-2-3-1-2, he doesn't miss a step. The audience is loud and frank. They're not polite, though they're appreciative when they like the entertainment. They clank their tobacco knives against their worktables as applause. Then it's our turn to start dancing.*

Cándido and Alberto dance Narciso's Yoruba inflected piece, Yambao e Mi, *which first mystified me in Finland. This audience knows all the references; they send up a cry in response to the strange, staccato chant that accompanies the dancing. There's a part where Cándido has to count backwards. The audience yells out random numbers, trying to confuse him. It works! Cándido loses his place and everyone laughs. They are so involved, so mischievous, so unlike the well-behaved, jaded crowds of New York City.*

After the performance, a factory representative leads us to the lunchroom. We are given a heavy meal of rice, beans, pork, avocado, some sweet sticky thing,

In the first stage of production at the Partagás cigar factory, tobacco leaves are sorted and graded for quality (July 1997). On the wall in the background on the left is a photograph of Raúl Castro. On the shelf on the right is a pencil sketch of Che Guevara.

Photographer David Garten as a ringer rolling cigars on the factory floor at the *Real Fábrica de Tabacos Partagás*, July 1997. Photograph by Santiago Pérez.

and warm refresco. *This is more food than any of us has eaten in one sitting for a long time. The guys are thrilled to have pork, the Cuban food of preference, and I am happy to hand it over. Cándido has developed the habit of mooching food off me at every opportunity. I tell him he can finish my lunch only if he behaves in rehearsal tomorrow. He assures me that he will, smiling devilishly as he spears the greasy meat off the metal tray. Cuban dancers are as opinionated and boisterous as Cuban audiences. Cándido and his cohorts have not internalized the passive obedience bred into many professional dancers. They offer unsolicited advice and violate the sacred hierarchies of the studio. Their informality is startling, and at times annoying, but not negative; they contribute creatively and spontaneously in ways that have been suppressed in their northern counterparts. So I know Cándido won't behave. He'll complain, swagger, interrupt to correct my Spanish, and dance dazzlingly.*

Once we have reveled in the unfamiliar sensation of fullness, we waddle down the steps to the lobby. The somber factory representative presents each of us with several loose cigars. These tokens of appreciation are most valuable to nonsmokers. By nightfall the dancers will have traded them for food, milk, rum and who knows what else. Because I am a foreigner I am invited to see the official cigar store, where only hard currency is accepted. It is dark, wood paneled and plush, just the sort of boy's club atmosphere you'd expect. Narciso accompanies me, but he is not officially allowed to buy anything. I am stunned by the prices, which would probably delight a serious cigar smoker.

My brothers will have to do without the real thing. Sorry guys, I'm being paid in pesos.

In the early '90s, Narciso still rehearsed his small company in the Teatro Nacional studios of Danza Contemporánea. Identification was often checked at the door, so Narciso introduced me to the higher-ups at Danza. These administrators walk a thin line between art and bureaucracy, trying to balance the Ministry of Culture, the Communist Party, and the Creative Urge. The novelty factor of a *yanqui* choreographer seemed hard for them to resist, and they invited me almost immediately to teach class and come back to choreograph for them — without compensation, of course. Cuban money seemed to have no value; barter was the currency of choice.

Danza's Artistic Director Miguel Iglesias stepped in with gallant immediacy to help change my tourist visa to a working visa that would be valid for several months. He asked Isidro Rolando, the company *regisseur* and a prize winning early member of Danza, to help. Although it was probably not in his job description, Isidro cheerfully led me to the nearby office of EscenArte, a national arts agency. EscenArte is located in a particularly stunning old mansion on Calle 4, in the Vedado neighborhood. Many ornate houses that were private homes before the Revolution have been transformed into government offices. In EscenArte's cool unlit foyer, curving stairs swept upward toward a dusty skylight. Antique mirrors and high ceilings suggested the grandeur of another time. But the *compañera* at the desk, with her brusque bureaucratic overload, was planted firmly in the present: "Wait here until *el jefe* can see you." And so we waited. And waited.

After a long while we were directed to an inner office. An older man in a khaki uniform greeted Isidro warmly, offering fresh coffee and asking only a few questions. "We don't get a lot of North Americans working with our Cuban dancers. What do you think of them?" I answered honestly that the dancers were spectacular. "In Cuba we have the best dancers, don't we?" he agreed, handing over a new visa, "Good for three months." It was becoming clear that in Cuba most rules were made to be broken — by those with the right connections.

Narciso's experience with EscenArte has frequently been more frustrating. Though still the official booking agent of many of the Revolution's performing artists, EscenArte remains years behind the rest of the world of performing arts presenters in terms of technology and time frame. But as far as my visa was concerned, EscenArte was a paradigm of efficiency. Danza, operating with the blessings of the state, could clearly pull more strings than Narciso. Flying solo, his small company operated without official recognition at that time, neither state supported or controlled. In the 1990s, independent artistic organizations were almost unheard of in Cuba; it's surprising that Narciso's endeavor was even tolerated.

Danza Contemporánea Studio, Havana 1992

Yesterday after rehearsal the whole of Danza filed into the studio for a regularly scheduled Communist Party meeting. One of the young soloists, Myrna, is the proud Party representative. She opened the meeting in a loud, clear voice, "Bienvenidos, welcome, and thank you for coming, compañeros. Remember, this is our opportunity to participate as socialists in improving our work life." Almost the whole company was present, although Narciso says not all of them are Party members. The dancers displayed varying degrees of enthusiasm, as attending Party meetings is an obligation, not a matter of personal belief or activism. Once the floor was opened they took turns talking about food shortages and transportation difficulties.

"Claro que we're late to class all the time," explained Regla, a compact soloist with the high cheekbones of a Masai princess. "When the buses finally come they're so crowded we can't get on them. I don't like to rehearse without taking class, por tu vida, but I can't leave home before my kid goes to school."

As the dancers murmured their agreement with the obvious, I realized that many of these dancers have kids! Despite the wide availability of birth control pills and free abortion on demand, despite the dwindling food supply and the high divorce rate, pregnant women are all over the place. These are wanted children. Cuban dancers have children mid-career. Even Alicia Alonso did.

Women in contemporary Cuba may be expected to have children, but they are also expected to continue their life's work. It helps that cultural tradition assumes that grandparents and extended families will help to raise these kids. Daycare is free, as is the University. Artists have permanent positions, pensions and a sense of security dancers in the States can only dream of. If these Cuban dancers get pregnant and fat and out of shape they may lose a role … but not a job. They can always come back next season. Most significantly, they know their kids will receive free health care and education. No one tells them to "get a real job" in order to raise their kids.

I think of my dancing peers at home, ears glued to the biological clock, juggling injured knees with hormone production. Flexibility and fertility decline simultaneously. It takes us so long to establish a vaguely secure life style within the arts; we often wonder aloud whether our last dance and our last ovulation will occur simultaneously. In the States, female dancers assume we have to choose, waiting until the last possible minute to conceive, whereas Cuban women assume they'll have kids and keep dancing. And doing the dishes, the laundry and the cooking.

The topic turned to coffee. The dancers always complain vehemently about the company brew, which like all coffee these days, is being stretched with chicory. Accustomed to the rich dark twang of pure Cuban beans, the dancers disapprove heartily. (I still prefer it to Starbucks' three-dollar espresso.) Some of the more zealous comrades noticed I hadn't left the studio. Realizing I'd overstayed my welcome, I checked the canteen to see if there was any chicory coffee left.

Chapter 9

Color

Cuba's soul is *mestizo* (half-breed), and it is from the soul, not the skin, that we derive our definite color. Someday it will be called "Cuban color." — Nicolas Guillén, 1972

    Coppélia is the renowned ice cream store and gay cruising spot near the Hotel Habana Libre. Only the Cubans would name their ice cream after a ballet. In the early '90s Coppélia still served customers in pesos, but the wait could be well over an hour. With hard currency I was able to walk past the long line and order as much ice cream as I wanted. I was also able to invite Cuban guests to join me — if I paid for them in dollars.

    In some locations the presence of Cubans was discouraged or even prohibited, but the rules were in flux (as is often the case) and not always entirely clear. Occasionally I went to the rooftop pool at the Hotel Capri, which boasts a great view of Havana's white-tiled roofs, the Hotel Nacional (built by Al Capone), and the bay. Some foreign medical students I'd befriended introduced me to the Capri pool, its great view and tasty *mojitos*. Cuba educates many foreign doctors, especially Africans, whose countries subsidize their education. In the '90s foreign students were expected to use Cuban-issue vouchers in place of the hard currency they received from their families or governments. These vouchers were used for goods within Cuba while, ostensibly, the Cuban government made use of the students' hard currency abroad.

Hotel Capri, Havana: 1992

We've been waiting for several hours for Narciso to join us at the rooftop pool. As it turns out, Narciso has been downstairs, where he's been told that he is not allowed to go to the pool because he's Cuban. But Narciso is insistent; finally the bartender gets a call from the lobby and asks me to come to the phone. I verify

*huffily that Narciso is the person the African students and I have been waiting
for. Finally Narciso is allowed to come up. He is furious.*

*A rising talent respected at home and abroad, Narciso must rely on the kind-
ness of foreign friends to enjoy the fruits of Havana. No amount of legal pesos
could buy him a drink at the Capri. Indeed, Cubans are not allowed up to the
pool without a foreign escort. Narciso is modest and polite, yet proud and endearingly macho. He is clearly uneasy taking favors where he should be the host. We
drink mojitos, the rum and crushed mint going down easy in the delicious dusk.
I feel a pang for the brilliant, emasculated choreographer, humbled by what I
have come to call "dollar apartheid."*[1]

This is not the picture of Cuban socialism that Narciso anticipated, nor
the one he was educated to expect. Yet Narciso has said repeatedly that for
the most part the Revolution has worked in his favor. "I am black, I come
from Guantánamo, and my family before me had no other tradition, no hier-
archy that could have otherwise helped me achieve what I have achieved. I
have done something with my talent, my work, my dedication, my intelligence — who knows — with the strength of having an objective in life."[2]

The question of racial advancement in Cuba is beyond the scope of this
study, but some understanding of the ongoing debate is worthwhile. I will
not attempt to provide a broad overview, but instead to contextualize comments made on this topic by friends and colleagues over the years. After the
incident at the Capri pool, I asked Narciso if it would have been easier for
him to get upstairs if he had been white. He said no. The students we were
socializing with were black Africans, and they had no trouble gaining access
to the pool; Narciso maintained it was a matter of dollars (and foreign student
scrip) versus pesos.

Narciso's view of race relations provides a specific, personal perspective;
he does not claim to speak for anyone but himself. He has remained a committed socialist, albeit one with a worldly view and a hidden stash of dollars.
He embodies some of Cuba's best social policies, but he is a realist. Having
worked in Europe, Latin America, Japan and the United States, he also enjoys
a wider perspective than most of his countrymen on this and other issues. He
believes that the Revolution afforded him tremendous advantages that would
have been unavailable to him in pre–Revolutionary Cuba, or elsewhere in
Latin America, as a black man and member of a poor rural family. Narciso
credits his talent and hard work with the success that he has achieved. Through
educational opportunities offered to every Cuban, he developed his intellect
and artistry, building an international career. He would seem to agree with
his countryman, Pedro Pérez Sarduy, who has written:

> What Cubans, and especially black Cubans, have achieved in Cuba, through
> sweat, blood and tears, are not handouts.... We're winning for ourselves the

"human identity" that has been James Baldwin's great obsession and was denied us for so long.[3]

While studying at La ENA Narciso was not steered toward Afro-Cuban folkloric performance, although he dances it very well. Instead he was welcomed into the multi-racial ranks of the contemporary dance company built on Cuba's multi-cultural dance tradition. This speaks to the mandate of the Cuban modern dance form, and to Narciso's own fluency as an artist. It also reflects a certain fluidity in terms of Cuban racial constructs.

Historically the national independence movement strongly influenced concepts regarding race relations in Cuba. This movement exploited abolitionist ideals to its own ends, stifling dialogue about the true conditions under which Afro-Cubans lived after emancipation. Fearing a slave revolt like the successful Haitian Revolution next door, Cuban elites reframed ideas of race, promising equality they never delivered. Several scholars have noted that the Cuban ideals of cultural leniency and mobility, of a culture based on merit and not race, discouraged pan-Africanist sentiment or unity.[4] The shape of race relations in Cuba became different from those in the rest of Latin America, not to mention the United States. Whether manipulated or authentic (and probably both) what continues to emerge is an orientation of Cuban identity toward nationhood as opposed to race.

Narciso speaks of himself as an artist first, a Cuban second, and only rarely in relation to his dark skin tone. His wife, Idalmis, has clear Asian features. She often uses a pejorative colloquialism, *un chino atrás*, which refers to having a Chinese person behind you. It denotes bad luck. This sort of self-derogatory reference may be a way to acknowledge and respond to internalized oppression. As Daniel writes, Cubans "consider themselves first of all to be Cuban, and only incidentally to be *negro, mulato, chino, indio*, etc."[5]

The prevalence of inter-marriage, the ubiquity of people of all skin colors in positions of authority, and the quality of basic daily interactions all suggest that race relations in Cuba are decidedly different from those in the United States. The overt manifestations of distrust and division that mark so much of the current racial climate in the U.S. are not evident on the surface in Cuba. But difficult issues lurk in the subtext. Scholar Carlos Moore reminds us of Castro's description of Cubans as "an Afro-Latino people"[6] while deconstructing El Comandante's motives and efforts:

> Essentially, Castro's speeches [directly after the Revolution] reconfirmed two permanent features of his approach to race relations: a commitment to an integrationist stance steeped in white liberal paternalism and a firm refusal to allow the racial question to escape that framework.... It was out of the question for Blacks themselves to define the content of their own oppression, or define the terms of their ethnic emancipation.... In other words, the government was

intent on banning discrimination based on race or color, while racism itself could remain a sort of discretionary ethical question.[7]

Shortly after the Capri Hotel incident in 1993, Narciso stated that most racism in Cuba had to do with "a white man who had lost his woman to a black guy." This inflammatory statement intrinsically incorporates several racial and sexual stereotypes. Interestingly, Narciso's view harks back to some of the iconography of Cuban black and *mulato* sexual prowess, and reveals a sort of internalized oppression/pride rooted in those biases. The term *mulato* is based on the Spanish word for mule, however in Cuba it has different connotations than it does elsewhere. Indeed, the *mulata* became a symbol of Cuban beauty and spunk in pre–Revolutionary times. Author Vera Kutzinski points to the "Cuban cult of the *mulata*,"[8] while Madeline Cámara Betancourt spells it out in her title: "Between Myth and Stereotype: the Image of the Mulatta in Cuban Culture in the Nineteenth Century, a Truncated Symbol of Nationality,"[9]

The mystique of the *mulata* is quite real in contemporary Cuba, where *café con leche*–colored women are celebrated. In Villaverde's classic novel of the *mulata*, *Cecilia Valdes*, a dark grandmother tells her light granddaughter, "You don't marry a black or a mulatto even if he has all the money in the world." In a twist on this theme of "lightening," when Creoles intentionally marry those whose skin is lighter than their own, Narciso advised me to find a dark man so my children would not be too pale. Nevertheless, Cubans still talk of "good hair" and "bad hair," good hair being straight and sleek, bad hair kinky.

In the studio of Danza where I spent many hours rehearsing, the in-house physical therapist called himself "Chocolate." He made a point of telling me I would never dance as well as a *cubana,* because I lacked the basic requirement of Afro-Cuban blood, and that my mouth was too thin, because I lacked *bemba,* or succulent black lips. These references reveal a complex dignity and anger, reactions to a history of inequality that has been examined more extensively elsewhere.[10] Narciso, whose dance company is racially mixed, has acknowledged that some dance professionals assume that whites are inferior dancers: "A black can be as racist as a white person in Cuba. I could say: I want my company to be all black, I don't want whites, they don't know how to dance, they have no rhythm, no swing."[11]

With the "re-conquest" by Spain taking the form of feverish investment on the island in the 1990s, Spanish men became the butt of a bitter running joke. More and more Spaniards were seen driving through Havana in rented convertibles, showing off their Cuban brides of mixed descent, women "prized for their exotic beauty."[12] By the mid–1990s this phenomenon was a common subject of Havana small talk. In 1996 Mario Aguila, former sound technician for Narciso's company, described a trend of economic disconnect between Cuban men and women. He did not perceive these cross-national marriages as *jinetería,* or hustling, per se. But Mario thought the stringent conditions of the Special Period had created a gap between contemporary Cubans, a new cold-hearted pragmatism in matters of romance and survival.[13] Contemporary novelists repeatedly tweak the image of the irresistible *cubana* of mixed heritage and mention her hypnotic effect on Europeans and Canadians. Pedro Juan Gutiérrez's *Dirty Havana Trilogy* and Zoe Valdes' *I Gave You All I Had,* two witty chronicles of the Special Period, both employ a sardonic take on this traditional imagery. Of course it is not just Creole women who attract gawkers and admirers from colder climes. Mario, resembling a *café con leche* matinee idol, left Cuba when he married a European, as did several of the male dancers mentioned in this book.

On later occasions, perhaps when he felt more comfortable discussing difficult issues with me, Narciso acknowledged other instances where he perceived racism in Cuban culture. In reference to the Cuban *telenovelas,* or soap operas (which are followed with less religious fervor than the blatantly racist Brazilian imports), Narciso pointed out that the heroes and romantic leads were always white, while the secondary characters and slaves were always black. When I reminded him of this statement during an interview, Narciso said:

> In general with television it is true that the soap operas have white protagonists — there is still that conformity. At the same time I think that there hasn't been anyone who applied their talent to changing this. If a writer wrote a script or a soap opera where the protagonist was black, I don't think that the Cuban state would stop it from being produced, just like the popular new *telenovela* about homosexuality.[14]

Narciso's belief in individual effort as the mechanism for change is noteworthy. After I had known him for several years, Narciso admitted to me what most students of Cuban politics know: the highest rungs of Cuban power are occupied almost exclusively by whites.[15]

Tom Miller, author of the seminal Cuba travelogue, *Trading with the Enemy: A Yankee Travels Through Castro's Cuba,* married a Cuban woman. Miller said one of his stepsons, who worked at a hotel, cited bribery as one way to find work in the state-sanctioned (vs. black market) tourist industry. Dark skinned workers, even if they graduated from Cuba's Tourism School, had it doubly difficult.[16] Cubans need hard currency in order to live decently, and jobs in tourism are highly coveted; the lack of access to those jobs creates another level of inequality. The idea that the tourist trade is biased against dark-skinned Cubans has been raised in literature, sociological studies, and cultural scholarship of the Special Period.[17]

The irony is not lost on Cubaphiles across the political spectrum. Again, a deep inquiry into the subject of race in Cuba is beyond the realm of this volume. I will add just a few notes from the perspective of a frequent participant/observer. Danza's outspoken Chocolate was the only person with whom I worked throughout the 1990s who ever suggested that my skin color made me different from my Cuban colleagues in any significant way. While working and talking at length with dancers in three different companies—the Cuban National Ballet, Danza, and Dance Company Narciso Medina—I noticed that pigment was discussed much in the same way as hair color, without much emotional weight. Skin color was mentioned most frequently to help identify someone whose name you might not know, for example, "the light-skinned tall guy," or "the dark girl with the blonde ponytail." Although Irma's mother disapproved of her daughter's boyfriend because he was dark-skinned, that perspective seemed to have a clear generational bias and was considered unacceptable among the dancers. For artists who grew up with and were educated by the Revolution, social ease and intermixing across ethnicities was the norm.

This anecdotal evidence is far from exhaustive, but it provides a contrast to my experience in the United States, where questions of race are often either inflammatory or uncomfortably unspoken. Even in the world of dance, where artists tend to associate according to aesthetic rather than ideological criteria, enormous issues of racial disparity continue. While the National Ballet is still much whiter than Cuba's two other national companies, it is significant that the BNC has produced some of the world's most celebrated ballet dancers of color.

Although I was often the lightest person in a group of Cuban dancers, the difference most commonly referred to was my nationality. When Lino Angel entered the studio to find me sweeping the floor, he exclaimed, "I never dreamed I'd see a yanqui cleaning a Cuban floor!" He did not mention the difference in our skin tones. The obvious gap between us had to do with the disparity between our passports, not our skin color.

Chapter 10

Keeping the Gods at Bay

Afro-Cuba is a survivor society. Its dances, which have been repeatedly outlawed, are survivors also.

Despite the disappointments and setbacks of the past decade, the strict racial divisions of pre–Revolutionary Cuba have given way to a changed social structure. This change is apparent in cultural production. While parity has yet to be achieved on many levels, the widespread acceptance of *Santería* is one indication of these changes. That *Santería* was censured through the Republican era, and at the beginning of the Castro years, has been documented. The Castro regime was initially resistant to the traditions of Afro-Cuba but — with characteristic pragmatism — slowly accepted them. The Teatro Nacional has been credited with helping to legitimize Afro-Cuban forms of expression over the years, particularly after a mid–1960s move by the state, which prohibited initiation ceremonies of *Santería*.[1] That act was revoked in 1971, although it took some time for initiates to feel comfortable with open religious practice. The regime's seemingly schizophrenic actions were a public reflection of its conflict of interests: communist ideology vs. popular religious sentiment. Since the mid–'90s Cuba's attitude toward religion has softened significantly, the most famous symbol of that change being the Pope's 1998 visit to Cuba. With a more tolerant attitude toward religion in general, *Santería* is now openly practiced. The turnabout in official attitudes toward Afro-Cuban tradition is not just good internal politics; it's good business. *Santurismo*, tourist trade based on the lure of *Santería*, has become extremely lucrative. While some Cuban practitioners are swayed by the deep pockets of curious tourists, performing what the late Katherine Dunham dismissed as "fast and easy initiations,"[2] many other believers guard their heritage closely.

Dance has been central to preserving Afro-Cuban identity and cohesion. Repressed by Spaniards, Christians, the early republic, and for many years the Revolutionary government, the *cabildos* kept certain dances secret in order to protect their practice. Other dances were simply too sacred to be shared with outsiders. Even today the true rituals of *Santería* worship are infrequently photographed; most images we see are of public displays or theatrical renditions.

The *rumba* tradition has had a less tumultuous path. The Revolutionary government had relatively little conflict with those who expressed African heritage through the more secular dances of *rumba*. That tradition was put into national service with the Ministry of Culture's decidedly secular support of neighborhood dance and music events called Rumba Saturdays.[3]

The more sacred dances of *Santería* have played an interesting role in Cuban cultural outreach since the Revolution. The Conjunto Folklórico specializes in performance of these dances in their traditional — though secular and theatrical — form. For its part, *técnica cubana* incorporates elements of *orisha* dances into its melded contemporary style. Some have argued that the theatricalization of ritual dances has denuded them of their power.[4] The great anthropologist Fernando Ortiz was opposed to Afro-Cuban ritual dances being used in tourist settings precisely for that reason.[5] Marketed as entertainment, these dances have not been preserved intact in their ritual context. In Cuba this has both helped the dances survive and destroyed their integrity. Most dances performed for the media, or within tourist settings, are constructed so as to be safely secular. These dances were redesigned to appease the audience's need for tradition, and at the same time not to offend the *santero* or the *santo*. Katherine Hagedorn explains that, "these ritual traditions were recontextualized in order to satisfy more fully their new revolutionary function: the uplifting, informing, and dignifying entertainment of the Cuban people."[6]

None of these dances are danced as they were in Africa centuries ago, or even as they are danced in Africa today. Yet even as these dances are being performed for uninitiated audiences, their religious context is being revived. Those who perform sacred dances theatrically have created a manner of keeping tradition alive. While this is not a pure repository of their ritual form, it has allowed dancers to pass knowledge from one generation to the next, seeking out those who would learn more while instructing those who can carry on. In other words, without theatrical, secular and carnival performance, certain Afro-Caribbean dances might have perished altogether during times when ritual practice was actively repressed. The path of these dances from their "pure"[7] ritual state in Africa, through embodied memory, past prohibition at the hands of church and state, all form part of a process that transforms dance practice according to the tenor of the times. Dance history is rife with examples of dances that have veered away from their traditional form and purpose, swayed by practical, religious, political and geographical pressures. In contemporary Cuba, the pressing realities transforming folkloric dance may have less to do with religious repression than they do with the market economy.

Omitting the Secret Ingredient

> A deity's supreme requirement is that one among the faithful become his "horse" by means of trance, so that he can come down among mankind and dance.— Gisele Cossard (1970)

Divine union is sought through *orisha* dancing. The divinity is said to enter the body of its acolytes and cause them to dance in a way that is distinctly characteristic of that god. Possession trances are central to the efficacy of Afro-Cuban rituals. A possession trance is an individual trance brought on with the help of a group that includes a leader, or *apkwon*, musicians, sacred drums, and other believers. Erupting in fast, uncontrolled movements, these dances externalize the state of possession, in a way sharing or exhibiting the god's presence to the group. The dancer, or trancer, embodies the deity in behavior and gesture. Channeling Elegguá, for instance, a believer might snatch someone's snack; ridden by Changó, the trancer might stomp the floor until it shakes.

> In possession, then, dance is a representation of the gods, in other words theater — sacred theater, but also theater that one enacts not only for oneself, but also for others.— Erika Bourguignon (1968)

Santería practitioners worship an alternate reality, one that their children are exposed to from an early age. Just as children observe and imitate dance moves, they also learn to recognize and accept the erratic gestures of possession. Most Cubans have witnessed *creyentes,* or believers, falling into trance. In sacred settings they give up their resistance and "let it happen," reigniting body memory that has been observed, sought, and developed over time. Scholars have written that the group — the *apkwon*, drummers, spectators and trancers — and their expectations have a huge impact on the proceedings.[8] These expectations and beliefs structure the behavior of the trancers, much like a hypnotist's commands to his subjects. This speaks to the significance of cultural learning and group worship, and to the deep connection many Cubans have to their African traditions.

"Possession trances are above all culturally stylized performances and experiences," writes Gilbert Rouget in his book, *Music and Trance*. "It's sacred theater, but also theater that one enacts not only for oneself, but also for others."[9] The use of the terms *performance* and *theater* here is intentional: by going into trance the trancer is publicly exhibiting his or her faith and connection to the deity. This is not to say it is not real from the empirical point of view, but rather that the group expects and seeks the transcendence of "bringing down the god." Context is essential to the ease and depth with which a person will allow him or herself to fall into trance. So is ritual preparation. Orishas are summoned with special altars, "toques" or events in their honor, the sacrifice of their favorite elements, like cigars, rum, cornmeal, and fruit.

To bring on trance practitioners use stylized, rhythmic movement, exertion, hyperventilation, as well as changes in balance and spatial orientation. They incorporate sensory stimuli like music, heat, symbolic scents or noises. They intensify and narrow their attention, seeking patterns previously observed and experienced. They call on their knowledge of the identities and characteristics of the deities they want to call down. Sometimes, along with the leader, they will drink rum or smoke a cigar, which are always first offered to the *orisha* and the ancestors. A large ingredient in these sacred acts is preparation for an altered state — whether by fasting, praying, building an altar, or consciously summoning the deity.

Practitioners of *Santería* understand that certain settings are sacred and others profane. The same auditorium could be ordinary one day and sacred the next, consecrated by the use of the ritual *batá* drums. It is not appropriate to go into trance in a non-ritualistic setting, such as a theatrical presentation. Performing a sacred act in a non-sacred location de-sanctifies it.

Since ecstatic union is the basis of *Santería*, performers have reconfigured sacred dances, making them "safe" for secular consumption. In order to perform in theatrical contexts, the Conjunto Folklórico altered many orisha dances to avoid offending the deity or "calling down the god."[10] The Conjunto and smaller folkloric groups have subtly altered sacred dances for secular use. Particular rhythms are left out, certain songs are edited, key elements are omitted. Ritual preparations, such as the "feeding" of the drums and offering rum to the ancestors, are not practiced. Sacred *orisha* rituals include more improvisation in terms of the interplay between the leader, the batá drums, and the participants. Creativity gives the proceedings more divine potential. Someone seeking a transcendent ritual prepares for an altered state; conversely, when dancers bypass sacred practices they help differentiate the performative context from the religious.

I am not an expert or even a practitioner, but I have tried to open my mind and honor the sacred dances I have witnessed over decades, in Cuba and in other cultures as well.[11] Essentially, it seems that entering into trance has to do with preparation and intent. The intent is either to participate in a ritual ceremony or to put on a performance. Like a cook omitting a secret ingredient from a recipe, dances are altered subtly for secular use.

What they leave out is the heart, the sacredness. — Consuelo Annon[12]

In teaching *orisha* dances to tourists and non-believers, Cuban practitioners separate *orisha* movement from religious context. Though teachers often explain the significance of certain gestures and steps, the transmission is informational rather than spiritual. There is essentially one way of dancing for and with *creyentes* [believers] and another way for those who admire or practice the music and dance separately from the religion. In secular settings there is no sacred intent, no ritual preparation. And the most sacred danced rituals are not shared.

Dancers practice these dances with different intent and purpose. Rehearsal for a sacred ritual is rehearsal of *function*; rehearsal for a theatrical performance is rehearsal of *form*.

So what happens when the god mounts the dancer without invitation?

The Feast of Changó, Havana 1994

The Feast of Changó, one of the most "feared and respected"[13] deities in the *Santería* pantheon, is simultaneously the feast of Santa Barbara, as the two are syncretic images of the same deity. In December of 1994, Narciso and his company produced a *peña*, or street performance in honor of this feast. It consisted of a stylized representation of a Santería *toque*, or ritual. Here is the "text" of that highly unusual performance:

The festivities take place in the street and on the patio outside #487 Calle 8 in Vedado. This building, once home to Jose Marti's mother, now houses the studio Narciso has built in his former residence. I am living in the building and my apartment, conveniently located next to the stone porch, serves as the performers' backstage, green room and dressing room. The entire neighborhood turns out. Entertainment is sorely needed since food, clothing and gasoline rations are at a low. Marlene Carbonell, now a principal dancer in the company, is using my electric hotplate to make a traditional offering of cornmeal for the orishas. *Dressed as Yemayá, the goddess of maternity and salt waters, Marlene is careful not to spill cornmeal on her blue and white costume.*

The porch has been equipped with a set of bleachers transformed into a makeshift altar. Marlene brings out dishes of the cooked cornmeal to adorn the bleachers/altar, adding to the offerings of flowers, bananas, and candles provided by other dancers and residents. Neighbors gather around, adding personal contributions to the arrangement. The feast happens to fall on one of the first nights of Hanukkah this year. In my role as visiting inter-cultural company representa-

A neighborhood performance on the steps of the Academia de la Danza and apartment building on Calle 8, December 3, 1999. Tomas Guilarte as Oggún, Narciso Medina as Changó, Omar Yirat as Elegguá. Jolena Alonso, a choreographer and former student of the academia, watches the proceedings from the left.

tive, I light a candle and recite the B'rucha *in Hebrew. This elicits curious whispers from the audience.*

Lino Angel, compact and energetic, dances the role of Elegguá. Dressed in red and black, the child god and trickster Elegguá "opens the roads;" as such it is he who begins all orisha *performances and ceremonies. Lino plays his part well. As I sit by the side of the stage, he chooses me as his foil, teasing and threatening me simultaneously as he embodies the mischievous deity. The dance of Elegguá intrigues neighbors and passers-by who join the audience. By this point the crowd has grown to include some foreigners, among them an American documentary film team and a group of French tourists. After the roads are opened the other deities make their appearance on the porch that is our stage. As the mother of the* orisha *pantheon, Yemayá, Marlene invokes the hypnotic undulations of the sea, weaving a polyrhythm, dancing 2/4 against a 3/4 beat.*

In his role as savvy impresario, Narciso drums up interest in his company by calling on local customs, religion, and imagery. Using song and dance familiar to a Cuban audience—much more familiar, in fact, than the relatively obscure art of modern dance—Narciso expands his audience base, creating a neighborhood event, and probably recruiting a few new students. This theatrical presentation of folkloric dances is not meant to substitute for real religious ritual. Narciso, a pragmatic Diaghilev of Cuban dance, doesn't try to "bring down the god" with his performance. Instead, as Changó, thunder thrower and King of the orishas, *he woos the crowd with strength and aplomb. Stomping the ground in his bare feet, reaching toward the sky to hurl an invisible thunderbolt, Narciso embodies Changó despite his threadbare red and white costume and paper crown. Laughing and voluptuous, Yamilé Socorrás joins Narciso onstage as Ochún, resplendent in an old lamé unitard and a skirt of yellow and white. The goddess of fertility, linked syncretically to Cuba's patron saint la Virgen del Cobre, Ochún is also Changó's lover and a famous flirt. The duet between these two is a crowd pleaser with gender caricatures taken skillfully to the extreme.*

The young and talented Cándido Muñoz, a schoolmate of the stellar ballet dancer Carlos Acosta, is a virtuosic firebrand in Narciso's troupe. Tonight he dances the god of iron and war, Oggún. Cándido is convincing as the imperious deity, using his machete to slice the air with menace. As it turns out, Cándido is a practicing believer in Santería, a creyente. *Still relatively inexperienced as a performer, Cándido crosses the line from performance to ritual. While this does not usually happen without many other ritual practices in place, trance or "bringing down the god" is something Cubans take quite seriously. For the most part they admit that possession is, by definition, beyond their absolute control. As Cándido dances with more and more fervor, his eyes take on a wild sheen. At first it is unclear what is happening, but soon it looks like Cándido is being "mounted" by the god, falling into trance. We in the company can't tell if he's acting or losing control. But he's onstage and we are off; we watch nervously as he steps into the crowd, playfully threatening the audience.*

There is a bald Frenchman in the crowd, smoking a cigar and looking unimpressed. Cándido spots him and without missing a beat takes the cigar and puffs dramatically on it, evoking laughter and annoyance. It's a good cigar, the kind sold only to tourists for hard currency. This is part of Cándido's politically subversive intent: he would not bother to grab a Cuban cigar available for pesos at the corner bodega. Eyes growing wilder, Cándido-Oggún passes his machete across the smoker's bald pate. To our astonishment, he draws blood. Cándido has crossed many boundaries by this point: religious, professional, sanitary and diplomatic. The Frenchman is enraged. His companions hold him back from pummeling Cándido who continues to dance triumphantly, still being "ridden by the god." The victim's friends noisily drag the bleeding man away, ostensibly to get a tetanus shot at the hospital exclusively for foreigners. The crowd, uncertain which parts of this spectacle have been played for their enjoyment, loves it.

Lino reappears as Eleggúa, whose job it is to end as well as begin the dancing. Lino tries to close the show with a semblance of normalcy, which requires great discipline on his part. Backstage, Narciso furiously shakes Cándido out of his trance, delivering a lecture on professionalism, illusion and reality. Cándido admits sheepishly that he had not been in control. What's not clear is who had been. For those who believe, the strength and presence of the orishas *is undeniable. Cándido knows he's gone too far, but he is too disoriented, and truly surprised at his own actions, to argue. For Narciso the impresario, the inviolable rules separating theater from reality, theater from religion, and professional conduct from self-indulgence, have been violated. His company is not supposed to provide a religious experience, but a folkloric and theatrical one. Never should a dancer cross those lines, not to mention assault an audience member.*

The event has been an artistic disaster, but a promotional blockbuster. The neighborhood buzzes for days with juicy details involving a foreigner and the toque, *or touch, of Oggún.*

Narciso's company had inadvertently created a Happening in the '60s tradition, or what Merce Cunningham would call an Event. Even more so, it had created an exciting neighborhood scandal involving a foreigner carrying hard currency and the intervention of irrepressible local deities. While Narciso was adamant that the mistake should not be repeated, what resulted was a tremendous mixture of performative realities: that of the professional dance troupe putting on a show; a free and popular street performance; agit-prop theater in which political realities and economic inequity incited aggression between real-life players; and a blurring of the divisions between ritual practice and folkloric recreation.

This story serves as an extreme example of the hybrid nature of Cuban modern dance. While Narciso's *toque* was based on traditional dances, it was performed by a troupe of modern dancers, those much more accustomed to, and interested in, bending the paradigms of theatrical performance. A folkloric troupe would be unlikely to make such a glaring mistake, neglecting to take precautions believers must take to keep ritual practice separate — and protected — from theatrical presentation. In this instance, not only were the boundaries that normally separate genres blurred, but the "fourth wall" between audience and performer was transgressed. It is not unusual for practitioners of *técnica cubana* to intentionally, and at times riskily, place themselves outside the traditional range of both Western theatrical dance and folkloric re-creation. While the company learned its lesson and did not repeat that particular gaff, Cándido's *faux pas* exemplified the experimental spirit of Cuban contemporary dance.

It was also a profoundly political moment.

In many ritual settings those who go into trance are released from normal expectations of behavior: responsibilities, gender roles, and the need to be appropriate. These can be very compelling reasons to give in to the lure of possession. Not surprisingly, at the time of his transgression Cándido was an angry young man. He was angry at his country, and at foreigners he resented for staying in luxury hotels where they enjoyed the fruits of his lush homeland while he and his cohorts stayed hungry. Under the guise of Oggún, Cándido was able to express his rage.

It's impossible to know whether Cándido actually went into a trance. Marlene, who danced Yemayá, says she will never forget that evening:

> That was the best era of our company — unforgettable! We were so young, with the desire to eat the whole world, to conquer everything.
> Cándido went into ecstasy, with a huge emotional charge, an immensely powerful internal moment. He touched the sky with his hand in that moment![14]

Asked if she believed Cándido was in trance, Marlene answered, "No; I don't believe in that stuff." But then she added, "Cándido did ... and he still does! For Cándido it was as if he had the god Oggún inside him."

Chapter 11

Ramiro Guerra:
Técnica De-contextualized

While the Conjunto Folklórico had an obligation to find balance between the sacred, traditional and secular, *técnica* had no such mandate. Elements of Afro-Cuban dance were integrated into *técnica* in a post-modern manner: de-contextualized and still ripe with significance. Just as a contraction from the Graham technique could be incorporated into a sequence with ballet steps and flamenco arms, so would the new technique include a spinal ripple or gesture from the lexicon of *orisha* movement. The understanding was that the audience would recognize the allusion without expecting a traditional ritualistic or religious outcome.

On a spring evening in 2006, Ramiro Guerra and I shared a leisurely meal at an outdoor restaurant near the Malecón.[1] He explained that he was surprised when, in the early days of the company, the Cuban audience often inferred references to *Santería* that were not intentionally placed in his dances:

> They said, "Oh! The dogs of Chango!" The public saw that because they are believers—you know most Cubans are. So they saw things [in my choreography] that I had not thought of, because they have their own perceptions—very much their own. I offered them one thing, and they saw something way beyond that, something in accord with their sentiment and their relationship with nature, with the gods, with the traditions.... They saw things I had not dreamed of.

The legacy of Afro-Cuban dance, including the dances of *Santería*, is woven into *técnica* as part of an expressive, integrated whole. The shape of that whole continued to transform in the early years, incorporating diverse dance knowledge that Guerra and his colleagues consciously chose to include in the new Cuban form. He explained:

> We have a tradition, those of us from the islands, of looking outside ourselves and then transforming what we find. Martí studied abroad, and later he became

the intellectual leader of Cuba. All those generations of writers, Carpentier and others, became who they were abroad. I did this also; I left. I traveled far from Cuba because it was very limited to study here. Then I brought back everything I learned. I made it my own, and I related it to the problem of being Cuban. And with that I built an audience.

Guerra said that initially he and his collaborators were strict about what was and what was not part of *técnica*. But over time, based on his observations of the dancers, and his study of "how the Cuban body moves," he made conscious additions, alterations, and refinements. Guerra used the iconic Graham contraction, but sparingly.

> Graham is very percussive, Graham contractions are difficult for Cuban dancers; our bodies are very undulating, even to the extreme. Graham used the pelvis and shoulders to arrive forcefully in certain positions. This creates the emotional impact of her technique. But not the Cuban technique. We travel in and out of the contraction less percussively. We adapted Graham for the Cuban body.

Guerra gave credit to Cuban folkloric dance for much of the movement of the torso and pelvis. "The use of the pelvis is highly developed in our dances. It's instinctive for us. And all of the upper torso work is not only like this," he demonstrated, rippling his spine forward and back at the table, "but also in torsion," he said, spiraling in his chair.

> It's elaborated with the head, the shoulders. I made one piece, to Garcia Lorca's poem "Lament for Ignacio Sanchez Mejia," which had five minutes of just turning. With the head spinning. It was very dramatic.

Laughing, Guerra went on:

> There are mysteries of the dance and culture. The human being functions with the body. How many things have we created with the body? How many things can the body create? We have built the world with the body, with our hands and with our voices. So many possibilities. And now we have genetic code to complicate our lives more!

Impishly energetic, Guerra returned to the elements of the Cuban style, acknowledging that the training in *técnica* has become increasingly powerful over the years. As a scholar he has traced countless dance influences back to their roots:

> African priests and priestesses who arrived as slaves in Cuba reconstructed the drums and the songs of their ancestors. They carried in their blood the rhythms and dances created by their people. Here in Cuba there have been a lot of studies, important studies by Don Fernando [Ortiz] to determine which parts of Africa our people came from, and what parts of our island they were taken to.

Ladling more crispy *tostones* onto his plate, I wondered about the source of a recurrent hand gesture in *técnica,* one that seems to echo the twirling wrists of flamenco *floreo.* I asked Guerra about flamenco influences in Cuba and in *técnica.* The Maestro gave his answer an historical twist, reminding me that "pure" flamenco is a hybrid form that combines ancient influences from far-flung sources:

> Of course, slavery existed in Spain before it existed in the Americas — the rhythms of Africa were already mixed into the music of Spain. You see, flamenco has origins in India, from some tribes along the Ganges. And in Spain popular dance and flamenco were also influenced by the sensuality of the Cuban body. For example the *sarabande* and the *chaconne*, which I have studied, were very sensuous dances originated by the black slaves in Cuba. *Sarabande* is a word used among the Bantu people here, it's a religious rite. When the Spaniards returned from the New World and landed in Cadiz, they danced the *sarabande* and the *chaconne*. Spanish authorities banned the dances as licentious, and the dancers went to jail if caught! Gruesome.... Later these dances were transformed into dances of the courts, but then they were stripped of any sexual allusion.

Guerra mimed a courtly posture before going on to cite more characteristics of Cuban dance. He spoke briefly of improvisation, which plays an important role in the choreographic process. Often highly trained dancers experience some inhibition when first asked to move spontaneously. Conversely, most Cuban dancers exhibit great freedom when inventing movement on the spot.

> Improvisation comes from popular dances, and from African tradition. We are very conscious of rhythm; we can do one rhythm with our hands and another with our feet, and this comes in part from flamenco.

Seizing my opportunity, I brought the conversation back to flamenco, trying to localize the source of one of my favorite gestures in *técnica*. His answer was professorial:

> Today in Cuba some dancers are consciously combining flamenco with Cuban elements. For example, there is the *rumba flamenca*, where dancers combine and exchange rhythms from the Americas and Spain.

"But at beginning of the *técnica cubana* did you put in this arm?" I interrupted, twirling my wrist above the rice and beans.

> No ... it had nothing to do with the Spanish dance. I studied the Spanish dance when I was in Spain, but never used it in *técnica*.

"Then where does this comes from?" I persisted, showing the *floreo* again.

> It was something from the choreographer Victor Cuellar, from his piece called *Panorama* in which he did something like that. It was purely choreographic.

"So you were not like Martha" I asked, "insisting that the technique had to be exactly the way you said it was?" We had arrived back at Martha Graham. Guerra shook his head and smiled.

At first, I was, yes. But it began to change; it changed with the bodies of the dancers. Everyone contributed, including the teachers. These embellishments were not invented in the classroom. They were created as choreography, and then returned to the classroom. They became part of the code. Unknowingly, unwittingly, parts of the choreography stayed in the style.

Teachers and choreographers have introduced eclectic dance elements over decades, refining and enriching the technique.

"Yes," Guerra confirmed. "Everyone contributes."

Once in practice, the elements are no longer teased apart. Instead they flow together in the service of the choreography. Technique is the language; but context, composition, music, costumes, and stagecraft provide the meaning. I asked him a question about *cubanidad,* using the popular academic jargon of "national identity."

> I have been in these meetings of intellectuals where they discuss identity. My generation, we didn't have to study identity [laughs]. We didn't have to study it — we were who we were! And now you have to publish books to decide what is identity. And at the conclusion of these very interesting books they say that you can't talk about identity — exactly what we are talking about — because the world has become too compact, and we are all dependent upon one another. A style that came out yesterday, young people see it on television or at the cinema, and they have to possess that same style tomorrow. Everyone does the same thing. To have identity now is very difficult.

Eager to study some iconic works of the Cuban style, I asked the Maestro if I might copy a few of his archival videos. I had struck a chord. In addition to having no working elevator, he had no internet access and nowhere to copy videos or DVD's. At the television department of the university, where the maestro customarily had his videos copied, all the video equipment was broken. The ubiquitous bureaucracy — which makes importing basic electronic equipment next to impossible — rankled him. He raised his voice, bemoaning the red tape that binds up every aspect of Cuban life.

> No one understands it. It's surreal. You have to beg for permission to bring in equipment the Ministry already gave you permission to bring! It's confusing, irritating. Can I or can't I? There is no rhyme or reason. No, it is the way it is. Then — no one knows why — it just changes! It's created huge insecurity in everyday life, in social life.

Yet within this context of change and conflict, Cuban modern dance had continued to flourish. I asked Guerra about the Special Period, when I encountered a vibrancy in Cuban dance that belied the economic struggles of the time. He felt that the creativity I witnessed in the 1990s was built on a dance tradition firmly established in earlier decades.

It came from before. There was no dance creativity in the '90s; it was already finished. By then people had it in their bodies, there were already dancers in the school who had assimilated the technique. The decade of the '60s was when all of that was created. By the '70s there was a cultural counter-reaction. People lost their way. I lost my way. Of course I did, because I dedicated myself to writing.

I respectfully disagree with Guerra on one point: I witnessed great creativity during the Special Period — admittedly not in the creation of a new dance form — but in the incorporation of that unusual form into dances that spoke to contemporary experience. The basis for the art form had been established in the first decades of the Revolution. It's unlikely that *técnica* could have been created during the Special Period, when there was little room for expansion or invention; but once *técnica cubana* existed, it gave generations of dancers a language with which to express their experience. Guerra acknowledged that the arts were hardy:

> The Special Period was a powerful psychological blow to the minds of all Cubans. It was a tremendous ordeal. But we had already created much of our culture, forms of expression that nothing could destroy.

With the building blocks of a clearly Cuban modern dance form in place, Guerra's students, and their students, were able to create a body of work firmly planted in Cuban thematic material and dance tradition. *Técnica* was not forged amid the economic and social chaos of the 1990s, but during those difficult years the state-sponsored schools continued training dancers well versed in the Cuban style and technique. The numbers of practitioners grew, and a new generation of choreographers, including Narciso Medina and Marianela Boán, used the language of Cuban modern dance to interpret the world around them.

The power and lure of the Cuban modern dance form lies in its specificity; it provides for particularities of bodies, traditions and ways of moving that are clearly Cuban. Cuban intellectuals, politicians and artists have struggled for centuries to define *cubanismo,* "a certain way" [*de cierta manera*][2] of being. This undeniable Cuban-ness reflects a self-concept that is consciously separate from Spain, from the rest of the Caribbean, and from the United States. *Técnica cubana* is a small but articulate part of that effort. Choreographers continue to transform their movement language in ways that make it current and relevant, building on a path of resilience and creativity. Cuban modern dancers are a small counterforce to global hegemony, embodying a homegrown art form that thrives on exploring what it is to be Cuban.

Maestro Guerra and I walked carefully down the buckling sidewalk back to his building. We slowly climbed nine flights of stairs, the last three in the dark. In his apartment, where the crumbling walls are lined with books and dance posters, we spoke for a few more hours, until the seasoned gentleman saw that he had tired me out. He sent me home in a *turistaxi* with a signed copy of one of his many books, *Coordenadas Danzarias,* a fascinating discourse on dance of the twentieth century.

Chapter 12

Modern Dance: A Hearty, Subversive Hybrid

Although Western theatrical dance has rarely been subjected to rigorous socio-political scrutiny, it is nonetheless a social practice which is inevitably and profoundly political. — Elizabeth Dempster[1]

The role of modern dance has often been to awaken, agitate, poke fun, or polemicize. In contrast with ballet, which seeks to uphold tradition while (hopefully) expanding it, modern dance is eternally pushing at aesthetic, behavioral and cultural boundaries. And often, with more or less efficacy, it has included social or political content.

Significantly, *técnica cubana* straddles the divide between Western theatrical dance and "non–Western dance forms."[2] The reason for this is its hybrid nature, its grounding in the aesthetic and socio-political context of modernism, and the inclusion of African diasporic movement in its fundamental dance language. Building on the Western dance tradition, Cuban modern dance frequently addresses the audience from behind the proscenium, in theatrical productions that maintain the audience/performer divide. Yet that convention has been ruptured by choreographers such as Guerra, Medina and Boán, all of whom have been known to present site-specific work in non-traditional settings ... by Western dance standards. Medina occasionally uses the street in front of his studio as a performance space, a format that is based in both ritual and street theater. And of course, Guerra's ill-fated *Decálogo del Apocalipsis* was created for the exalted Plaza de la Revolución, though it was never performed in that location or any other.

Dance is a relatively obscure setting for social and political criticism. As discussed earlier, the decorative reputation and opaque nature of dance provide choreographers with both freedom and limitations. The exigencies of the Special Period inspired several important developments in the repertoire of Cuban modern dance: as polemic, practice, and commodity. While reams have been written on the economic, cultural and literary transformations that occurred in Cuba during this era, very little is available in the way of modern dance documentation, much less analysis. Interpreting dance language within a theoretical perspective requires a cross-disciplinary approach. Dance scholarship has developed with a strong reliance on dance journalism, where some of the best dance writing still occurs.[3] Coming late to the academy, often through the gymnasium door, dance scholarship has grown out of a strong association between documentation and analysis. Dance theorists often meld visual descriptions of dancing with explorations of the work's significance. This mixed approach focuses on the "text" of the dance — the choreography — as distinct from, and in addition to, specific performances by particular dancers. Fundamentally, and problematically for many viewers, the text of the dance cannot be divorced from its medium, the body. Current dance theory highlights the historical, social and political contexts in which the dance was made as well as when it was presented, with nods to literary, post-colonial and performance theory. It provides an examination of often-unexpressed preconceptions about the body, the gaze and the implications of movement.

The idea of "reading" dances is not new, yet it has only recently entered the academy. The inter-dependence of dance theory with other disciplines reflects dance's nature as an ephemeral form that resists notation, verbal description, and reliable repetition. It also speaks to the ongoing perception of dance as an art practiced primarily by women and homosexuals, enduring low pay and questionable legitimacy. Dance has often been seen as a pursuit not deemed worthy (until quite recently and among specific populations) of serious scholarship. Yet this underdog position of dance in the arts and academia outside of Cuba is surprisingly different from its ascending status within Cuba. "In Cuba," according to la Señora Alicia, "ballet is a high career."[4]

Modern dance is not in the same category as the highly established ballet, especially in Cuba. But from periods of relative security to times of economic difficulty, modern dancers have situated themselves as artists within the greater Cuban society. This position gives them a certain sense of place. They know that their chosen practice has value.[5] While the average dancer's economic holdings may be as paltry as the next person's, his or her socio-cultural capital is strong. Dancers perceive themselves as important members of society, building on those many years of training and preparation, empowered by a social contract with a society that sees their contribution as valuable. This may not seem like much, but to a North American dancer it represents an enviable sense of cultural validity.

It is possibly that this sense of validity and purpose helped to give dance a voice in the difficult years of the Special Period. Dancers and choreographers felt they were fulfilling certain needs in a troubled society: entertainment, escape, emotional involvement, and at times, social commentary. Dance, at its best, gives form to that which is already known, but is as yet unexpressed. Everyday experience can be re-imagined with humor or absurdity. Deep discontents, pathos and satire can be shared in the dark auditorium, on the traveling theater cart or the open plaza. The primal medium of the body, articulate beyond words, can evoke both thought and feeling. The dancer trains the body and then gets out of the way, allowing a finely developed kinesthetic intelligence to take over. The viewer has an empathic experience, a sense of participation in the flying leap, the embrace, the fierce contraction. This is different from the particular joys of a well-made play, where the experience is tightly connected to language. What dance creates, then, is a physical/ visual/kinesthetic experience in dancer and audience. It teaches us to recognize what we know without knowing we know, using the forms of expression that are most basic to every human: gesture, emotion, and movement. With these direct links to the psyche, the right creative dance-maker can communicate almost anything.

Dancers use words that are linked to spoken language: we speak of dance "vocabulary," "phrases," and "combinations," the latter being like paragraphs of movement. Different dance languages are not usually combined; in traditional texts we still see divisions between the languages of ballet, modern, and folkloric dance, which frequently refer to similar movements and rhythms by different names. For example, "waltz," "*balancé*," and "triplet" all refer to essentially the same step in 3/4 time, using social, ballet and modern dance terminology respectively. Contemporary dance forms plumb the past and the present to create new idioms, combining a mixed vocabulary while using new syntax. This symbolic system continues to evolve; emerging choreographers and performance artists are constantly reinventing the rules.

Dance is often referred to as a universal language, but the context and symbolism that make dance readable are often decidedly local. Narciso Medina's *La Espera* is a piece that is modest in conception and execution. Nevertheless, it successfully crystallizes a particular moment and mindset in Cuban history. *La Espera* explores a fundamental experience of the Special Period: the act of waiting.

Women's Work: Polemical Pliés

While Medina often reaches beyond the confines of theatrical convention, his eagerness to connect to both his subject matter and his audience on a socio-political level reflects his forebears in modern dance. After all, his mentor

Ramiro Guerra studied with some of the great choreographic iconoclasts for whom sexual and class politics were favorite fodder for dance-making. Early in the 20th Century, Isadora Duncan led an effort to reform the physical constraint women endured in everyday clothing. By the 1930s, a time of great creativity in American and German modern dance, the form was intimately linked to social activism. Modern dance became both a symbol of and a rallying point for the growing Leftist movement. "To ask how to create revolutionary dance was to ask how to choreograph revolution by engendering an avant-garde."[6] Dance in some ways provided impetus, or *movement*, to the growing movement, in effect embodying the revolutionary impulse.

While the old modern dances were literal in their reference to social causes, they were expressionistic in their form. Graham's seminal *Chronicle* is a masterpiece of anti-war visual poetry, a dance in solidarity with victims of the Great Depression and the Spanish Civil War. In 1937 critic Henry Gilfond noted that *Chronicle* depicted "the looming horror of a universal catastrophe and its moral breakup."[7] To see this work today is to understand it in a timeless context: the vulnerability of innocence, the call to arms, the resistance, the perseverance of women left behind, the mindless compulsion of violence. While not narrative, the dance still "speaks," that is, it creates its own non-verbal text that communicates volubly.

Graham had many progressive contemporaries and acolytes, such as the firebrands Sophie Maslow and Anna Sokolow, who addressed issues pertaining to social injustice without concern for ladylike behavior. They in turn influenced generations of dancers, spreading the gospel of concept-based dances bearing little relation to the tales of sylphs and princesses popular in the nineteenth century. Modern dance became individualistic and expressionistic in form, striking a chord in a public tired of fairy tales. There was a hunger for extreme psychological drama, for a connection to contemporary life, and for an art that reflected the new World and its heterogeneous population. These tastes were satisfied by Graham's powerful renditions of ancient Greek myth, by the progressive subject matter of the New Dance Group, and by Katherine Dunham's celebration of Afro-Caribbean themes within concert dance.

Dance scholars have linked the aesthetic development of the art form with political and feminist trends that surfaced in the early twentieth century.[8] Early modern dance was female-driven, while other modern (not to mention classical) art media were most decidedly not. Radical dance grew out of the feminism of Isadora Duncan, and matured with the social consciousness of Martha Graham. Pioneering modern dancers and their postmodern counterparts challenged the prevailing aesthetic and societal status quo with their onstage innovations. Their dramatic offstage personae often contributed to this endeavor. These dancers chose a markedly different trajectory from those who pursued a traditional ballet career. They worked barefoot and often for free, baring their hearts and occasionally their breasts. If they titillated their audience, so be it: their goal was not to embody beauty for its own sake, but to explore ideas of consequence. They eschewed traditional lifestyles and cultivated connections to other "free spirits" and "bohemians."

In Cuba, modern dance has often pushed the socio-cultural envelope. Guerra fought the good fight as a young male dancer in an oppressively macho system, and later as a choreographer and writer (one of his recent essays is titled "Dance: Menace and Resistance"). Medina played with gender assumptions in his evening-length *Ultimos Exitos del Fin del Siglo* (Greatest Hits of the End of the Century), creating militaristic movement for a corps of muscled women and costuming two hunky male dancers in pink tutus and brassieres. *Danza Voluminosa* [Voluminous Dance] is a company of very full-bodied dancers, one of several emerging groups in Cuba that experiment with preconceptions about aesthetics and sex roles.

The Language of Emotion[9]

> For the modern dancer, dance is an expression of interiority — interior feeling guiding the movement of the body into external forms. Doris Humphrey described her dance as "moving from the inside out"; for Graham it was a process of "making visible the interior landscape." — Elizabeth Dempster[10]

Duncan showed her emotion in raw form, dancing to release women from their physical restraint, to embody the Marseillaise and celebrate the Russian Revolution. Graham squeezed emotion into a highly disciplined and stylized theatrical package, decried by early critics as "ugly dance." One might also say the traditionally female characteristic of emotion feminized the form. In both its emotional transparency and the gender of its founders, early modern dance went against the Modernist grain. While contemporary dance remains a language of emotion that can portray quiet intimacy or communal connection, it has largely diverged from the feminist/activist profile of its early days. The feminine strength and vulnerability that built the form reflect a paradigm that was slowly inverted by the rise of male choreographers. Today, perhaps unsurprisingly, most professional contemporary dance companies around the world are run by men, as are most ballet and folkloric companies.

The prominence of male dancers in Cuba, as discussed in previous chapters, is now legend. While Ramiro Guerra's early pre–Revolutionary performances were greeted with disdain and homophobia, he ultimately led the way for the success of such dancer/choreographers as Eduardo Rivero, Lesme

Grenot and Narciso Medina. Through intimate subtlety or grand gestures, men in modern dance embrace a certain clarity and range of feeling that is less revealed in other forms. The *danseur noble* of classical ballet must remain stoic in both love and defeat, while the flamenco dancer must exhibit self-assurance and machismo at all times. In contrast, the modern dancer — male, female, gay, straight, or transgendered — is allowed to express a full spectrum of emotion through the thinking/feeling, strong/vulnerable body.

Dance artists such as John Kelly and Richard Move have taken the sexual politics of dance into a new arena, challenging the very idea of gender. This is not surprising, considering that the art form has always attracted progressive thinkers and practitioners of alternative lifestyles. There is great freedom allowed in dance's admittedly outside-the-mainstream milieu. This may have something to do with the fact that despite a few glossy television ads, modern dance has never been very commercial.

> The fact that modern dance, unlike some other theatrical dance forms, was not "big business" allowed it to disregard many of the discriminatory practices of stage and screen, where "morals" clauses often caused performers, including dancers, to remain deeply closeted.[11]

Contemporary dance can be decidedly provocative. The polemical, prodding and even subversive roots of classic modern dance are central to its form. Yet by putting ideas into motion, dance can be specific without being mimetic or literal. In critical circles, there is much discussion about the representational aspects of dance. Graham said, "dance does not represent; it is." Isadora Duncan said, "If I could write it, I wouldn't have to dance it."[12] Dance speaks its own language, and it does so in ways that words cannot. The postmodern bias in modern dance has been against the literal or narrative, dances that do represent, telling a story in the manner of *Swan Lake* or *Coppelia* (or my own choreodrama, *SH'MA*). In contrast, several contemporary Asian dance forms retain their narrative function, while experimenting with music, theatricality and structure. Currently the pendulum in Western concert dance is swinging back to narrative work after decades of "pure" and "abstract" choreography. George Balanchine, the father of the plotless neoclassical ballet, felt that dance is never truly abstract since the body is always unmistakably human. Guerra has written that dance and sensuality cannot be completely divorced, as the body is the tool of both dance and sex.[13] The dancing body will always be someone's body, no matter how disguised it is by yards of fabric, lighting, movement invention, makeup or convention.

Elements of dance language remain stable across genres: when a boy takes a girl's hand in any dance style from folk to ballet to the most abstract postmodern, audiences make certain assumptions. (The interest for the dance-maker often lies in shaking up those assumptions.) There is inherent, if culturally rooted, meaning in gestures and interactions of dancers on the stage, even without the reliance on character, music, or plot. The communicative effectiveness of a dance depends not only on its text, but on its production values, lights, costumes, etc., and most importantly, on the performance given, or *embodied*, by specific dancers.

Narciso Medina instinctively situates himself somewhere in between the dance world's shifting camps of "dance for dance's sake" and dance with a message. The debate, although it continues in Cuba as it does elsewhere, seems to be of little interest to him. Narciso uses a postmodern grab-bag of influences and dramatic devices. He gives himself license to reveal emotion directly or shield it in irony, to pursue a narrative line or forego storytelling in favor of kinesthetic exploration, to make socio-political references or invent surrealistic flights of fancy.

In the choreography and performance of Narciso's *La Espera*, the experience of being Cuban during the Special Period is encapsulated onstage, projected onto and manipulated by the body of the dancer. He himself is the "page" on which his concepts are written, and the physical restraint he exhibits in this particular dance speaks to the constraint and frustration of the Special Period. *Técnica cubana* was developed with the support of an emerging regime. Yet, in keeping with the experimental and non-conformist nature of modern dance itself, *técnica* has retained the expressive tools and the emotive power to question aspects of life under that regime.

La Espera: The Wait

The best performances allow audiences to see past stylized movement, well-trained bodies and theatrical trappings, and instead create empathy with the kinesthetic experience of the performer. In *La Espera* the viewer experiences an intentional sort of frustration that is both the subject and the result of the material shown. We are distracted by the dancer's virtuosity, by his beauty, and by his odd appearance and costume. It would be easier — that is, more enjoyable — to watch a dancer such as Narciso "really dance" than to see him stand onstage endlessly repeating what is essentially a boring and redundant series of activities. And here lies the basis of the work itself. Narciso subjects his audience to an experience much like his own: that of a Cuban waiting for the bus.

In the Special Period the *guagua*, or bus, often took the form of a truck engine pulling a trailer with a hump in the middle, hence it was not-so-affectionately called a *camello*, or camel. The *camellos* always came late and packed to capacity; once they finally arrived they often broke down by the side of the road. The bus came to represent the travails of a people already under duress.

Here is the sequence, or text, of *La Espera* (based on live performances and recordings viewed from 1991 to 2006):

La Espera: The "Text"
Sirens whine before the curtain opens. A man (Narciso) sits in a pool of light in the center of the stage, his head dropped between his knees. He leans on an old tire that supports a post on which hangs a bus stop sign. He slowly, painfully, stands. Holding onto the post with one long arm, he inches one foot away, his body making a long diagonal from toes to fingers. His hand stays in contact with the post for what seems like a long time. The stage space is lit to reveal only a small circumference around the sign. Finally his fingers detach from the post as he slowly describes small circles with his foot. He makes similar small circles with his

Narciso Medina "crucified" on the bus stop in his solo work *La Espera* [The Wait/Hope], Havana 1992. This work takes a surreal look at the transportation crisis of the Special Period. Photograph courtesy of Compañía de la Danza Narciso Medina.

hand, which dangles listlessly from his lifted right elbow. His whole body seems to hang from the acute angle of this awkwardly raised elbow. He looks defeated, exhausted, strangely without purpose. His head droops toward his knee, which creeps upward. Finally, he grabs his knee and stands upright, leg hooked over his arm. His other arm shoots upward; now he hangs as if suspended from his own hand. The soundtrack, constantly changing, clicks into the sound of Radio Reloj (Clock Radio), the Cuban station which intractably tells the time, second by second, in a voice of forced cheer. Narciso swings his lower leg to the ticking of Radio Reloj, telling time with his dangling limbs. His hand, now swinging from his lifted elbow, punctuates the sound of ticking seconds.

Changing positions slightly, he lets his fingers wriggle uselessly. A circle of white light defines and limits the space around the bus stop sign. He pulls his

The *camello* [camel], the double-length bus *habaneros* loved to hate, April 2004. The Washington-style *capitolio* building is visible in the background.

body away from center stage where the sign is standing, inching toward the periphery of the lighted circle. He slides out, then pulls back. We now can see that one foot is clad in a white sneaker, the other foot is bare. He is oddly pathetic, like a sad clown. He begins to step sharply, moving to every tick of the second hand. The music becomes cacophonous, interlaced with radio voices that are hard to decipher.

Laughter is heard.

The odd figure assumes a flat-footed balance, one foot suspended limply, arms curved above his hanging head. He descends slowly to the floor, then jumps surprisingly into an air turn, lifting his legs tightly underneath him. Suddenly he is lying on the floor again. It is not clear how he got there. He lifts his head to the sound of corny stringed music, which is quickly followed by the honking of car horns. He struggles to his feet, turns, falls into a heap. Without warning he begins a lithe circle: he vaults from the floor perched on one extended arm, jumps and spins, repeating the movement until he has encircled the signpost at the outermost rim of light. This sequence, reminiscent of capoeira, is the one moment that reveals the true virtuosity of the dancer, the one hint that more is possible. This airborne circle suggests an un-mined virility of movement. Other than this brief explosion, the force seems to have been squeezed out of this broken figure.

Potholes and Che on Calzada de Infanta, near the corner of Calle Zanja, Centro Habana, October 1995.

A half phrase of Michael Jackson's singing blurts through the sound collage, followed by voices screaming. Narciso steps on his own foot, reaches across his body, falls to his back and twists from side to side, kicking his legs parallel to the floor. Somehow he is standing again, pivoting in and away from the post, always within the circle of light. Finally he rests, balancing on one foot, both arms lifted softly above. Slowly he reaches the gesture leg out, slides toward it and turns. Once again his arms dangle above his head as his legs form a twisted base. Down to the floor, rolling again and then shaking, he slowly returns to standing, repeating the motif of small circles with the elbow and foot, this time jiggling his limbs slightly. Suddenly he turns, reaches, pulls his arms abruptly inward and spins. He jumps into the air, turning just as the music expresses forced gaiety. As he lands the accompaniment changes again, this time to strains of Ennio Morricone's film score from The Mission. *The lights switch to red and he extends his left leg to the side, reaching tentatively with his foot. We hear a choir sing "Ave Maria" as the sad figure turns slowly, his elbow up again, his foot lifted and leg bent. Now both arms are above his head, elbows bent, hands dangling. He opens his chest upward — his first gesture toward the level high above his body — as if seeing the space above his head for the first time. Sliding one leg across the other, he moves behind the post, with jerky arms and slow turns. It looks as if he is going to stay there, blocked from view, but then he plunges to a shoulder stand, traveling to the side of the bus stop.*

Clambering to his feet, he returns to the elbow motif. He grabs his leg again, swinging it in time to the clock ticking, a reprise of Radio Reloj in movement but not in sound. Now he turns and sees the sign as if he has not seen it before, as if he's just now acknowledging that it is in fact a bus stop. As the refrain of "Ave Maria" comes in, he steps lightly onto the tire at the base of the signpost. He takes his eyes out into the distance; for the first time his visual focus becomes external rather than internal. He seems weak as his knees bend together, his elbow lifts and his hand dangles in that familiar defeated gesture. On the third "Ave" he reaches his right arm up and, instantly, he is suspended on a cross. He hangs there, arms draped across a horizontal piece of wood, legs folded together uselessly. As soon as the familiar image registers on the eye, the stage goes black. Quickly the lights bounce up, bright red. We see him again for just a moment, crucified and drenched in scarlet.

Blackout.

La Espera: The Context

The first time I saw *La Espera* was in Finland, in 1991, at the Kuopio Dance Festival where I met Narciso and his troupe. I was unimpressed by the choreography and did not understand the piece at all. I found the other works on the program much more engaging and impressive in choreographic structure, performance values, and audience impact. It was not until I stayed in Cuba for three months, working and living with Narciso's company and using public transportation, that I learned to appreciate the piece. In Havana *La Espera* was perceived in an entirely different manner than it was abroad. It reflected the direct experience of the viewer, not just the artist, and found resonance in the daily lives of audience members.

Significantly, *La Espera* externalized the internal experience of both dancer and viewer. The wait for the bus during the Special Period was often so exaggerated that it ate up a significant part of everyone's day. Every day. The lack of transportation and unavailability of gasoline became familiar refrains, excuses for everything from work absences to the paucity of available produce. (Produce was often unavailable anyhow, as the best items were sent directly to the budding tourist industry or exported for hard currency. But this didn't mean the transportation crisis wasn't also blamed for the fact that no mangoes were available to Cubans in Cuba during mango season.[14]) By the mid-'90s bicycles had become incredibly popular and increasingly hard to procure. A new shipment of Chinese bicycles could be the hottest news item of the week, and stories of rampant bicycle theft became legend.

Prior to 1990 bus service in the capitol was less than perfect, but it was

Bicycles are big business in Havana. A *ponchero* fixes tires with a "Barrio de la Revolución" sign in the background, May 1998.

not bad enough to be a major topic of conversation, a political talking point, or a source of inspiration to artists. With the fall of the Soviet Union and the marked drop in the availability of gasoline, transportation within, to, from, and out of Havana became increasingly problematic. For a population accustomed to basic services, these changes were emblematic of the Special Period. Like the decrease in food rations and household items such as toilet paper and soap, the hours-long wait for the bus defined the new era. Here Tom Miller describes the situation in 1990:

> Fewer buses were on the streets; a shortage of spare parts and fuel kept the rest garaged…. Erratic and reduced oil deliveries from the Soviet Union coupled with upheavals in petroleum production and supply from the Middle East further threatened the country's already dwindling reserves. The new long-range program of island self-sufficiency encouraged beasts of burden and bicycles rather than internal combustion engines…. Day by day Cubans were becoming increasingly aware of the situation their country foundered in.[15]

Transportation questions came to define activities, possibilities, and all aspects of work and personal life. Coming from New York, I was completely unprepared for this. An example from my own efforts to get around Havana will illustrate the situation better than any statistic.

El Quixote de La Habana, 1992

One day after rehearsal Narciso and I visit a neighbor who sells bootleg gas. We fill up Narciso's old red Lada and set off to find the elusive Ernesto Márquez, pronounced "Mikey," a.k.a. El Quixote de La Habana. "The perfect composer for your piece," Narciso assures me. We drive through neighborhoods that are eerily quiet, not a light burning or a radio playing. They are enduring their weekly fuel-saving blackout, another nifty feature of the Special Period. Narciso explains that we are, happily, spared this inconvenience because his house is on the same electric grid as the hospital two blocks away. That does not mean that the water always runs, however.

We putter past the blocky Soviet embassy and up once-flashy Fifth Avenue, with its little parks and chipped statues, to a neighborhood called Playa. We arrive unannounced at Márquez' second story apartment. Tall and gaunt, Márquez ushers us into the middle of a jam session. He gestures for us to sit and listen to his latest creation. A cool melody floats above scalding rhythms. Márquez looks up conspiratorially from his keyboard, showing off his licks. I am the only woman in the room and the only North American within miles. The men make a big fuss of offering me rum and cigarettes. I take the rum. Narciso and I stay late as the sun sets pink and purple and Márquez agrees to collaborate on my new ballet.

The next afternoon Márquez and I work happily, losing track of time during our first recording session. It becomes clear at 10 P.M. that there is no way for me to get from Márquez' Playa studio back to the Medinas' Vedado apartment. "Mira," he explains patiently, "We have a transportation crisis in Cuba. Buses take hours, and they stop running when it's late." His guitarist friend who moonlights driving an ancient Pontiac has disappeared into the night. Márquez' neighborhood is not one with hotels and turistaxis waiting outside. I suggest calling a cab, but Márquez reminds me that you can't call a cab without a phone. Calling a cab is not a familiar activity for him. He looks at me like I'm from another planet. I find it absurd and frightening to be unable to move around a capital city alone.

There is no running water in his apartment, nothing to eat, and hardly any light. Márquez chivalrously gives me his bed. He is so rich in music, so poor in everything else. It makes his hospitality seem all the more heartfelt.

The next morning I eke out a little coffee from the tin. It takes me awhile to figure out how to ignite the ancient gas burner. Finally I light it and make a pot of chicory coffee. It isn't very good by Cuban standards, but Márquez makes a big deal out of drinking it.

He dutifully accompanies me on the long, strange trip to the Plaza de la Revolución and the Teatro Nacional. Murphy's law is the law of the land. The wait for the bus seems never-ending. When the camello *finally arrives, it is packed to bursting. People hang out of the open doors, sticky with sweat. Márquez and I push our way onto the bus, a seemingly impossible feat. Inside it's so crowded there's no need to hang on, since there's no room to move or fall. We go about ten blocks before the bus breaks down, or runs out of gas. No one knows for sure. We pile off the injured* camello, *dutifully cramming out the doors to wait on the street for another overflowing bus to arrive. Another* camello *finally comes by, but it is so full that the driver doesn't even stop. People on the ground yell and shake their fists as the bus resolutely continues with its overload. I think about the piece Narciso danced in Finland,* La Espera, *"The Wait," where he crucifies himself on a bus stop. I finally get it.*

Márquez curses his country's poverty and flags down a passing car. He instructs me not to speak, lest my foreign status become more obvious than it already is. The vintage car is packed with people too, and we sit almost on top of each other. I keep my head down, handing Márquez a dollar for the driver. Like black market activity of all kinds, the business of bootleg transportation is booming. It's officially illegal for Cubans to be in possession of dollars. Nonetheless, many find ways to acquire fula, *the exclusive currency with which to acquire goods available only in the* diplomercados. *The dollar is both illegal and essential.*

Miraculously, we arrive at the Teatro Nacional moments before I am scheduled to teach my first company class at Danza. There are no musicians available to accompany the class. Perhaps they had transportation problems of their own, but unlike us, they didn't have access to the spare yanqui *dollar.*

A later instance illustrates that the problem had not much improved over several years.

The Suburbs: Alamar, 1996

Narciso has invited his dance company to a party at his home in Alamar, a seaside housing project outside of Havana. (Now that the company has become successful and is bringing in touring income from abroad, the government has awarded the Medinas with a new house. But still no phone.) After a leisurely day at the beach we gather our things to go back to town. Yamilé Socarrás has left something behind, so a few of us stay to wait for her. We lag behind the others, whom we see boarding a bus to Havana at the bus stop near the highway. We walk through the heavy heat slowly, wondering whether we just missed the last bus of the evening. We stand waiting for what seems an interminable amount of time. There is no light, no bench, and no indication if or when another bus will appear. There are plenty of mosquitoes. After two hours a bus finally arrives. This, I am told, is standard: the uncertainty, the lack of alternatives, and the waiting. We make it back to Havana late at night, finding our way home together through the dark but noisy city. We make the most of our jolly company, but it would be quite different as a daily commute or as a person (i.e. woman) traveling alone.

At times this constant crisis of transit bordered on the surreal. In this context, the subject matter and dreamlike tone of *La Espera* have deep resonance. The dancer transmits a metaphysical — and quotidian — anxiety. If we are all waiting, what is the meaning and purpose of our wait?

Decoding the Dance

In *La Espera*, freedom of movement is severely limited. This becomes especially clear given the glimpses of airborne and virtuosic steps that are almost immediately squelched, replaced by the languid, repetitive tropes of inertia. The audience feels a kinesthetic empathy with the dancer, whose body longs for expansion. The subtle control developed through *técnica cubana* is here used to contain the kinetic impulse. The dance can be read as a metaphor for the lack of freedom of movement Cubans experienced both inside the country and in attempting to travel outside the country.

Narciso enjoyed, and continues to enjoy, the privilege to travel extensively as an artist. He owned a car at the time he premiered *La Espera*, and as such was among the elite who had access to private transportation. Nevertheless, as noted previously, gasoline was strictly rationed in the early '90s, and on many occasions Narciso ran out of gas while running production errands like retrieving props or costumes. We had to push Narciso's car up the formidable hill of Paseo after Márquez and I premiered our piece at the Teatro Nacional. It became a running, though bitter, joke between us that cars need gas just like dancers need food. Of course at that time Cubans had neither. Because Narciso could rarely get the gasoline or repair parts the Lada needed he often took, and continues to take, public transportation. So do his family and company. Dancers were continuously late or absent to both rehearsals and performances due to the transportation crisis. Despite the advantages he has acquired as a recognized artist — most notably his access to hard currency — Narciso has long lived and worked with reliance on the ubiquitous *invento cubano*. He has never been divorced from the realities of the daily struggle, or *lucha*, in Havana. That being so, he was in a good position to represent the experience of a Cuban Everyman, which he does in *La Espera* more than in any other piece of choreography in his repertoire.

The restriction and repetition of the steps and gestures in *La Espera* evoke the powerlessness of this Everyman. His body, capable of flight, is lulled into a sleepy torpor. He perseverates like an obsessive compulsive, repeating the same useless gestures — the dangling of the arm, the circling of the lower leg — until he gives in to gravity and entropy, stretching out on the floor. Despite this resignation, he bounds upward again, springing off the floor and turning in the air before returning to his prone position. Just once, he leaps around the bus stop pole in an expression of weightlessness. Some part of him, perhaps his subconscious, wills his body to move. He does so against logic, for there is no tangible gain in this activity. It is followed by more torpor.

What this suggests to this viewer is an internal fortitude that persists despite the beating down of repetition, of waiting, of the simplest chores made difficult. This character, representative of the Cuban people during the Special Period, maintains an undeniable resilience. *Esperanza* means "hope" in Spanish; the verb *esperar* means "to wait" OR "to hope." The play of words suggested by the title reflects the possibility of change, of deliverance: the hope that the bus will come, that the economy will improve, that the situation will change. Narciso, as noted earlier, is a Socialist raised and educated by the Revolution. He has not, to this day, given up on the Revolution or its goals despite specific criticisms of the system expressed in his art and in private conversation. Narciso maintains his belief in certain aspects of the society and system that have given him advantages he insists he would not have had elsewhere.[16] This is reflected in the way the dancer bounds back in this piece, gathering his strength and reaching, jumping or turning when there is little reason for him to do so. The wait is unbearable, but hope persists.

The dance does not spell out these streams of thought. In contrast, it dips into the surreal, with music shifting unexpectedly and a sense of the suspension of time. There is nothing literal or linear in the choreography. Narciso states a movement motif, then another, then a repetition, a variation, then a pause ... all without a sense of organic kinesthetic connection. That is to say, there is no physical syntax such as fall and rebound, concentric circles, paths through space, or any other choreographic or physical logic that might suggest the sequences presented. There is a randomness to the movement that has its own logic. It implies a certain chaos theory of dancing, a starting and stopping, an embrace and rejection of the floor, a statement and re-statement of themes that go nowhere. This in itself is a very clear choreographic choice. It works against the ideas of presentation, theme and variation, the use of developed technical skills to transcend physical limitations. It makes the audience suffer the tedium of a bad rehearsal, repeating the same movement over and over without the sense that improvement is imminent. The rhythm and energetic lags in the movement are tied inextricably to the meaning of the dance.

The final sequence of *La Espera* comes as a true surprise. The dancer has "danced around" the bus stop pole for at least four minutes before actually looking at it. After the third repetition of the words "*Ave Maria*," he evokes a deep-seated image of suffering by assuming his place on the cross. In the context of early 1990s Cuba, a traditional Christian reference in dance was quite rare, much rarer than it might be since 1998, when the Pope visited Havana for the first time in decades. In *La Espera* these aural and visual allusions are jarring. They are out of context in a society that seldom — at least publicly — refers to the symbols of the Church. In some ways Narciso was able to make this allusion precisely because the political and cultural sway of the Church in Cuba were so minimal at the time. (If he were to have made a sardonic reference to *Santería*, for example, his audience would have been much less forgiving.) As it was, Narciso surprised — and delighted — the public by equating the trials of his Cuban Everyman to those of the Christ. Medina's usage of imagery is subversive. He suggests that Cubans have waited long enough, that the people are being crucified on the cross of delayed gratification, "without hope and without dreams," in the words of fellow dancer Tomas Guilarte.[17]

At the same time, the work's ending employs such overstatement, and relies on such theatrics, that it introduces an element of parody. Narciso waits until the last moment to show his card; it is a trick of theater, complete with a surprise ending dependent on the use of a disguised prop. This sacrifice is how the person waiting *feels*, but it is a sentiment, not a reality. This is the bus, after all, not Roman rule. For this reason the piece draws laughs from the crowd, in addition to sighs of recognition and applause. Narciso's Everyman is exasperated with the wait—he is exhausted by it, driven to desperation—and the viewer's identification with this character is the source of the work's black humor. It taps into the *zeitgeist* of a particular moment, expressing the legendary angst of long waits for the *camello*, for goods at the *bodega*, or bread at the *panadería*. In creating this small piece, less than five minutes long, Narciso created new iconography for the Special Period.

Chapter 13

Personal Perspectives

Cuba, like its dance and dancers, continues to change almost as quickly as the winds at Varadero. Once a beach for rich tourists, this highly touted resort became a popular getaway for hard-working Cubans during the flush days of the Revolution. Even in the early '90s, Cuban families took vacations on the exquisite white sands of Varadero, enjoying the clear and deliciously warm water which stays shallow far out into the ocean. Today it is once again a tourist resort. Having passed through several stages of access and lack of access for Cuban nationals, it has all come down to money once again: those who have dollars can frolic on the famous beach, those who do not cannot.

The beach has entirely different contours than it once had, and the swank new hotels are owned and operated by international corporations in partnership with Cuba. For those who visited years ago, when modest kitchenettes housed large groups of average earners, the manicured landscape is almost unrecognizable. But the crystalline waters of the Caribbean retain their enchantment, emitting their timeless siren call even as the winds continue to change.

Having introduced many dancers in these pages, it seems reasonable to follow up with a few of them, to take a closer look at their art, their politics, and their personal choices. As the Special Period passed into the New Millennium, a distinct malaise swept over the Cuban dance world. Many dancers, no longer convinced things would get better at home, took advantage of touring opportunities to defect.

Others, like my dear friend Mildred Gonzales, left concert dance for cabaret, where more money could be made. Mildred sang and danced in Varadero until she met a Canadian and married him. She waited over a year to get permission to move to Canada, where she has learned to drive a car, teach Zumba, and shovel snow.

Jineteras y Jineteros: Hustlers

At this point we must address another icon that emerged in the Special Period and continues to this day: the hustler, or what Cubans call the "jockey" or *jinetero/jinetera*. As the nineties went on and the Special Period became less special and more of a permanent condition, changes in Cuban morals and morale emerged. At the beginning of the 1990s, evidence of prostitution was scarce. It existed, but it was cloaked, discrete, and often denied in conversation. By the turn of the century, hustling had become a common way of life. An equal opportunity employer, *jineterísmo* caters to sexual fantasies of all flavors, and has had a devastating effect on Cuba's social fabric and self-esteem.

Narciso's neighbor, Vivian, was very popular in the early '90s, despite (or perhaps because) she was the local representative of the CDR, the Committee for the Defense of the Revolution. Her popularity had a lot to do with her possession of the building's only phone and television, at a time when obtaining government permission for a personal telephone was next to impossible. (Interesting trivia: Cuba has one of the first telephone systems built anywhere. Unfortunately, that original system is largely still in use.) Vivian had frequent visitors and was able to keep up with local gossip. Vivian held a job as an economist, wore a uniform, and took her CDR position seriously. She made a point of telling me that "before the Revolution, I would have had no choice but to be a prostitute. Now I am an educated professional and my daughter will go to college."[1] She gave me a stack of books about Che Guevara. I dutifully carted these back to the small apartment I shared with the Medina's, to the great amusement of Idalmis.

"*Que linda*, Cuba" (how beautiful, Cuba), Idalmis would say, as she worked the outdoor pump, filling a bucket with water to flush the toilet.

By the late nineties, sadly, Vivian had come to expect less of the Revolution. Her lofty goals had come crashing down, along with her own social position and her loyalty to the CDR. Vivian had discarded her uniform, and her husband, and had spent several years caring for her senile mother and oversexed daughter, Cabinda. Cabinda was named patriotically, for a province of Angola, where Cubans had fought and died for communist ideals on a distant continent. Despite her earlier conviction that Cabinda would have a brilliant career, Vivian had become actively involved with a new enterprise. She was helping Cabinda find a rich foreigner to marry. In the words of a popular song by La Charanga Habanera, they were actively seeking "*un papirrici, con wanikiki*," which translates loosely as a Sugar Daddy. Vivian is now living in the Dominican Republic with her daughter and well-heeled son-in-law.

Jineteria. One of the most unsettling aspects of Cuba's economic down-

Tomas Guilarte and the author in rehearsal for her piece, *BarrigaBestia*, in the loft studio of the Academia de la Danza Narciso Medina, April 2000.

turn is the resurgence of prostitution. Over time, Castro made the canny move of legalizing the possession of hard currency. What was illegal one day for Cubans — owning dollars — was suddenly legal. Ironically, the currency of the *yanqui* imperialist became Cuba's legal tender. Drowning in the wake of lost Soviet subsidies, Cuba looked to international tourism as a lifeboat. Small businesses began to crop up, encountering fewer restrictions. One of the most lucrative businesses was the oldest profession. Women who had been trained as doctors and mathematicians began to support their families the old-fashioned way. When Castro was asked about the "thousands of young women who had flocked to the cities to tease love and money out of visiting Spaniards and Italians, he remarked that at least they would be the healthiest and best-educated prostitutes in the world."[2]

This change cuts deep into the heart of Cuba's self-image, based legitimately on years of social progress. Women's advancement, while faster in the professional world than in the home, had been a significant marker of the Revolution.

> One of Fidel Castro's first dramatic gestures after taking power was to close the brothels of Havana, which were humiliatingly associated with *yanqui* imperialism and its emasculation of Cuba's men. In the new Cuba, women would be firm pillars of society, never again forced to work as housewives, maids and whores. Women were organized into a mass organization, the FMC (Federation of Cuban Women), whose founder and president, Vilma Espín, fought in the Sierra Maestra with Fidel Castro.... The national desire to transform gender relations was serious, radical, and wide ranging.[3]

The reversal of this feminism was deeply wounding and disorienting. By the late 1990s, however, pragmatism had set in. The optimism of the Revolution's early years, of Che's "new man"[4] and the overzealous sugar cane harvest, the disastrous *zafra*, had been replaced by the *invento cubano*. Cubans who had grown up supported by a net of social services learned to string together a living by any means necessary. This was not without its humor or self-reflection. In Pedro Juan Gutiérrez' *Dirty Havana Trilogy*, a novel that lampoons the difficulties of the Special Period and caricatures the denizens of Havana, a character states, "Thirty-five years spent constructing the new man and now that's over ... now we've got to make ourselves into something different, and fast."[5] Indeed, Cuba of the late 1990s had devolved to resemble Cuba of the mid–1950s, filled with foreign investors, sex tourists, and big spenders smoking fat cigars.

Waylaid in Havana 1998

At the end of a short visit working with Narciso's troupe, my evening flight from Havana to Montreal is cancelled. Cuba and Canada share daily flights and diplomatic relations, but tonight this Canadian charter airline is going nowhere. After several hours of waiting—yes, even foreigners must wait in Cuba—the entire planeload of travelers is loaded onto a bus. We are transported to the Marina Hemingway, a ritzy tourist attraction crammed with foreign yachts and air-conditioned tour buses. I have never actually been inside the Marina before, although I've driven past and heard about it for years. It's a bit far from the center of town, and off limits for most Cubans. The dock is loaded with beautiful boats. The luxurious vessels hail from all over the Caribbean, Mexico and South America. A few are identified as North American, which is logical considering the proximity, and illogical considering the law. The site boasts Papa Hemingway's name, but exhibits little of his grit or salty character.

After several attempts on the lobby phone, I succeed in calling my husband in New York and my friend Mildred in Havana. I try to figure out how to spend my windfall extra evening in Cuba with her, but the charter company is adamant: we are to remain at the Marina because our flight could leave at any time. Cubans who do not work at the Marina are not allowed to enter. So Mildred and I make do with a long phone call—she is among the few and fortunate who have a phone—and I resign myself to an evening of the divided Cuba that most tourists experience. We are instructed to go to the dining room, where a hearty meal is served. I cringe at the amount of food we foreigners waste, and think of how the strapping lads in Narciso's company would devour this feast if given the chance.

Sitting at my table are two Canadian men who strike up a conversation about their visit. One of them has been to Cuba before, and he waxes poetical about the beauty and availability of the women. The other man complains that Cuban "girls" are gold diggers and that he got tired of them asking him to buy shoes and food for themselves or their kids. I stifle a nasty comment, trying to glean as much anthropological information as possible. What is this species, that preys on poverty-stricken women for cheap sex, complaining if they share their need for nutrition or footwear? These men are unabashed, as if it is their droit de seigneur to enjoy a sexual holiday, free of the stress of human interaction. I am surprised that they feel comfortable speaking this way in front of me, as I am clearly female and ostensibly not here for the meat market. Nevertheless, they act entitled and unapologetic, as if Cuba and its women exist exclusively for their enjoyment.

I excuse myself loudly. Even though I've been hungry for weeks, I've lost my appetite.

Of all the dancers I knew and worked with, only one was ever suspected of working the street. She did not last long in Narciso's company; that behavior did not fit into the self-concept the dancers had constructed for themselves and their environment. Most dancers seemed to have found an internal locus of control, steering themselves away from such demeaning work. This may be in part thanks to the elevated position they enjoyed — in terms of status if not salary — a status associated with their professional identity as artists. Contemporary, folkloric and ballet dancers pursued opportunities to earn hard currency while touring abroad, giving them additional incentive to stay focused on their artistic achievement. I cannot speak to the experience of cabaret or hip-hop dancers, as my contact with them was minimal and they are not the focus of this study. But most concert dancers, those trained in the schools of art and performing on the nation's stages, maintained a sense of pride and purpose as members of a society that valued their contribution, even if that society could no longer truly take care of anyone.

Centro Habana 2006

Back in Havana for the first time in several years, I invite some friends out to eat. Marlene is an accomplished dancer; our friend Mildred, a lovely performer, now has a delightful little boy. We choose the Café Paris, a tourist spot with live music in Habana Vieja. It's right around the corner from the festival de danza callejera, *a popular outdoor dance festival where we are hoping to see a performance of Danza Combinatoria. The bouncer who stands in the open doorway flirts with Marlene and assures us the food is good. We squeeze through the tables and settle down to dinner. The bouncer walks by and cracks a joke. The band isn't bad, and several tourists get up to dance. We smile at them, but continue gossiping furiously until*

Choreographer and dancer Marlene Carbonell in La Habana Vieja, March 1999. Marlene is now working as a dancer and instructor in Spain.

we finish our food. As we get up to leave, Marlene shows off a few fancy steps. I join her timidly. Suddenly the bouncer steps in, picks Marlene up, and carries her out the door. I interpret that surprising move as a suave prank, the sort of impromptu choreography we dancers might do with each other. Mildred has a similar impression. But Marlene experiences it quite differently. Marlene is a beautiful mulata, *with the lithe build and honey-colored skin so highly prized by poets and pervs alike. Marlene is convinced that her appearance led the bouncer to assume she was a* jinetera. *"I am an artist, not a prostitute!" Marlene yells furiously, oblivious to the staring passers-by and the wide eyes of Mildred's child. "I can't accept how Cubans are being insulted by other Cubans!" she berates the bouncer directly. He apologizes softly and claims that he would never mistake Marlene for a prostitute. Still fuming, she is unconvinced. She says that it has happened to her before, because of how she looks and the fact that she dresses in nice — admittedly tight — clothes. The bouncer looks sincerely sorry, and repeatedly tells her he meant nothing by it. But Marlene will not be assuaged. She stalks off, joining the crowd jostling for a glimpse of dancers on the raised stage of the outdoor festival.*

Hustling has entered the consciousness so deeply that Cuban rap songs blithely refer to jineterísmo *as a way for Cubans to make ends meet.[6] It has entered Marlene's consciousness so deeply that it does not matter whether the insult was real or imagined. She feels branded by her own people, as much as by the ubiquitous and voracious Other. She plans to leave her mother, her home, and her soloist position in a celebrated dance company behind. She plans to defect.*

The crisis of the Cuban economy has become a crisis of identity. Some of the most laudable goals of the Revolution — and some of its most significant accomplishments — have become casualties of a perfect economic storm. The fall of the Soviet Union, the persistence — and periodic tightening — of the U.S. embargo, the reliance on tourism, the collapse of a series of profit-making initiatives, and the fraying of the social safety net have left many Cubans feeling they have no alternative but to sell their bodies. None of the rampant jokes about Cuba having the world's best-educated and healthiest prostitutes can ease the sting. Men, women, and children work the streets of Havana much as they did a half-century before. The tragedy is that many have known another way of life, and they recognize how profoundly that life of decency and self-respect has slipped through their collective fingers.

Narciso's View

In April of 2006 Narciso Medina and I sat down in his office at the Teatro Favorito, turned on the voice recorder, and cranked the air conditioning to mask our voices as we spoke. Over the near-deafening whir of the old machine, we had a long discussion about race, revolution, and Cuban dance. I believe that Narciso answered my questions frankly and without feeling the need to self-censor, or to protect himself from government censure. We had worked together for 14 years at that point, we'd long had open conversations about our respective cultures and countries, and Narciso had become very secure and successful in his career. The state had not only finally given him a phone for his home in Alamar, but they'd given him a crumbling old movie theater, the Cine Favorito, that he'd converted into a stage for dance. Narciso has always known that I write for publication, and that I would ask his permission to publish anything that might compromise him. But Narciso did not indicate reticence of any kind, even though we broached some thorny issues. We spoke frankly, as we have so many times in so many contexts over the years. Easy communication is the essential glue of collaboration. It didn't hurt that I'd lived with his family in a tiny apartment without running water while his wife was pregnant, that I knew his mother and he knew my father, and that we have long shared key moments of our lives as well as crises in our careers. I trust that Narciso spoke to me truthfully.

Narciso describes himself as a socialist,[7] but he can be critical of the Cuban regime. His wry commentary can be straightforward in conversation, or subtle in his dances. He has not always been supported by the state, in fact, he began the first independent dance academy in Havana in 1993. This was not only unprecedented but also risky. As a small business, charging the public directly for services the company offered, the new academy was changing the paradigm. While the government did not offer financial support, neither did they close him down. The state seemed to sit back and watch, waiting to see what this well-known dancer and fledgling choreographer would do in the tiny studio he created out of his tiny apartment.

At the beginning, most of Narciso's dancers continued to work with the big companies, moonlighting with him while collecting their state-subsidized salaries from Danza Contemporánea or the Conjunto Folklórico. Company members became skilled teachers as well as performers, and they were paid with monies the company earned for their efforts. Narciso charged a small fee for open classes and performances. He created a new model for Cuba, sidestepping the state system of education in order to offer dance experience to those who might never dare audition for the official schools of art. Classes were organized according to age and skill; anyone who wanted to dance could find a class to take. This small foray into the market economy was highly unusual at the time, and Narciso wasn't quite sure how it would work or how far he should go. Luckily, he had worked abroad extensively with Danza, and he'd studied the way companies from Finland to Peru navigated the seas of small business. While some other small enterprises were squelched, Narciso interpreted the state's turning a blind eye as permission to continue. "There was an opening for business in 1993," Narciso explained in his Favorito office, "or if you will, private enterprise," he clarified, employing what was in Cuba a highly unusual phrase to describe his highly unusual project. The softening of official Communist Party policy was a change employed on a case-by-case basis. Narciso was a good bet — he was a known talent with a celebrated work, *Metamorfosis,* and though he frequently toured internationally, he always came home. The early company cobbled together teaching and touring gigs, paying the dancers out of the income they produced. There was no grant money or private financial support to be had, but in the early days Narciso worked under the organizational umbrella of the Fundación Pablo Milanés. The great

Cuban singer, Milanés, didn't contribute financially to the company, but his name and good will helped the nascent troupe navigate bureaucratic hurdles. Once Narciso began to tour more extensively with his small company, the government started taxing his touring income not only as an individual, but as a company. But it wasn't until 1997 that the Compañía de la Danza Narciso Medina was first subsidized by the government. This meant that from that moment all the dancers who achieved professional level in the company received their salary from the state.

Narciso is now back within the circle of artists admired and affirmed by the regime. He has entered this protective circle several times in his career: young talent from the provinces, rising star in his class, principal dancer in a national company. He's also exited the ring of approval and taken some risks with his career: breaking away from Danza, booking tours to

Narciso Medina in the barrel used for *Metamorfósis* while on tour with his company, Middlebury, Vermont, May 7, 2003.

Europe as an independent dancer, touring with his independent company, housing a North American in his home, and creating a small business without seeking prior approval. He does not seem afraid to say and do what he believes.

In ways, Narciso's experience has been optimal: he represents what is successful about the Revolution's educational and cultural policies. His perspective is that of a man who would have probably spent his life cutting cane in Guantánamo had it not been for the opportunities the Revolution provided. He has seen enough of the world to appreciate his position. When two of his dancers defected during a U.S. tour in 2003, Narciso was terribly shaken. He told me privately that he "could not wait to leave Miami, arrive at home and kiss the ground in Cuba."[8] Narciso's lifestyle surpasses that of many Cubans. Dark and noisy as it is, he has his own office in his own theater where he runs his own company. As we sat there in 2006, he said "dancers and artists are privileged people in

Cuba." Although he has complained to me over the years about many things in his country, they have generally been the sort of rules his mentor Ramiro Guerra calls "surreal,"[9] such as the prohibition against DVD players entering the country. But Narciso has never had the content of his work restricted by government forces. While self-censorship is always a possibility, I have seen works of his that surprised me in their sexual and political content. In fact, it was not until his tour to the U.S. in 2003 that he was compelled for the first time to costume male dancers in shorts — instead of the simple jock straps they have always worn — for *Metamorfosis*.

Marlene Carbonell (foreground), Narciso Medina and Ariel Vasquez on drums, rehearsing Medina's neo–Africanist fantasy, *La Musica del Cuerpo*, Middlebury, Vermont, May 7, 2003.

Sitting in his office

in Centro Habana, Narciso obscured the sound of his voice in order not to be heard by others in the building. Although he is frank he must continue to be discreet, to follow certain rules, and to pay his taxes. The system that produced him gave him many opportunities; it also taught him his neighbor could be a spy or a counter-revolutionary. In the course of our conversation he made statements that were decidedly personal, and may not (disclaimer) represent the beliefs and feelings of others:[10]

> I don't believe in racism. I don't believe in racism because we all have the same social rights. Unconsciously [racism] has been instilled in people, in the black, in my race. We have to achieve the consciousness that we can be as brilliant, that we have the same capacity in our brains, as any white man. At least in Cuba. Because the problem isn't institutional. We all go to the same university, we have the same rights.
>
> I think it is all a question of talent. If you have talent and you work, if you are intelligent and you make progress, then you have a good chance of realizing your dreams and yourself. I am black and I enjoy an artistic level and artistic conditions that are as good — who knows, better — than most white men. When I say that there is no racism that means it depends on the person and his work, his capacity, his education. It's not to say everything will be this way for everyone.

Narciso implied that there is a distinction between institutional or legal practices and the way racism may play out in society at large. His comments are informed by his experience within the Cuban system, and his exposure to other cultures when traveling and working for extended periods in other countries. Though his perspective may not coincide with that of some scholars, it carries the weight of personal testimony, albeit that of someone educated by the Revolutionary system. While he has been brought up as a socialist, and he has benefited from the socialist system, his worldliness makes him anything but naive. He acknowledges that his position reflects his success, and not the common experience:

> There is a group of artists in Cuba who, according to their talent, their accomplishments, and the success of their work, have become personalities in Cuban culture. These people get special consideration from the Ministry of Culture, and from the point of view of the state. They get a lot of consideration which, truly, is not given to other sectors. They can freely have Internet and e-mail, they can communicate perfectly with the world. If an artist has already reached a level of success and perspective through their work, through their talent, this opens many doors and possibilities.

In the course of our discussion I mentioned the incident that had occurred with Marlene and the bouncer at the Café Paris. At that time Marlene was still dancing in Narciso's company. His response to that story was as follows:

Unfortunately we don't have a label that says, "I am a principal dancer, I'm famous and I go on television." So how do they evaluate you? By your clothes, your carriage. And truly, in all the world they evaluate you like that, right away. I know a lot of people who suffer this sense of being discriminated against. Which is not to say that when I go into the street the police don't stop me because I am black. Because they do, they stop me.

The truth is that our country has fallen into a lot of vice. It is unfortunate. It is a problem of stereotyping. If a white guy puts on a pair of torn jeans, it's cute. It's the style. If a black guy does it he's a delinquent. So what do I do? I'm sorry, but I don't wear torn jeans, because I don't want to experience that bad treatment. It's psychology. If I go with you [a foreigner] to eat or dance, I use psychology. I know how the *jineteros* act and I don't act that way.

Narciso is not blaming the victim, but he does suggest that Marlene's behavior and dress may have exacerbated a problem that already exists. He does not see the situation in simple terms, nor is he blind to the Revolution's failings. He has learned to work the system, and to make the system work for him. He is far from average, but he embodies what the Revolution fervently tried to accomplish. Coming from what had traditionally been Cuba's lowest sociological level, Narciso has risen to the top by virtue of his ability and the education provided him. He has made the most of opportunities his father's generation never enjoyed, and built his career on excellent training his family could never afford had they lived elsewhere. The ironies of post-millennial Cuba are not lost on him.

Cuban society now is divided between people who have a higher standard of living and people who don't. The equality that they wanted, the dream of achieving that, now, well … this was not what the Revolution envisioned. They wanted everyone to be equal. In a way they maintain that with education and health. They have raised everyone's salaries, but not to the level of what things cost in the farmer's market, or what it costs to take a taxi. Transportation is one of the gravest difficulties, a situation that really hits home. In family life, in the home, truly there are differences. I don't want to say "classes" because of the associations, but there are different levels of society.

Narciso admits that he enjoys privileges that are unusual among ordinary Cuban citizens. He has earned access to special advantages because he thrived under the Revolutionary system, with its free and excellent education and its belief in national artistic development and dissemination. Though he frequently went abroad, he always came home. Narciso proved a good cultural ambassador, a proven artist with a love for his homeland. His way of life, his prized telephone, his car without gas, his theater with crumbling walls, and most coveted, his freedom to travel, are all awards he has earned as a Revolutionary success story. I would argue that his willingness to speak his mind is in that category as well. Narciso is a golden child of the Revolution, pretty damn close to Che's dream of the New Man.

Regardless of what one thinks of the concept of "national identity," or whether the phrase was ever actually uttered behind closed doors in the early days of the Castro regime, it was a fundamental precept in the decision to promote Cuban culture. Whether or not it is a legitimate idea, in terms of individuals or their cultural production, is a fascinating discussion being conducted outside of these pages. In the case of Narciso, there is no doubt that he has benefited from the solid cultural, societal, and economic value placed on dance as an agent of Cuban national identity — *cubanidad, cubanía,* or a "certain manner" of being.... The Revolution made a significant investment in national culture as a unifying influence across socio-cultural differences. Without that commitment, *técnica cubana* might never have gotten off the ground, let alone soared. The same could be said for Narciso.

Yamilé Breaks My Nose: Hospital Carlixto Garcia 1994

One of the advantages Cuban artists enjoy is the guarantee of free and excellent health care. As our country has struggled with the question of providing universal access, and North American artists frequently squeak by without insurance until they are in dire need, it's interesting to look at how medical care is provided elsewhere. At the National Ballet and Danza Contemporánea, physical therapy and injury prevention experts work onsite. When dancers need health care that is not directly connected to injury or fitness maintenance, they go to the free clinics and hospitals staffed by well-trained doctors. In recent years those hospitals have operated without essential medicines, and at times even without running water. Meanwhile, Cuba keeps turning out doctors and medical innovations whose praises are sung throughout the Third World. Imagine what they could accomplish if they had the resources they needed....

My respect for Cuban physicians has a personal basis. Here is one of several forays I took into the health care system:

Rehearsing in the small loft studio on Calle 8, I step in close to correct Yamilé's turn. She flies around, smacks me in the face, and we hear a loud "crack." Instantly I'm down, screaming for ice. My nose begins to swell, and it hurts. The dancers tell me I need to go to the hospital. The phones are out, so we can't call a cab and it's too far to walk. We decide to take our bikes.

We wait on several lines, in several waiting rooms. Although I am officially supposed to go to the foreigner's hospital, where payment is expected in hard currency, no one sends me there. Ostensibly because I'm working in Havana, but probably because no one in Cuba follows the rules.

Photographer David Garten was walking down the street in *El Cerro* (a Havana neighborhood) in May 1994, when the man on the right said hello. David was invited inside this workplace, where food was being prepared for the workers in a seed distributorship.

I meet the Otorrino, *the ear and nose specialist. He's super cute. In order to get an x-ray of my nose without my having to transfer to the special hospital for foreigners, he gives me a Cuban name, "Zenaida Mendez." While we're waiting for the results of the x-ray, he tells me that he can't afford a bicycle. If he worked in the tourist industry for hard currency he'd be better off. But he loves medicine. He tells me the joke about the doctor who pretends he's a waiter because he has delusions of grandeur. He shares his sandwich with me, and it is a gourmet delight by Special Period standards. I ask where he got ham and cheese, rare delicacies in these lean times. He has his sources, he smiles.*

My nose isn't broken, the Otorrino *determines, it's just fractured. Promising to attend our next performance, he gives me a prescription for painkillers and anti-inflammatories. Yamilé fills the script for me since Zenaida Mendes does not exist.*

When all is said and done, parking our bikes costs more than my medical care.

Diaspora of Dancers

"The '90s were a difficult time, but people still had the desire to create," Marlene explained in March of 2008. "If an artist wants to make a work, they'll do it alone, with three dancers, in a tiny space, wherever and however they can." She was still, reluctantly, in Cuba. No longer dancing with Narciso, she was now dancing with the cabaret-inflected company of Santiago Alfonso. During a break from rehearsals on the upper floor of the Centro de la Danza in Centro Habana, Marlene stretched her long body on the floor of an empty studio. We could hear music floating up from the lower level where Marianela Boán's company, DanzAbierta, continued to work diligently, even though their founder was no longer in Cuba.

"This crisis has influenced all of us," Marlene said, alluding to the debilitating hardships that persist in Cuban life. "There are many artists who stopped creating. Many went away. Marianela left, Lidice [Nuñez] left, Rosario [Cárdenas] left — maybe not forever, but she does more abroad than she does here. In Cuba everything is so hard, just getting the theater is a struggle." Marlene described how she spent a year preparing a dance work, and on the day she was supposed to move into the theater she discovered the space had been reserved for a series of meetings. It took another year to find a place to debut the work, but by then they were making something new, and the first work was not shown. "And then, you may have the theater, but the dancers defect," she added. Since theaters are government property managed by the Ministry of Culture, decisions are made from the top down. Narciso had a similarly frustrating experience when he published his book about the creative process, *El suspendido vuelo del ángel creador*.[11] He arrived at the Teatro Mella for an event coinciding with the book debut only to discover the ballet company was using the theater. And the national ballet always takes precedence.

"I was determined to apply for a choreographic scholarship in Montreal," Marlene recounted. "I didn't care how much the application cost to send, I was motivated. I made the work, did the project, made the video, transferred it to DVD, and translated the application into English. But when I went to send the package, they wouldn't let me send a DVD through DHL." This sounds like another nonsensical restriction of the kind Ramiro Guerra lamented. "When I finally got it in the mail, everything arrived after the deadline. Another application I sent to California arrived empty, with the package torn." Marlene went on to mention a point that was particularly inflammatory at the time of this conversation, lack of internet access. "If I could use the internet, if I could get the information to them somehow, if I could rely on the mail...." Marlene had no recourse. "All of the doors were closed to me. It slipped out of my hands. But then I tried again, with another choreographic competition in Canada. I put in the same effort, getting the theater, getting people to help me, running here and there. But it was the same thing. I went to the Ministry and asked if they could help me and they said no. I asked why. They said, "Canada? Forget it. What are you going to accomplish with Canada?"

By the time we had this conversation, Marlene was desperate to get out of Cuba. She explained how she had received several offers to dance in Europe, but in order to get an exit visa she needed the permission of her boss, choreographer Santiago Alfonso. This concept was beyond my comprehension, so she explained it several times. As the director of a company where dancers received government salaries, Alfonso had the authority to approve or deny a dancer's right to travel. Marlene assumed the decision was based on whether the director felt he could trust her to come back to Cuba. This was not simply a question of whether or not he'd give her time off from work. Major decisions about Marlene's life and career were in the hands of a man for whom she'd been dancing for less than a year.

Indeed, many of Cuba's best dancers have left their home behind. Aside from all of the luminous ballet stars working internationally, defection, legal migration and lucrative long-term gigs abroad have thinned the ranks of accomplished contemporary dancers. Cándido Muñoz, Lino Angel, Yamilé Socarrás, Ivan Rodriguez and scores of others have moved to Europe. Ramón Ramos Alaya settled in the Bay Area; Mildred Gonzales is still in Canada. Narciso's daughter Dislaidys, all grown up now, became a popular reggaeton teacher in Tokyo. Manolo Vasquez teaches abroad at every opportunity, as does Tomas Guilarte, who now directs the school at Danza Contemporánea. "Even Narciso is practically never here," Marlene opined.

Finally a door opened for Marlene. In 2010 Alfonso gave her permission to dance in Spain. When her flight left Madrid to return to Cuba, she was not on board.

Chapter 14

International Influence

From *Súlkary* to *El Decálogo del Apocalipsis* to *La Espera*, Cuban modern dance has evolved eloquently. In fact, the contemporary element has emerged more powerfully as the country moves into a new stage: pragmatic global dissemination of Cuban culture. As Cuba exports more and more *cubanidad*, its cultural ambassadors are exposed to a smorgasbord of new ideas. Simultaneously, they serve as strong artistic examples for those they encounter abroad. Dancers of the early *Conjunto de Danza Moderna* were most likely to be exposed to artists from the Eastern Bloc and Latin America. Today, artistic exchanges with Europe, Asia, Canada, Central and South America are increasingly common. Due to the embargo and the paucity of internet access, it is still hard for Cuban dancers to keep abreast of trends happening in the United States, but dancers of all nationalities (including a few North Americans) now travel to the island, bringing choreographic and somatic practices with them. There is a certain permeability to the culture that was not the case in the early years of the Revolution — or the early modern dance movement. Contemporary Cuban dancers continue to be hungry for outside information, for exposure to artistic developments around the globe.

Economic constraints, in addition to customs restrictions on media and equipment entering Cuba, continue to limit even the electronic access artists have to international work. Videos of foreign companies are rare and highly coveted. Due to the degeneration of equipment at the national arts academies, it is difficult for dance teachers to copy videos to share with their students. During a research trip in 2006 I tried to buy a copy of the famed Danza piece, *Súlkary*. I recruited Narciso's company manager and administrator, as well as the Film Institute, ICAIC, in securing a copy for which I would have paid hard currency. While this fundamental piece of Cuban dance history exists on videotape, it was virtually impossible to find, dub or purchase a recording. In this context, it is easy to imagine how difficult it would be to obtain copies of foreign dance videos or DVDs. Cuban dance remains isolated

Two (North) American symbols of Cuba: a 1957 Chevrolet and 1948 Dodge, on the Barrio Chino, Calle Galiano at the corner of Calle Zanja, in Centro Habana, June 2004.

on the island, relying on personal encounters as the primary source of new ideas and cross-pollination. But the need for growth and innovation remains strong, pushing Cuban dance artists to strenuously seek expansion and inspiration.

Fortunately, contemporary Cuban dance is becoming more widely known in international circles, no doubt benefiting from the increased renown of Cuban ballet and Afro-Cuban music. Danza Contemporánea de Cuba offers intensive workshops for foreigners, as does the Conjunto Folklórico, and various smaller companies. Manolo Vasquez, master teacher from Danza Contemporánea, has taught briefly at Stanford University and extensively across Latin America. Dancers from the ranks of Cuba's modern dance companies now live, teach and perform in Spain, Finland, Denmark, Italy, and Japan. A few Cuban modern dancers have recently come to live in the U.S.

In 2007 a group of Canadian dancers traveled to Havana where they hoped to take class with Narciso's company. At first they were quoted a price of $15 per person per class. When Narciso's wife and company manager, Idalmis, realized that the visitors were "dancers not tourists," she insisted that the classes would be free. "For us this inter-cultural exchange with dancers and universities is extremely important," Idalmis explained.[1] What this illustrates is not only an artistic curiosity fed by cross-cultural exchange, but a new kind of marketplace *savoir faire* which Cubans have developed over the last two decades. Like many cultural producers, Idalmis is keen to cultivate international partnerships. These contacts build the bridges that lead to work abroad.

DanzAbierta has always had an international bent. Artistic Director Marianela Boán incorporated varied movement tropes from the beginning, actively creating what she calls *danza contaminada* [contaminated dance]. Boán often invited foreign choreographers to teach company class while in the process of

setting work. Gabri Christa, originally from Curaçao, was a natural choice to work with the young company. Christa notes that her own work "always dealt with Caribbean influence as well as fusion" in dance vocabulary.[2] Just as Guerra described flamenco *floreo* accidentally finding its way into the practice of *técnica*, Christa explained that certain movements, exercises, and gestures remained in the

The Committee for Defense of the Revolution (CDR) is everywhere, November 2001.

mix, becoming part of DanzAbierta's company class. Though Boán was trained in *técnica,* and Guerra considers her one of his protégés, she made a conscious choice to explore movement that differed tangibly from *técnica cubana.* Conceptual theatrical investigation remains a hallmark of DanzAbierta. Boán left Cuba to work in the United States, and later to direct a company in the Dominican Republic. "Now, more than ever," says Boán, "my body is my country."[3] Guido Gali, her former assistant, became artistic director, bringing DanzAbierta to Jacob's Pillow in Massachusetts in 2011, where they showed a dramatic film/dance performance by the Spanish-born Cuban resident, Susana Pous. Fusion remains central to the company's self-concept.

Marianela Boán, Marlene Carbonell, Ramón Ramos Alayo, Lidice Nuñez, Arturo Castillo, Rosario Cárdenas, George Céspedes, Jorge Abril, Santiago Alfonso, Rafael Olivera, Tangin Fong, and Eduardo Rivero are just a few contemporary Cuban choreographers, on and off the island, who continue to experiment with and enlarge upon their training in *técnica cubana.* All Cuban dancers were and are exposed to high quality work — the classical repertoire of the National Ballet, the rich Afro-Cuban traditions of the Conjunto Folklórico, the contemporary pieces of Danza, and work by visiting artists — but only those who travel abroad are acquainted with full scale productions by contemporary European, Asian and North American companies. While not all Cuban choreographers have had extensive international exposure, they do have a solid foundation on which to make aesthetic choices. They have been prepared technically and artistically to explore and create, rather than to simply recreate foreign work, add a little *cubanía*, and call it their own.

As he matured as a choreographer, Narciso began to lace his choreography with global cross-references. While presenting at the 1991 Kuopio Dance Festival in Finland, Narciso first viewed performances by the troupe Sankai Juku. This was his initial exposure to the Japanese contemporary dance form Butoh. Over time Narciso began to work with tropes from that style: shaved heads and powdered bodies, exaggeratedly slow movement, and stark theatrical imagery. In the last few years Narciso has worked for long periods in Japan. His continued exposure to the technique and aesthetic of Butoh has moved his work in unexpected directions. The results are a far cry from *La Espera* in plasticity, theatrical sophistication, and style. Narciso's ability to impose a novel physicality onto a variety of theatrical structures rests squarely on the thorough preparation and solid technique he acquired through *técnica cubana*.

Dancing in the street: a performance on the porch outside the Academia on Calle 8, Vedado, 1996. Lino Angel is seen front left. Photo courtesy of the author.

Medina's astute choreographic use of unfamiliar movement and imagery has been enhanced by his extensive exposure to varied dance forms. In addition to Butoh, he was also greatly influenced by European *tanztheater* he witnessed at festivals throughout Europe. Medina's ongoing interest in a rich variety of dance has informed his work in myriad ways. In his 1996 *Ultimos Exitos del Fin del Siglo,* (Greatest Hits of the End of the Century) Medina's interest in theatrical and technical innovation, as well as contrasting movement styles, produced an exceptional piece. In *Ultimos Exitos* male and female dancers worked separately. The two male dancers, big muscular *machos* dressed in pink tutus and bras, danced together with their arms entwined through a wooden bench. As guest artist, I played a floaty eccentric, dancing on and off the bench manipulated by the male dancers. A phalanx of women dressed in dark simple clothes executed sharp athletic movements in unison. While Narciso was still working with limited technical resources in the theater, he made the most of what he had. Large drapes of fabric hid and revealed dancers in unexpected configurations. Physically and conceptually, the work revealed influences far flung from *técnica*. It included the stylized gesture and gender-bending of *tanztheater*, and an operatic sense of scale. It also incorporated pseudo-military precision, and what I was flattered to hear Narciso call "*el impulso de Suki.*" What he was referring to here was not my own invention, but a use of the off-balance, fall and rebound, and energetic impetus that were greatly developed in the work of Doris Humphrey, Charles Weidman, and José Limón. As a visiting instructor and choreographer, I found that those principles of movement were often underdeveloped in Cuban dancers, so I emphasized them in my classes. Narciso found it easier to refer to that particular movement impulse through the shorthand of using my name. Far from being unusual, such personal exchanges of movement knowledge are basic to the transmission of both choreography and technique. Dance relies on a tradition of personal coaching, modeling, and intense scrutiny. This malleable context is perfect for intercultural exchange. Steps, rhythms, ideas and inspirations are traded in the studio. Often the only shared language is the codified French of ballet, but dancers are adept at communicating kinesthetic information. Such collaborations are not only central to preserving dance forms, they are essential to their evolution and transformation.

Fortunately *técnica cubana* continues to thrive in Cuba, where dancers of sublime versatility graduate every year. As those dancers make contact with artists from around the world, their contribution to the art of contemporary dance is becoming more visible internationally. From Lima to London, Trinidad to Tokyo, dance practitioners and scholars are slowly becoming more aware of the grace and vigor of this formidable technique.

Re-shaping the Rep

In response to the economic and artistic need for international contact and local support, the repertoires of Cuban modern dance companies have shifted over the years. These changes continue to alter the way Cuban dance companies make art and do business. While internally devoted to innovation and an evolving contemporary aesthetic, companies such as Danza Contemporánea and Compañía de la Danza Narciso Medina began to find ways in the late 1990s to attract both local and foreign crowds. Relying on established repertoires that included familiar pieces such as *Súlkary* and *Metamorfosis*, these companies tried to build a new local following by featuring visiting choreographers, music by contemporary bands, and site specific works in unusual locations. Conversely, in order to attract foreign touring contracts, they emphasized the *cubanía* of their product, using music that played up traditional arrangements, choreography based on Cuban themes, and references to Cuban archetypes or the *orishas*.

Narciso brought three pieces to New York in 2003 at the invitation of the Guggenheim's Works & Process series. When picking the touring repertoire, he made a conscious choice to include a piece that reflected more of the Cuban folkloric element than the contemporary.[4] This work, *Musica del Cuerpo*, relied on vocal and percussive music generated by the dancers themselves. "We included steps and rhythms that come from our roots in Afro-Cuba," Narciso stated during an onstage interview at the Guggenheim, "but the songs and steps and even the words were actually invented by the dancers." (This may be another touch of subversion or parody by the Afro-Cuban choreographer. Disinterested in authenticity, he is concerned more with impact, creativity, and significantly, marketability.) The public seemed to appreciate the contemporary works on the program. These included a world premiere commissioned by Works & Process, set to live music by New York composer Joel Diamond, and the tried and true *Metamorfosis*. But the New York crowd responded most ardently to *Música del Cuerpo*. Cuban iconography exists firmly in the North American psyche; this piece clearly appealed to the public's desire for a Cuban experience. It didn't matter to this audience that the dance and pseudo-ritual in *Música* were inventions; Narciso candidly revealed that fact before the piece was shown. What mattered was the *cubanía*, the beat, and the irrepressible enthusiasm of the attractive and accomplished dancers. The piece fit into the North American public's image of the exotic Other, fulfilling an expectation of what is and should be Cuban dance.

As suggested earlier, I see Cuban contemporary dance as a potential diplomatic tool. It could help thaw a Cold War leftover — the rocky relationship between Cuba and the U.S.

Dance could truly be the new ping-pong!

Selling the Moves

Cuban companies continue to create revenue by attracting foreign students to residential study sessions, as well as by offering dance workshops as part of their touring packages abroad. During the Special Period they gave workshops in modern dance, but increasingly began to include courses in Afro-Cuban folklore and Cuban social dance. Whereas they once defined themselves almost exclusively by their contemporary edge, they slowly began to capitalize on the exoticism of more recognizable Cuban tropes. They played these expectations up when marketing performances and workshops toward visiting foreigners and presenters. While touring the East Coast of the U.S. in 2003, the Compañía de la Danza Narciso Medina led a sold out *salsa* workshop at Sandra Cameron Dance Center, one of the largest ballroom schools in New York. They packed a crowd into a small studio in Maine, where they gave a workshop in *orisha* dances. However, when the company conducted a workshop featuring their true specialty, Cuban contemporary dance, only a small group of modern dancers at Middlebury College in Vermont showed up to participate.

Dance companies have, if anything, become more adept at giving the audience what they want. In 2006, for example, Narciso gave the Havana premiere of his work *Bandoleros*, set to *reggaetón* music, a cross between rap and reggae. He acknowledged that he headlined the piece in his spring season precisely because the novelty of *reggaetón* might bring in young audiences. He theorized that once inside the theater they would be exposed to, and hopefully drawn toward, the less accessible aesthetic of modern dance. As many an impresario before him, Narciso was altering his image at home in order to reflect a current trend and bring in a new crowd. This was a sensible response to the fact that in 2006 many of the local clubs catering to a Cuban clientele were playing *reggaetón* instead of traditional dance music. Meanwhile, tourist clubs continued to play *salsa* and covers of the Buena Vista Social Club.

This internal/external divide is part of the equation of cultural commerce: one version of Cuban culture sells abroad and within the tourist industry, while yet another continues to evolve and appeal to Cubans themselves.

Ironically, Narciso began the *reggaetón* piece while working as a guest artist in Japan. He has worked in Tokyo extensively, bringing other Cuban dancers with him for extended residencies in colleges and private studios. He has a large following to which he teaches Cuban modern, folklore, and *salsa* classes. *Reggaetón* began to eclipse the extensive *salsa* boom that had become a phenomenon in Japan in the late '90s, sending many Japanese dancers to Cuba for *salsa* workshops. By 2006, *reggaetón* was marketable enough for Narciso to produce a Japanese-language instructional video featuring his daughter Dislaidys, now a company member with her own career in Japan. Narciso is very successful in Tokyo, where he banks on his teaching skills as well as the exoticism of his *cubanidad* in both dance style and persona. This reflects what both Esther Whitfield and Yvonne Daniel have noted as the "commodification of the self,"[5] a sort of export-only version of Cuban culture

Omar Yirat at la ENA (National School of Art), in the Cubanacán neighborhood of
Havana, in the section of the campus meant to be the ballet school. Damaged by
flood in 1965, this area was never completed, never repaired, and left to be reclaimed
by nature, March 2000.

that has become increasingly common since the late 1990s. While Narciso's own dance interests may range from Butoh to *tanztheater* to *cha-cha-cha*, he is most able to market himself abroad as an ambassador of Cuban culture. This includes giving the audience what they expect even as he expands their aesthetic, and his own definition of what Cuban modern dance is, and might become.

The Ever-Changing Dance

Cuba exists in a post-colonial context, manifest in its explosive artistic expression. Many contemporary Cuban dancers eschew purist aesthetics and nationalist dogma, while retaining fierce pride in their culture. Playing with the frameworks of post-modernism, these dance-makers enjoy the freedom to pick styles and quotes from any historical period, geographical source, or genre. Combining panoramic stylistic allusion with post–Special Period pragmatism, Cuban dancers embrace formats, philosophies and techniques from all over the world. Some reject the idea that Cuban dance must remain exclusively Cuban in order to fulfill revolutionary objectives or a sense of cultural superiority. Instead, these dancers favor a constantly evolving definition of contemporary dance, layering borrowed artistic influences on their rich indigenous base. This includes artistic entrepreneurship: learning how to market themselves in a changing economy where their state salary is no longer sufficient. From incorporating foreign movement tropes into their dances, to experimenting with theatrical innovation, to using novel sources of musical inspiration, to offering workshops that appeal to specific groups of tourists, to captivating audiences with their prodigious skills, Cuban dancers are becoming an increasingly visible part of the dance world at large.

In philosophy, practice, and subject matter, contemporary Cuban dance invites constant growth, dialoguing and developing in tandem with the ever-changing Cuban society and, whenever possible, its global counterparts.

Epilogue: 2011

*I spend a day preparing a package for Cuba. A friend of a friend has been
e-mailing me for advice on her first trip. I tell her to take bug spray, antihistamines,
sunblock, tampons, eye drops, sun-dried tomatoes, peanut butter and dried milk.
I warn her not to bring American traveler's checks but assure her she can use those
bought in Canada. I set her up with private salsa classes at Narciso's school and
give her a few phone numbers. I convince her not to travel light, as she originally
planned; I pressure her into carrying as much as she can, with the intention of
giving it all away.*

 *As payment for my wisdom I exact space in her overweight luggage. Because
of the embargo it's still impossible to send supplies to Cuba through the mail. So
I start the familiar process of putting together an ad hoc First World care package.
I try to negotiate a prescription for baby asthma medication for a friend's son. It's
a long shot, since my doctor can't examine a baby who's in Cuba. I buy baby
aspirin and vitamins, hair ties and grown-up vitamins (with and without extra
iron). I go through my bottles at home: Vitamin E for Vivian's cysts, bottles of
unfinished prescriptions for Marnia's brother the physician, minerals for Tomas.
He claims he can feel the difference when he takes them. I doubt it, but even a
placebo is better than nothing. I soak labels off the bottles and include them inside
the Ziploc bags. Just in case the customs officials get suspicious. Of course I don't
seal any of the letter envelopes. That would make their job too difficult.*

 *Narciso, Yamilé, Cándido, Beti, Irma, Alberto, Vivian, Mildred, José Manuel,
Carlos Jr., Viengsay, Alihaydée, Marlene, Mario, Juancito, Pedro, Ramón, Manolo,
la Señora Alonso, El Negociante and El Quixote, all the folks I have known in
Cuba have helped me become who I am. They gave me their time and belief, their
spins, their jumps, their secrets, their rum, their laughter and their music.*

 *For Cubans, music and dance are like food and water. Cuba, that enigmatic
island, has shared its feast.*

Chapter Notes

All translations are the author's unless otherwise noted.

Introduction

1. http://www.treas.gov/offices/enforcement/ofac/sanctions/t11cuba.pdf. Accessed June 10, 2007. The United States Treasury Department Office of Foreign Assets Control posted the following warning on their website:

"Part 515 (the 'Regulations') were issued by the U.S. Government on 8 July 1963 under the Trading With the Enemy Act in response to certain hostile actions by the Cuban government. They are still in force today and affect all U.S. citizens and permanent residents wherever they are located, all people and organizations physically in the United States, and all branches and subsidiaries of U.S. organizations throughout the world. The Regulations are administered by the U.S. Treasury Department's Office of Foreign Assets Control. **The basic goal of the sanctions is to isolate the Cuban government economically and deprive it of U.S. dollars** [emphasis added]. Criminal penalties for violating the sanctions range up to 10 years in prison, $1,000,000 in corporate fines, and $250,000 in individual fines. Civil penalties up to $55,000 per violation may also be imposed."

2. Mousouris, 2002:57.

3. From Fidel Castro's speech in January 1990, quoted in "Período Especial," Ministerio de las Fuerzas Armadas Revolucionarias (MINFAR), June 29, 2000. http://www.cubagob.cu/otras _info/minfar/periodo_especial.html, Accessed April 10, 2007 (translation, Horacio Cocchi).

4. "The name "tanztheater" refers to a performance form that combines dance, speaking, singing and chanting, conventional theater and the use of props, set, and costumes in one amalgam. It is performed by trained dancers. Usually there is no narrative plot; instead, specific situations, fears, and human conflicts are presented. Audiences are stimulated to follow a train of thought or to reflect on what the tanztheater piece express. It has been described as a new twist on an old form: German Expressionism." Langer, Roland. "Compulsion and Restraint, Love and Angst," *Dance Magazine* 58, no. 6 (1984).

Prologue

1. Lyrics by Camilo Sesto.
2. Electronic communication, September 22, 2011.

Chapter 1

1. Guerra, 2000:162.
2. As quoted in Chasteen, 2004:119.

3. As quoted in Chasteen, 2004:154.

4. Author unknown, *"No hay virilidad?" El Palenque Literario* 3, 1888, 473–74.

5. See Daniel, 2005:119.

6. Crypto-Jews are otherwise known as *marranos*, or hidden Jews, those forced to convert to Christianity by the Inquisition. In some cases certain elements of Judaic observance found their way into daily life, often without the participants fully understanding the source of their "family" traditions.

7. As quoted in Chasteen, 2004:156.

8. Chasteen, 2004:192.

9. According to Daniel, "Carabalí in Cuba most often refers to the Ngbe and Ekpe secret societies which were centered on the Calabar region of southeastern Nigeria during the height of the transatlantic slave trade." 1995:172.

10. As of this writing this remains the policy regarding Cuban artists performing in the U.S. As with all travel and economic restrictions involving Cuba and the United States, all things are subject to change at any moment.

11. The letter writing campaign was spearheaded by the U.S.–Cuba Cultural Exchange. Full disclosure: I am on the advisory board of this organization.

Chapter 2

1. Heredia, 1998:139.

2. Ortiz, 1947:98.

3. See Ortiz, Fernando. *Cuban Counterpoint; Tobacco and Sugar.* New York: A. A. Knopf, 1947. The concept of Transculturation is also explained below:

> "The Cuban historical experience provides yet another illuminating example to contrast with the North American melting pot. Cuban culture developed as various exogenous cultures (primarily Spanish and African) met and mingled. There were only creoles. The *indígenas* disappeared entirely early on. This situation prompted Fernando Ortiz, a Cuban lawyer, folklorist, and historian, to develop the idea of transculturation to depict the Cuban experience of mixture [97–103; Coronil]. Transculturation differed from acculturation in stressing that all cultures change in a situation of contact; it involves a simultaneous loss and acquisition of culture and, in the case of Cuba, it is a matter of a continuing, creative flux, never a finished synthesis. The Cuban example thus did not indicate assimilation to a cultural or ethnic dominant standard as was the case in the U.S., nor did it have a teleology of whiteness as did other parts of Latin America." Stewart, Charles. "Syncretism and Its Synonyms: Reflections on Cultural Mixture." *Diacritics*— Volume 29, Number 3, Fall 1999, 40–67.

4. Suchlicki, 1986:4.

5. Rogozinski, 1999:52.

6. Rogozinski, 1999:38.

7. Rogozinski, 1999:43; This phrase, with a long history on the island, is used today by the U.S. Treasury Department to describe the illegal expenditure of U.S. dollars in Cuba. It is also the title of a popular book on Castro's Cuba by author Tom Miller.

8. Suchlicki, 1986:75.

9. The term Third World is politically and emotionally loaded for many residents of this ill-defined space. Here are two perspectives:

> "Gayatri Chakravorty Spivak explains that the term 'Third World' was initially coined in 1955 by those emerging from the 'old' world order: 'The initial attempt in the Bandung Conference (1955) to establish a third way — neither with the Eastern nor within the Western bloc — in the world system, in response to the seemingly new world order established after the Second World War, was not accompanied by a commensurate intellectual effort. The only idioms deployed for the nurturing of this nascent Third World in the cultural field belonged then to positions emerging from resistance within the supposedly 'old' world order — anti-imperialism, and/or nationalism....'"

"KumKum Sangari argues that the term 'Third World' not only designates specific geographical areas, but imaginary spaces. According to Sangari, 'Third World' is 'a term that both signifies and blurs the functioning of an economic, political, and imaginary geography able to unite vast and vastly differentiated areas of the world into a single 'underdeveloped terrain' (217). Sangari is critical of the way 'Third World' is used by the West to indiscriminately lump together vastly different places."

http://www.english.emory.edu/Bahri/ThirdWorld.html. Accessed April 8, 2007.

10. Choreographer Marlene Carbonell, speaking from the post–Colonial and Revolutionary perspective of the present day, made this comment during rehearsal of her dance, *Entre Dos Aguas*, in which she incorporated specific modern dance and *orisha* dance tropes; April 21, 2006.

11. Williams, 1970:122.

12. Quiñones, 2001.

13. Perez, 1998:109.

14. Suchlicki, 1986: 30.

15. Suchlicki, 1986:59.

16. Perez, 1995:125.

17. Perez, 1995:145.

18. Chipaumire, 2000:37.

19. Suchlicki, 1986:79.

20. Quoted in Pérez Sarduy, 2000:1.

21. Mintz and Price, 1976.

22. Hagedorn (2001:243) goes on to note that "the religious and performative activities of *cabildos* were gradually curtailed throughout the 1880s by the civil government until they became mostly social clubs."

23. "Syncretism" has come to refer the melding of Catholic saints with indigenous or non–Christian deities. Below are more definitions and discussions of the term:

> "*Syncretism* is [a] term with a controversial past and an uncertain present, and the following genealogical consideration attempts to use an awareness of past conflicts and prejudices to generate a creative theoretical response in the present.... The term *syncretism*, originally coined with a positive sense by Plutarch in the first century AD [*Moralia* 2.490b], acquired overriding negative connotations in the seventeenth century.... *Syncretism* became a term of abuse often applied to castigate colonial local churches that had burst out of the sphere of mission control and begun to 'illegitimately' indigenize Christianity instead of properly reproducing the European form of Christianity they had originally been offered.... In the New World a much more positive attitude toward the concept of syncretism has long prevailed among social scientists.... The anthropologist Melville Herskovits, for example, considered syncretism a valuable concept for specifying the degree to which diverse cultures had integrated [see also Apter]. It was not a bridge leading to religious relapse, but rather a stage (for African Americans and other minorities) on the road toward the ideal of cultural assimilation and integration." Stewart, Charles. *Syncretism and Its Synonyms: Reflections on Cultural Mixture. Diacritics* — Volume 29, Number 3, Fall 1999, 40–67.

24. Browning, 1995:29.

25. Daniel, 2005:125.

26. Hagedorn, 2001:115.

27. Chasteen, 2004:92.

28. Wurdemann's *Notes on Cuba*, originally published in 1844, is excerpted in Pérez, Louis A., Jr., 1992: 152.

29. Quoted in the documentary film, *Havana Nagila: The Jews of Cuba*.

30. De la Fuente, 2001:293.

Chapter 3

1. See: John, Steven Sándor. Permanent revolution on the Altiplano: Bolivian Trotskyism, 1928–2005. New York: CUNY, 2006.

2. Perez, 1995:253.
3. Pérez-Stable, 1999:36.
4. Suchlicki, 1986:109.
5. Perez, 1995: 288.
6. Perez, 1995:287.
7. Perez, 1995:295–301.
8. As quoted in Perez, 1995:305.
9. Several sources are used for these legends, including personal interview with Narciso Medina, 1996.
10. Full disclosure: I am on the board of this organization.

Chapter 4

1. Martinez Heredia, 2002:140.
2. Mousouris, 2002: 61.
3. Daniel, 1995:41.
4. Mousouris, 2002:57.
5. Hagedorn, 2001: 140.
6. Mousouris, 2002:57.
7. Chasteen, 2002:67.
8. Guerra, Ramiro. *La Danza: Amenazas y Resistencias.* Unpublished manuscript, personal communication, 2010. Used with permission of the author. Translation by Mildred Gonzalez.
9. http://www.dccuba.com/index.php?option=com_content&view=article&id=47&Itemid=28 and http://cuba.alivepages.com/cultura/danza.html accessed Sept. 13, 2011.
10. http://www.cubaminrex.cu.
11. Guevara, Ernesto Che. "Man and Socialism in Cuba." Letter to Carlos Quijano, Editor of *Marcha.* Montevideo: March, 1965. Translation, Margarita Zimmerman. http://www.marxists.org/archive/guevara/1965/03/man-socialism-alt.htm accessed May 12, 2010.
12. Guevara, Ernesto Che. "Man and Socialism in Cuba." Letter to Carlos Quijano, Editor of Marcha. Montevideo: March, 1965. Translation, Margarita Zimmerman. http://www.marxists.org/archive/guevara/1965/03/man-socialism-alt.htm accessed May 12, 2010.
13. Prieto, Abel. Cuba's National Literacy Campaign *Journal of Reading,* Vol. 25, No. 3, Education in *Cuba: 1961–1981,* and http://www.workers.org/2007/world/cuba-0111/ accessed May 11, 2010.
14. Franco, 1967:278.
15. Pajares, 1993:28.
16. Mousouris, 2002:57.
17. Quoted in Pérez León, Roberto, 1985:6.
18. Guerra, quoted in Pajares, 1993:80.
19. Quoted in Pérez León, Roberto, 1985:12.
20. *Historia de un Ballet (Suite Yoruba).* DVD. Dir, José Massip. Havana: ICAIC, 1962.
21. Quoted in Mousouris, 2002:62.
22. According to Honour and Fleming (2002) Soviet Constructivist painters "enjoyed a brief honeymoon of official recognition," (829) receiving support and encouragement from the Russian Revolution of 1917. Constructivism is described as having goals that were "primarily social, utilitarian and materialist. The artist's mission was to express the aspirations of the revolutionary proletariat and enhance the physical and intellectual conditions of society as a whole..." (830). While the avant-garde aesthetic that was further developed by the Constructivists represented a new use of artistic techniques, it was not in itself a new technique for creating art. The techniques employed were not created intentionally as an expression of Constructivist thinking, though the pervading internationalist style — especially in architecture — was put to use with a conscious social agenda.
23. "The media coverage on the closing of the Graham center was quick to note the importance of such a loss. But there has been little commentary on how or why an institution of such stature was allowed to fail as a result of financial difficulties. The past several years have witnessed a gutting of public funding for the arts, with the largest source of federal support,

the National Endowment for the Arts and the National Endowment for the Humanities, having had their already inadequate levels of funding frozen for several years now. The inadequacy of public funding and the difficulties faced by artists in trying to attain such support have produced an increasing dependence on the benevolence of private institutions." Grant-Freidman: 2000.

   24. Duncan quoted in Kirstein, 1985:266.

   25. Guerra, quoted in Pajares, 1993:81.

   26. Dance companies from as far afield as China, Brazil and Germany have built on North American modern dance forms to create their own models.

Chapter 5

   1. Daniel, 2005:119.

   2. Mousouris, 2002:57.

   3. Bénitez-Rojo, 1992:11.

   4. Personal interview, Havana, April 2006.

   5. In studying national rhythms and national dances, John Charles Chasteen refers to cultural theory: [Dance] "is a social practice — a *habitus*, to use the valuable conceptualization of Pierre Bourdieu. Bourdieu uses the term to describe an enveloping web of behavioral habits that give structure and stability to social interactions. Few things exemplify the function of *habitus* more aptly than social dance." Chasteen, 2002:67.

   6. Chasteen, 2002:69.

   7. In Cuba Yorubans came to be called *Lucumí*. Their deities are known as the *orishas*. Priests and priestesses are known as *santeros* and *santeras*.

   8. Stephens, unpublished: 24. Included with permission of the author.

   9. Daniel, 1995: 35. Also see Daniel's *Dancing Wisdom* for specific dance elements from distinct African sources.

   10. Ortiz, 1947:103.

   11. Mintz and Price (1976: Chapter 1) suggest that all African-American culture is distinct from African culture, and results from the changes in cultural, social, and religious practices brought on by the trauma of the Middle Passage and the transformative years that followed.

   12. See Hagedorn, González-Wippler, Farris Thompson, and Murphy.

   13. Stephens, unpublished: 24.

   14. Brandon, 1993:55.

   15. Daniel, 2005: 141.

   16. Brandon, 1993:55, and Murphy, 1988:27.

   17. Brandon, 1993:58.

   18. Daniel, 2005: 141.

   19. Daniel, 2005: 141.

   20. Brandon, 1993:1.

   21. Jaima Chevalier's *La Conquistadora* (2010) is an insightful volume on Santa Fe's iconic Marian statue. Chevalier gives several telling examples of Native American practices syncretized into the adoration of this most Catholic of images.

   22. Dr. Robert Stephens, personal interview, August 4, 2003.

   23. The term "santéro" can refer to priests and priestesses of Santéria as well as to initiates and believers.

   24. Hagedorn quotes Carlos Aldama Pérez, a *batá* drummer with the *Conjunto Folklórico de Cuba*: The Arará songs were supposed to be played with Arará drums, but the only Arará drums were in Matanzas, because that's where all the Arará people are. So when the Matanceros [people from Matanzas] came to Havana to visit, they taught us the rhythms and we played them on the *batá*...." See Hagedorn, 2000:124.

   25. This phrase, commonly used to describe ecstatic union during trance dance, has been documented by Dunham (1983) and other scholars.

   26. Daniel, 1995: 17–19.

   27. Daniel, 1995: 17–19. Daniel links rumba to African dances as described by Fernando Ortiz and Rogelio Martinez-Furé, whom she cites as the "current authority on Cuban dance traditions."

28. Daniel refers to this as "a Cuban creole concept of proper body orientation." Daniel, 1995:74)
29. Daniel, 1995:72.
30. Chasteen (2004:13) uses the term "dance-of-two" which he translates from the original Portuguese. Attributed to Edmundo, *O Rio de Janeiro do meu tempo.*
31. See Daniel (2005), Chasteen (2004) and Emery (1988) for descriptions for possible historical sources of hip movement in dances of the New World.
32. Chasteen, 2004:20.
33. Jonas, 1992:165.
34. Guerra, 2000:163.
35. See Chasteen's chapter, "Drums of the Epiphany" (2004).
36. Bennahum, Ninotchka, 2007:74–75.
37. Bennahum, Ninotchka, 2007.
38. Chasteen, 2002:73
39. See Chasteen (2002) and Guerra (2000).
40. Guerra, 2000:108.

Chapter 6

1. Wirth, 2005:138.
2. This assumption has been expressed to me in numerous conversations with dance critics and historians. It is not unusual in the mainstream and dance press, for example: Cuban Carlos Acosta's choreography included what the British *Independent on Sunday* (October 28, 2007) called "Soviet style technical demands...." Lisa Rinehart, *Dance Magazine* (Feb. 2007), referred to the "Soviet style" of the school designed by the Alonsos, with help from their Russian colleague Azari Plessetski: "In the 1960s Fidel Castro was intent on building Cuba into a force to be reckoned with, and a world-class ballet company was part of the plan. Alonso, a personal friend of Castro's, was charged with creating a ballet school in the Soviet style." What Rinehart does not specify here is that the "style" or more accurately, structure, of the Cuban school is distinct from the stylistic bent of the ballet being taught there. Rinehart is not alone in failing to make this distinction.
3. reviewofcuban-americanblogs.blogspot.com/2007/11/from-tellechea-newspaper-archives. html. Accessed March 10, 2007.
4. Cabrera, 1998:45.
5. Cabrera, 1998:15.
6. See: Chazin-Bennahum, Judith. *Dance in the Shadow of the Guillotine.* Carbondale: Southern Illinois University Press, 1988. Also see Souritz on Russia; and Roca on Cuba.
7. Souritz, 1990.
8. Souritz, 1990:43.
9. Souritz, 1990:3.
10. Personal communication, Havana, March 12, 2008.
11. Campoy, 2001.
12. For more on Cuban baseball see: Bjarkman, Peter. *A History of Cuban Baseball, 1864– 2006.* Jefferson, North Carolina: McFarland & Co., 2007.
13. Campoy, 2001
14. Alonso, 1993:20–21.
15. Alonso, 1993:21.
16. Campoy, 2001.
17. Alonso quoted in 1978 in Cabrera, 1998:18–19.
18. Fernando Alonso, personal interview, 1996, NYC.
19. Alonso, 1993:20–21.
20. Alonso, 1993:20.
21. Kisselgoff, Anna. "Two Guests Uncover a Different Side of Balanchine," *The New York Times,* May 15, 2004.
22. Based on personal interviews with Fernando Alonso, 1996, and BNC principle dancer, Viengsay Valdes, 2008.

23. Cabrera, 1998:23.
24. These letters can be read on the website of U.S.-Cuba Cultural Exchange: http://www.cubaresearch.info/uscubaculturalexchange.
25. Plisetskaya, 2001.
26. Alonso, 1993: 24.
27. Personal interview with Alicia Alonso, 2006, Havana.
28. Narciso Medina, personal exchange, Havana, 2006.
29. Acocella, 2006.
30. Kourlas, Gia. "Hot for teacher, Mikhail Baryshnikov moves Azari Plisetsky to the head of the class," *Time Out New York.* Issue 574: Sep 28–Oct 4, 2006.
31. Rinehart, 2007.
32. Cabrera, 2007, personal electronic correspondence.
33. Alonso, 1993:38; and Cabrera, 2007.
34. Guerra, 2000:162.
35. Email exchange, June 16, 2010.
36. Personal interview, June 1996, New York City. For more on the Jaffe/Carreño partnership, see: John, Suki. "José Carreño: Raising the Temperature at ABT," *Dance Magazine.* July 1997; and John, Suki. "Susan Jaffe; Strong Dancer Series," *Ballet/Tanz International.* December 2002.
37. Alonso, 1993:36.
38. Telephone interview, July 2000. Laura Alonso runs her own company in Havana, Pro-Danza, and frequently teaches in the United States.
39. Guerra, 2000:31.
40. See Guerra, *Eros baila: danza y sexualidad,* 2000.
41. Guerra, 2000:165.

Chapter 7

1. Pajares, 1993:101.
2. Herrero, 1987:176.
3. See Roslyn Sulcas in *The New York Times*: http://www.nytimes.com/2011/05/17/arts/dance/danza-contemporanea-de-cuba-at-joyce-theater-review.html?scp=5&sq=danza&st=cse and Claudia La Rocco http://www.nytimes.com/2011/05/12/arts/dance/danza-contemporanea-de-cuba-review.html?scp=3&sq=danza&st=cse.
4. Johnson, Robert. "Cuban dancers enchant in first U.S. trip" *The Star-Ledger.* May 16, 2011.
5. Ilene Diamond, May 25, 2011; telephone conversation.
6. Guerra, quoted in Pajares, 1993:81.
7. Guerra, quoted in Pajares, 1993:80.
8. Guillermoprieto, 2004:268.
9. Daniel, 1995:43.
10. Tomás and Marnia Guilarte, personal interview, 2000,Santa Clara, Cuba and Narciso Medina on several occasions.
11. Telephone communication with dancer/choreographer/filmmaker Gabri Christa, Sept. 8, 2011.
12. Ibid.

Chapter 8

1. Daniel, 1995:55.
2. Burdsall, 2001:134.
3. Guerra, 2000:168.
4. See Mousouris, 2002.
5. Guerra, 2000:171.
6. Guerra, 2000:168.
7. Personal interview, Havana, April 20, 2006.
8. Guerra, 2000:168.

9. Mousouris, 2002:57.
10. Guillermoprieto, 2004:233.
11. Guerra, 2000:174.
12. Castro's speech *Palabras a los intelectuales* has been the subject of ongoing debate ever since he delivered it in 1961. It is cited frequently as having a chilling effect on cultural production. Here are two perspectives:

> Polemical critiques of the Cuban Revolution's cultural policies often quote Castro's 1961 speech "Palabras a los intelectuales" as evidence of the oppressive dogma circumscribing intellectual production: *"dentro de la Revolución, todo; contra la Revolución, nada"* [Inside the Revolution, everything, against the Revolution, nothing]. The speech served as a basis for subsequent cultural policies, but it was a response to the crisis developing around *Lunes de Revolución,* and Cuban cultural policy in general. The crisis accounts in part for Castro's attempt to embrace all artistic views and forms under the revolutionary banner and to encourage only constructive criticism: *"el espiritu de la crítica debía ser constructivo, debe ser positivo y no destructor."*—Salah, Hassan, "Introduction: 'Origins' of Postmodern Cuba," *The New Centennial Review* 2.2, 2002, 1–17.

> In June 1961, in a famous meeting with some of the most important personalities of the Cuban intellectual scene, Comandante Fidel Castro (1961, 11) uttered a phrase that, because of its brevity, construction, and categorical nature, has functioned, from that moment until the present, as a summary of the Revolution's cultural politics: "Within the Revolution, everything; against the Revolution, nothing." Taken out of context and in the hands of circumstantial hermeneutists and exegetes, this versicle, part of a speech known since as "Palabras a los intelectuales" [Words to the intellectuals], proved to be extraordinarily polysemic, which allowed it to become the guiding principle for the successive periods and tendencies in struggle. The country's cultural and social life would repeatedly bring up many more specific questions that never got a well-developed, clear, and categorical answer: Which events and processes of Cuban social and cultural reality form part of the Revolution and which do not? How can one distinguish which cultural texts or practices act against the Revolution? Which act for it? And which simply do not affect it? Which social criticism is revolutionary and which is counterrevolutionary? Who decides what is the correct answer to these questions? How and according to what criteria is this decision made? Does *not* going against the Revolution imply silence on the social ills of the pre–Revolutionary past that have survived or on the ills that have arisen due to erroneous political decisions and unresolved problems of the revolutionary period? Doesn't being for the Revolution imply publicly revealing, criticizing, and fighting these social ills and errors? And so on.
> After the 1959 revolutionary victory, and especially after the 1961 proclamation of the socialist nature of the revolution, relations between the political avant-garde and the intellectual or artistic avant-garde—to use designations of the time—experienced strong but localized and passing tensions in matters of cultural politics (for example, in regards to the prohibition of the public showing of the Sabá Cabrera Infante film *P.M.* or the sectarianism of 1961–62). Nonetheless, the intellectual avant-garde widely adhered to the decisions and projections of the political avant-garde in all the other spheres of national public life. On the other hand, in September 1966 Roberto Fernández Retamar (1967, 186), one of the most outstanding thinkers of the intellectual avant-garde, still could present the critique of the politicians' errors as a duty that is consubstantial to the intellectual's adherence to the Revolution, and as a diagnostic and corrective factor that the "actually existing" Cuban politicians of the time took into account: "A theoretical error committed by someone who can turn his or her opinions into decisions is no longer just a theoretical error: it is a possibly incorrect measure. We have come across incorrect measures, and they pose a problem of conscience. The revolutionary intellectual is not really acting as such when applauding what he or she knows to be an error of *his or her* revolution; rather, he or she acts as a revolutionary in showing that an error has been made. The intellectual's adherence, if he or she really wants to be useful, can only be a critical adherence, since criticism is "the practice of judgment." When we have detected such errors of the Revolution, we have discussed them. This has been done, not only in the aesthetic sphere, but also with erroneous ethical conceptions that have been translated

into infelicitous measures. Some of these measures have been rectified and others are in the process of being rectified. And this has occurred, in some measure, because of our participation.... In some way, as modest as it may be, we contribute to the modification of this process [the Revolution]. In some way we *are* the Revolution." — Navarro, Desiderio. "In Medias Res Publicas: On Intellectuals and Social Criticism in the Cuban Public Sphere," *Boundary 2*, Volume 29, Number 3, Fall 2002 (187–203).

13. http://www.kirjasto.sci.fi/sartre.htm accessed September 25, 2011.
14. Luis, 2002:262.
15. Luis, 2002:262–267, explains the entire P.M. episode which led to the loss of many supporters on the international Left:

"With writers and artists such as Heberto Padilla, José Álvarez Baragaño, César Leante, Rine Leal, and [Guillermo] Cabrera Infante, *Lunes de Revolución* positioned itself as the cultural vanguard of the Revolution. Cuban Revolution was in a constant state of transition.... *Lunes* came eventually into disaccord with members of the Communist Party.... The most serious polemic occurred in 1961, with Sabá Cabrera Infante [Guillermo's brother] and Orlando Jiménez Leal's film *P.M.*, which was censored and confiscated.... The censorship was also an attack on *Lunes. P.M.* and *Lunes*, in their attempt to give culture a new direction, became victims of a transition that gave the Cuban Communist Party an increasingly powerful voice in the new government.... Cabrera Infante and *Lunes* attempted to champion openness toward culture, which included fostering those literary and artistic currents in vogue.... On April 16, 1961, the day before the Bay of Pigs invasion, Castro had declared that the Cuban Revolution was Socialist.... Castro's idea of consolidating the Revolution implied turning away from rebel friends, and accepting the help of the better-organized members of the Communist Party, even though they had not participated in the Revolution. The writers of *Lunes* had worked for the Revolution, but the historical climate had changed and Castro needed the Soviets in order to fight U.S. imperialism and remain in power. The political and cultural concepts promoted by the *Lunes* staff became incompatible with those [who] sought to control cultural production. *Lunes* was closed because of an alleged shortage of paper."

16. Loss, 2005:1.
17. Guerra, 2000:175.
18. Franko, 1995:9.
19. Pedro Valdés, personal interview, Havana, 1995.
20. For a more detailed explanation of the economic changes of this era see Chanan (2003) and Dominguez (1986).
21. Caminitzer, 2003: xxviii.
22. Eric Driggs expounds on the *libreta*:

"The *libreta de racionamiento*, or ration book, has been an integral part of daily Cuban life since its inception in 1962. With the collapse of the Soviet Union and of the heavy subsidies received by the Cuban government, the basic food basket offered by the ration system shrunk considerably, and has not rebounded to pre–Special Period levels. Presently, the monthly allotted food per citizen under the ration system is enough to last 7–10 days, provided that all the items included are available, a prospect which is far from certain given the irregular re-supply of the bodegas, or small neighborhood markets which distribute rationed items. For example, in the first trimester of 2003 the ration of basic hygiene products, a bar of soap per person and a tube of toothpaste between three individuals, were not available for several months in the capital." — Driggs, Eric. "Food Security and Nutrition in Cuba," *Focus on Cuba*, Issue 47, September 11, 2003. http://ctp.iccas.miami.edu/FOCUS_Web/Issue47.htm.

Chapter 9

1. Tom Miller (1992) and Susan Eckstein (2004) have also used the phrases "dollar apartheid" or "tourist apartheid" to describe similar phenomena.

2. Personal interview, Havana, April 22, 2006.
3. Sarduy, Pedro Pérez. "An Open Letter to Carlos Moore," *Cuba Update*, Summer 1990: 34–36.
4. For further discussion of these themes see Helg (1995), Chipaumire (2000), Daniel (1995), Chomsky (2000), and C. Moore (1988) and (2003).
5. Daniel, 1995:26.
6. Quoted in Moore, C., 1988:1.
7. Moore, C., 2003:422.
8. See Vera Kutzinski's *Sugar's Secrets* where she posits that, "*Cecilia Valdés* can be taken as a representative of a racialized and sexualized cultural iconography that offers an alternate mythic foundation: the Cuban cult of the *mulata*," 1993:21.
9. Betancourt, 2000:101.
10. See R. Moore, C. Moore, Valdes, Guttierez, Kutzinski, Miller, Betancourt, etc.
11. Personal interview, Havana, April 22, 2006.
12. Kutzinski, 1993:20.
13. Personal communication, 1996.
Behar, 2000:142, writes: "It is now considered a survival strategy to *jinetear* (literally 'jockeying'), the term used in Cuba for providing personal services, particularly prostitution, to tourists and foreigners."
14. Personal communication, Havana, 2006. Narciso was referring to the contemporary soap opera "The Dark Side of the Moon," which has broken ground by including sympathetic characters who are clearly homosexual.
15. See Adams, 2004:168, who writes:

> "Although there exists a significant body of literature documenting the under-representation of black Cubans in the island's most important governing institutions throughout the forty-four years of Fidel Castro's rule, these analyses have emphasized limited access to political power as the sole factor responsible for this state of affairs. However, this comprehensive analysis contends that with the aging of the Cuban Revolution, other factors such as low holdover and high replacement rates for blacks during periodic reshuffling of the political elite have become crucial, albeit unacknowledged, explanatory variables for the paucity of blacks among the country's leadership."

16. Phone communication, 2002.
17. See De la Fuente (1988), Pérez Sarduy (1998), and Aguirre (2002).

Chapter 10

1. De la Fuente, 2001:293.
2. Dunham, 1983:xii.
3. Daniel, 1995:117.
4. See Schechner (1990), Sweet (1983).
5. Hagedorn, 2000:127.
6. Hagedorn, 2000:67.
7. As a dance scholar I doubt that any dance practiced by more than one person can exist without hybridity of some kind, be it personal, kinesthetic or cultural.
8. See Bourguignon (1968, 2005), Cossard (1970), and Rouget (1985).
9. Rouget, 116.
10. Hagedorn, 2000:chapter 3. For informative and thorough explorations of the *Conjúnto Folklórico*, see Daniel (1995) and Hagedorn (2000).
11. I have had the good fortune to attend sacred dances in Cuba as well as on the Rio Grande Pueblos in my home state of New Mexico. Sources which have helped me to understand and contextualize what I have seen include: Consuelo Annon, Francois Blanc, Erika Bourguignon, Felicitas D. Goodman, Charlotte Heth, J. McClenon, Gertrude Prokosh Kurath, Antonio Garcia, Jill Sweet, and perhaps most importantly, the late Stan Steiner. Sources are listed in the bibliography.
12. Personal communication, April 2007.

13. González-Wippler, 1992:25.
14. Personal communication, Havana, April 2008.

Chapter 11

1. This sequence of quotes is taken from personal communication with Ramiro Guerra on April 20, 2006 and during a follow-up interview on March 12, 2008. Both interviews took place in Havana, at the same outdoor restaurant and in the Maestro's apartment.
2. Bénitez-Rojo (1992:11) uses this phrase to describe Caribbean-ness in general, but in this case I apply the term to being Cuban, which is a very "certain manner" of being.

Chapter 12

1. Dempster, 1995:25.
2. I put this in quotes as Native American, South American, and Cuban dance forms are geographically Western, but often excluded from histories of theatrical dance.
3. See, for example, Joan Acocella, Edwin Denby, Deborah Jowitt, Anna Kisselgoff, and Elizabeth Zimmer.
4. Personal interview, Havana 2006.
5. See Bourdieu, 1984:466. I am working here with Bourdieu's models of class structure and taste, what he refers to as "a sense of one's place ... a practical anticipation of what the social meaning and value of the chosen practice will probably be."
6. Franko, 1995:28.
7. Gilfond, Henry, "Martha Graham and Group." *Dance Observer*, January 1937, p. 6.
8. See Franko (1995), Dempster (1995), and Roger Copeland, "Towards a Sexual Politics of Contemporary Dance." Contact Quarterly Spring/Summer 1982, 45–50.
9. Title of the Dance chapter in Dr. Veronka John-Steiner's book on the creative process, *Notebooks of the Mind*. Full disclosure: the good Dr. VJS is my esteemed mother....
10. Dempster, 1995:28.
11. http://www.glbtq.com/arts/dance,2.html accessed June 10, 2011.
12. Kisselgoff, 1998.
13. See Guerra, 2000.
14. "The semi autonomous company [Frutas Selectas S.A.] selects the best fruits and vegetables produced by state-owned farms and state-controlled cooperatives and markets the products to the tourist hotels and restaurants.... Prices of products sold in the dollar stores are normally higher than those offered in other internal food markets.... Quality of products in the dollar stores is normally superior to those in the other internal markets." — Ross, James E. and Fernández Mayo, Maria Antonia, "Overview of Cuba's Dollar Food Market: An Exploration of the Purchasing and Distribution System," *Cuba in Transition, ASCE* 2002 p. 278. http://lanic.utexas.edu/project/asce/pdfs/volume12/ross.pdf.
15. Miller, 1992:48.
16. Narciso Medina, personal conversation, Havana, April 24, 2006.
17. Personal exchange, April 21, 2006.

Chapter 13

1. Personal interview, Havana, 1992.
2. Robinson, 2004:x.
3. Behar, 2000:141.
4. See Ernesto "Che" Guevara's *Socialism and Man in Cuba*. This article was written in the form of a letter to Carlos Quijano, editor of *Marcha*, a weekly published in Montevideo, Uruguay. It was first published March 12, 1965, under the title, "From Algiers, for *Marcha*. The Cuban Revolution Today."
5. Gutiérrez, 2001:99.

6. Fernandes, 2000:366.

7. The first time he said this to me was during a personal exchange, Havana, 1993. He has since reiterated this stance, as he did during this conversation in 2006.

8. Telephone conversation, 2003.

9. Personal interview, Havana, 2006.

10. The following passages all come from the interview I conducted with Narciso Medina April 22, 2006. It took place at the Teatro Favorito, the home of the Compañía de la Danza Narciso Medina in Havana. I have provided the translation, with assistance from Horacio Cocchi.

11. Though hard to find, this book provides a poetic glimpse into the art of dancemaking. Medina, Narciso. *El suspendido vuelo del ángel creador*. Ediciones Alarcos, Havana, 2003.

Chapter 14

1. Idalmis Arias, email communication, May 6, 2007.

2. Telephone communication, Sept. 4, 2011.

3. http://www.marianelaboan.com/Site%205/Home.html, accessed October 16, 2011.

4. Telephone communication, March 10, 2003.

5. Daniel (1995:117) and Whitfield (2001).

Bibliography

Acocella, Joan. October 16, 2006. "Talk of the Town — The Dancing Life: Master Class," *The New Yorker.*

Adams, Henley C. 2004. "Fighting an Uphill Battle: Race, Politics, Power, and Institutionalization in Cuba," *Latin American Research Review.* V. 39, Number 1, 168–182.

Aguirre, Benigno E. October 2002. "Cuba's Post-Castro Transition: Demographic Issues," Federal Research Division: Library of Congress.

Alonso, Alicia. 2000. *Dialogos con la danza.* Havana: Editoria Política.

Atkinson, Paul, and Martyn Hammersley. 1994. "Ethnography and Participant Observation." Denzin, Norman and Yvonna Lincoln, ed. *Handbook of Qualitative Research.* Thousand Oaks, CA: Sage.

Bastide, Roger. 1967. *African Civilisations in the New World.* London: C. Hurst & Co.

Behar, Ruth. 2003. "Foreword." Freedman, Diane and Olivia Frey, *Autobiographical Writing Across the Disciplines.* Durham: Duke University Press.

Bénitez-Rojo, Antonio. 1992. *The Repeating Island: The Caribbean and the Postmodern Perspective.* Durham: Duke University Press.

Betancourt, Madeline Cámara. 2000. "Between Myth and Stereotype: The Image of the Mulatta in Cuban Culture in the Nineteenth Century, a Truncated Symbol of Nationality." *Cuba, the Elusive Nation: Interpretations of National Identity.* Fernández, Damián and Betancourt, Madeline Cámara, eds. Gainesville: University of Florida Press.

Bethell, Leslie, ed. 1993. *Cuba: A Short History — Cambridge History of Latin America.* Cambridge: Cambridge University Press.

Bourdieu, Pierre. 1984. *Distinctions: A Social Critique of the Judgment of Taste.* Trans., Richard Nice. Boston: Harvard University Press.

Bourguignon, Erika. 2005. "Spirit Possession." *A Companion to Psychological Anthropology.* Oxford: Blackwell. Print.

_____. 1973. *Religion, Altered States of Consciousness, and Social change.* Columbus: Ohio State University Press.

_____. 1968. "Trance Dance." *Dance Perspectives 35 Autumn, 1968.* Print.

Brandon, George. 1993. Santeria from Africa to the New World: The Dead Sell Memories. Bloomington: Indiana University Press.

Brock, Lisa, and Cunningham, Otis. 1991. "Race and the Cuban Revolution: A Critique of Carlos Moore's *Castro, the Blacks, and Africa.* Pittsburgh Press: *Cuban Studies* 21.

Browning, Barbara. 1995. *Samba: Resistance in Motion.* Bloomington: Indiana University Press.

Burdsall, Lorna. 2001. *More Than Just a Footnote: Dancing from Connecticut to Revolutionary Cuba.* Quebec: AGMV Marquis.

Cabrera, Miguel. 1998. Ballet Nacional de Cuba: Medio Siglo de Gloria. Habana: Ediciones Cuba en el Ballet.

_____. 2000–2010. Historian of the Cuban National Ballet, Personal interviews and electronic correspondence.

Camintzer, Luis. 2003. *New Art of Cuba*. Austin: University of Texas Press.

Campoy, Ana. 2001. "Ballet: Cuba's Enduring Revolution — Prima ballerina Alicia Alonso and the National Ballet of Cuba." http://journalism.berkeley.edu/projects/cubans2001.

Chanan, Michael. 2003. *Cuban Cinema*. Minneapolis: University of Minnesota Press.

Chasteen, John Charles. Aug. 2002. "A National Rhythm: Social Dance and Elite Identity in Nineteenth-Century Havana." *Critical Studies: Music, Popular Culture, Identities*. 19(1): 55–73.

_____. 2004. *National Rhythms, Africa Roots: The Deep History of Latin American Popular Dance*. Albuquerque: University of New Mexico Press.

Chevalier, Jaima. 2010. *La Conquistadora: Unveiling the History of Santa Fe's Six Hundred Year Old Religious Icon*. Santa Fe: Sunstone Press.

Chipaumire, Nora. 2000. *Danza Moderna y Contemporanea: African Influences and the Effects of Communist Governance on Cuban Modern Dance*. Oakland: Mills College.

Chomsky, Aviva. August 2000. "Barbados or Canada? Race, Immigration, and Nation in Early-Twentieth-Century Cuba." *Hispanic American Historical Review*. 80:3 (415–462).

Clifford, James. 1997. *Routes: Travel and Translation in the Late Twentieth Century*. Cambridge, MA: Harvard University Press.

Clifford, James and George Marcus. 1986. *Writing Culture: The Poetics and Politics of Ethnography*. Berkeley: University of California Press.

Cole, Hohnetta B. November/December 1980. "Race Toward Equality: the Impact of Cuban Revolution On Racism." *Black Scholar* 3–25.

Daniel, Yvonne. 2004. *Dancing Wisdom: Embodied Knowledge in Haitian Voudou, Cuban Yoruba, and Bahian Candomblé*. Chicago: University of Illinois Press.

_____. 1995. *Rumba: Dance and Social Change in Contemporary Cuba*. Bloomington: Indiana University Press.

De La Fuente, Alejandro. 1998. "Recreating Racism: Race and Discrimination in Cuba's Special Period." *Georgetown University Cuba Briefing Paper Series*, vol. 18.

Dempster, Elizabeth. "Women Writing the Body." Ellen W. Goellner and Jacqueline Shea Murphy, eds. *Bodies of the Text: Dance as Theory, Literature as Dance*. New Brunswick: Rutgers University Press, 1994.

Domínguez, Jorge. Fall 1986. "Cuba in the 1980s." *Foreign Affairs*.

Driggs, Eric. September 11, 2003. "Food Security and Nutrition in Cuba," *Focus on Cuba*, Issue 47.

Dunham, Katherine. 1983. *Dances of Haiti*. Los Angeles: University of California Press.

Fernandes, Sujatha. 2006. *Cuba Represent! Cuban Arts, State Power, and the Making of New Revolutionary Cultures*. Durham: Duke University Press.

Franco, Jean. 1967. *The Modern Culture of Latin America: Society and the Artist*. New York: Frederick Praeger.

Franko, Mark. 1995. *Dancing Modernism/Performing Politics*. Bloomington: Indiana University Press.

Freedman, Diane, and Olivia Frey, eds. 2003. *Autobiographical Writing Across the Disciplines: A Reader*. Durham: Duke University Press.

Freedman, Russell. 1998. *Martha Graham: A Dancer's Life*. New York: Clarion Books.

Fryer, Peter. *Rhythms of Resistance: African Musical Heritage in Brazil*. Middletown, CT: Wesleyan University Press, 2000.

Gilfond, Henry. January 1937. "Martha Graham and Group." *Dance Observer*.

Graff, Ellen. 1997. *Stepping Left: Dance and Politics in New York City, 1928–1942*. Durham: Duke University Press.

Grant-Freidman, Andrea. "After 70 years in Operation, Financial Problems Close the Martha Graham Dance Center in New York City." http://www.wsws.org/articles/2000/jun2000/grah-j17.shtml.

Guerra, Ramiro. 2000. *Eros Baila: danza y sexualidad.* Havana: Editorial Letras Cubanas.

_____. 2000–2010. Personal interviews and electronic correspondence.

Guevara, Ernesto Che. 1969. "Socialism and Man in Cuba," Mallin, ed. and translator. *"Che" Guevara on Revolution: A Documentary Overview.* Coral Gables: University of Miami Press.

Guillermoprieto, Alma. 2004. *Dancing with Cuba: A Memoir of the Revolution.* New York: Pantheon.

Gutierrez, Pedro Juan. 2001. *Dirty Havana Trilogy.* New York: Farrar, Straus and Giroux.

Hanna, Judith Lynne. Fall 2004. "Cuban Dance on Street, Stage and Page." *Dance Critics Association News.* 11: 6–13.

Hagedorn, Katherine J. 2001. *Divine Utterances: The Performance of Afro-Cuban Santería.* Washington: Smithsonian Institute.

Helg, Aline. 1995. *Our Rightful Share: The Afro Cuban Struggle for Equality: 1886–1912.* Chapel Hill: University of North Carolina Press.

Herrero, Fernando. 1987. "Cuba y la Danza: El folklor trancendido" *Revista de Folklor,* Fundación Joaquín Díaz, v. 83: 176–178.

Holland, Dorothy, William Lachicotte, Jr., Debra Skinner, and Carole Cain. 1998. *Identity and Agency in Cultural Worlds.* Cambridge: Harvard University Press.

Honour, Hugh, and John Fleming. 2002. *The Visual Arts: A History. Sixth Edition.* Upper Saddle River, NJ: Prentice Hall.

hooks, bell. 1992. "Representing Whiteness in the Black Imagination," ed. Grossberg, Nelson and Treichler, *Cultural Studies,* Routledge Press, NY.

Infante, Guillermo Cabrera. 1994. *Mea Cuba.* New York: Farrar, Straus, Giroux.

John, Suki. Aug./Sept. 2002. "Carlos Acosta: Cuba Confidential." *Pointe Magazine.*

_____. 2002. "Cuban Modern Dance." *Caribbean Dance: From Abakuá to Zouk: How Movement Shapes Identity.* Susanna Sloat, ed. Gainesville: University of Florida Press.

_____. 1998. "Cuban Modern Dance." *The International Encyclopedia of Dance.* Selma Jean Cohen, ed. New York: Oxford University Press.

_____. September 5, 1995. "Dancing in the Dark: A New York Choreographer Works for Love in Cuba," *The Village Voice.*

_____. Jan. 20, 1998. "Get 'em While They're Red," *The Village Voice.*

_____. Oct. 9, 2005. "On Separate Coasts: A Sisterly Pas de Deux," *The New York Times.*

John-Steiner, Veronka. 2005. Personal Interview, Santa Fe, NM.

Kirstein, Lincoln. 1987. *Dance: A Short History of Classic Theatrical Dancing.* Princeton: Dance Horizons.

Kutzinski, Vera M. 1993. *Sugar's Secrets.* Charlottesville: University Press of Virginia.

Lakoff, George, and Mark Johnson. 1980. *Metaphors We Live By.* Chicago: University of Chicago Press.

La Rosa Corzo, Gabino. 1988. *Runaway Slave Settlements in Cuba: Resistance and Repression.* University of North Carolina Press, Chapel Hill and London.

Las Casas, Bartolomé. 1971. *History of the Indies.* Translated and Edited by Andrée, Collard. Harper & Row, New York.

LeCompte, Margaret, Wendy Millroy, and Judith Preissle, eds. 1992. *The Handbook of Qualitative Research in Education.* San Diego: Academic Press.

Leigh Foster, Susan, ed. 1995. *Choreographing History.* Bloomington: Indiana University Press.

_____. 1996. *Corporealities: Dancing Knowledge, Culture and Power.* London: Routledge Press.

Lindren, Gunnar. *Arabic Roots of Jazz and Blues,* http://www.unesco.org/imc/mmap/pdf/prod-lindgren-e.pdf.

Loss, Jacqueline. *Cosmopolitanisms and Latin America: Against the Destiny of Place*. New York: Palgrave Macmillan, 2005.
_____. 1 August 2003. "Global Arenas: Narrative and Filmic Translation of Identity." *Neplanta: Views from the South*. V4: 317.
Luis, William. Summer 2002. "Exhuming *Lunes de Revolucion*." *The New Centennial Review*, V. 2, # 2. 253–283.
Martí, José. 1973. *Cuba, nuestra América, los Estados Unidos*. Mexico: Siglo Veintiuno.
Martin, Randy. 1998. *Critical Moves*. Durham: Duke University Press.
Martinez Heredia, Fernando. 2002. "In the Furnace of the Nineties: Identity and Society in Cuba Today." *Boundary 2*, 29.3: 137–147.
Medina, Narciso. 1992–2006. Cuban choreographer, personal exchanges, Havana.
Miller, Tom. 1996. *Trading with the Enemy: A Yankee Travels through Castro's Cuba*. New York: Basic Books.
Mintz, Sidney, and Richard Price. 1976. *The Birth of African-American Culture, an Anthropological Perspective*. Boston: Beacon Press.
Moore, Carlos. 1988. *Castro, the Blacks, and Africa*. Los Angeles: University of California Press.
_____. 2003. "Silence on Black Africa," *The Cuba Reader*. A. Chomsky, B. Carr, and M. Smorkaloff, eds. Durham: Duke University Press.
Moore, Robin. 1997. *Nationalizing Blackness: Afrocubanismo and Artistic Revolution in Havana, 1920–1940*. Pittsburgh: University of Pittsburgh Press.
Morley, Iris. 1945. *Soviet Ballet*. London: Collins, p. 10.
Mousouris, Melinda. 2002. "The Dance World of Ramiro Guerra." *Caribbean Dance/ From Abakuá to Zouk: How Movement Shapes Identity*, Susanna Sloat, ed. Gainesville: University of Florida Press.
Murphy, John. 1988. *Santería: An African Religion in America*. Boston: Beacon Press.
Nochlin, Linda. 1988. *Women Art and Power and Other Essays*. New York: Harper & Row.
Netanyahu, B. 1999. *The Marranos of Spain: From the Late 14th to the Early 16th Century, According to Contemporary Hebrew Sources*, Ithaca, NY: Cornell University Press.
Ortiz, Fernando. 1947. *Cuban Counterpoint: Tobacco and Sugar*. New York: A. A. Knopf.
_____. 1920. "La fiesta cubana del dia de reyes" *Revista Bimestre Cubana*. XV: 5–26.
Padilla, Heberto. 1971. *Fuera del Juego: El "Caso Padilla" Cronologia e Informaciones*. Editorial San Juan, Puerto Rico.
_____. 1990. *Self-Portrait of the Other*. New York: Farrar, Strauss, Giroux.
Pajares, Fidel. 1993. *Ramiro Guerra y la Danza en Cuba*. Quito: Casa de la Cultura Ecuatoriana.
Pérez, Louis A., Jr. 1995. *Cuba, Between Reform and Revolution*. New York: Oxford University Press.
_____. 1999. *On Becoming Cuban: Identity, Nationality, and Culture*. Chapel Hill: The University of North Carolina Press.
_____. 1992. *Slaves, Sugar and Colonial Society: Travel Accounts of Cuba, 1801–1899*. Wilmington, Delaware: Scholarly Resources, Inc.
Pérez León, Roberto. 1985. *Por los orígenes de la danza moderna en Cuba: Premio crítica 1985*. Havana: Departamento de Actividades Culturales Universidad de la Habana.
Pérez-Stable, Marifeli. 1999. *The Cuban Revolution: origins, course, and legacy*. New York: Oxford University Press.
Pérez Sarduy, Pedro. 2000. *Afro-Cuban Voices: On Race and Identity in Contemporary Cuba*. Gainesville: University Press of Florida.
_____. Summer 1990. "An Open Letter to Carlos Moore," *Cuba Update*: 34–36.
_____. 1998. "Que tienen los negros en Cuba?" *America Negra*, 15: 217–28.
Perna, C.A. 2002. "Dancing the Crisis, Singing the Past: Musical Dissonances in Cuba During the Periodo Especial." *Journal of Latin American Cultural Studies* 11(2).

Plisetskaya, Maya. 2001. *I, Maya Plisetskaya*. New Haven: Yale University Press.

Quiñones, Rolando García. 2001. "International Migrations in Cuba: Persisting Trends and Changes," *SELA*, Caracas, Venezuela.

Robinson, Eugene. 2004. *Last Dance in Havana: The Final Days of Fidel and the Start of the New Cuban Revolution*. New York: Free Press.

Roca, Octavio. 2010. *Cuban Ballet*. Layton, Utah: Gibbs Smith.

Rogozinski, Jan. 1999. *A Brief History of the Caribbean, From the Arawak and the Carib to the Present*. New York: Penguin Putnam.

Rouget, Gilbert. 1985. *Music and Trance: A Theory of the Relations Between Music and Possession / Gilbert Rouget*; Translation from the French revised by Brunhilde Biebuyck in collaboration with the author. Chicago: University of Chicago Press. Print.

Said, Edward W. 1979. *Orientalism*. New York: Vintage Books.

Sartre, Jean-Paul. 1960. *Sartre on Cuba*. Westport, CT: Greenwood Press.

Schechner, Richard, and Willa Appel, eds. 1990. *By Means of Performance: Intercultural Studies of Theatre and Ritual*. Cambridge: Cambridge University Press.

Soto, Francisco. 1998. *Reinaldo Arenas*. New York: Prentice Hall International/Twayne Publishers.

Souritz, Elizabeth. 1990. *Soviet Choreographers in the 1920s*. Durham: Duke University Press.

Stephens, Robert. 2003. *Ceremonial Language in Lucumi Ritual*. Unpublished manuscript.

Stewart, Charles. Fall 1999. "Syncretism and Its Synonyms: Reflections on Cultural Mixture." *Diacritics*, Volume 29, Number 3: 40–67.

Suchlicki, James. 1986. *Cuba from Columbus to Castro*. Washington: Pergamon-Brassey's.

Sweet, Jill Drayson. 1983. "Ritual and Theatre in Tewa Ceremonial Performances." *Ethnomusicology*, Volume 27, Number 2: 253–269.

Taylor, Patrick, ed. 2002. *Nation Dance: Religion, Identity, and Cultural Difference in the Caribbean*. Bloomington: Indiana University Press.

Thomas, Deborah A. 2002. "Democratizing Dance: Institutional Transformation and Hegemonic Re-Ordering in Postcolonial Jamaica," *Cultural Anthropology* 17 (4): 512–550.

Thompson, Robert Farris. 1983. *Flash of the Spirit: African and Afro-American Art and Philosophy*. New York: Vintage Books.

Uriarte-Gaston, Miren. 2004. "Social Policy Responses to Cuba's Economic Crisis of the 1990s." *Cuban Studies*. V. 35: 105–136.

Von Martels, Zweder, ed. 1994. *Travel Fact and Travel Fiction: Studies on Fiction, Literary Tradition, Scholarly Discovery, and Observation in Travel Writing*. New York: E.J. Brill.

Valdéz, Zoe. 1996. *I Gave You All I Had*. New York: Arcade.

Villaverde, Cirilo. 1962. *Cecilia Valdes or Angel's Hill*. Sydney Gests, Trans. New York: Vantage Press.

Ward, Seth. Summer 2004. "Crypto-Judaism and the Spanish Inquisition," *Shofar: An Interdisciplinary Journal of Jewish Studies*. V. 22, No. 4: 167–169.

Welsh Asante, Kariamu, ed. 1996. *African Dance: An Artistic, Historical and Philosophical Inquiry*. Trenton: Africa World Press.

Whitfield, Esther Katheryn. 2001. *Fiction(s) of Cuba in literary economies of the 1990s: Buying In or Selling Out?* Boston: Harvard University.

Williams, Eric. 1970. *From Columbus to Castro: The History of the Caribbean 1492–1969*. New York: Harper and Row.

Wirth, Isis. Summer/autumn 2005. "Puntas que solo yo veo." *Dossier "Los Nuevos Rusos,"* *Encuentro*, 37–38.

Wright, Irene. 1970. *The Early History of Cuba*. New York: Octagon Books.

Index

Numbers in **bold italics** indicate pages with photographs.